'RED'ᶜ

RESEARCH HIGHLIGHTS IN SOCIAL WORK 21

Social Work

Disabled People and Disabling Environments

j

37

Disability Studies: A Reader
Stuart Carruthers and Jim Sandhu
ISBN 1 85302 198 X

Disabled People and Buildings
Ian McKee
ISBN 1 85302 207 1

Managing Disability at Work: Improving Practice in Organisations
Brenda Smith, Margery Povall and Michael Floyd
ISBN 1 85302 123 7

Information Technology Training for People with Disabilities
Edited by Michael Floyd
ISBN 1 85302 129 6

The Contributors

Michael Oliver

Dr Michael Oliver is Reader in Disability Studies at Thames Polytechnic. He has written extensively on issues related to social work and disability, having previously lectured in social work at the University of Kent and worked as a development officer for Kent Social Services. He is active in the disability movement and a member of the Management Committee of the Spinal Injuries Association.

Vic Finkelstein

Vic Finkelstein came to Britain in 1968 after being imprisoned and banned from South Africa because of his opposition to apartheid. He worked as a Senior Clinical Psychologist in the NHS, trained as a teacher and is now Senior Lecturer at the Open University. He is actively involved in a number of organisations of disabled people, has written widely on disability issues and carried out consultancy work for the United Nations and World Rehabilitation Fund.

Bob Sapey

Bob Sapey worked as a social worker in Cornwall, with disabled people since 1975, and since 1990 working as a training officer for Cornwall Social Services Department.

Nadia Hewitt

Nadia Hewitt worked as a generic social worker in Cornwall, with a special interest in work with disabled people since 1984 and is currently working as a planning officer in the Primary Care and Community Services Unit of Cornwall and Isles of Scilly Health Authority.

Patrick Phelan

Patrick Phelan has been Assistant Director: Social Work at RSB Leatherhead since 1985. Previously he worked in a variety of social work agencies since qualifying in 1962. He was Chair of the British Association of Social Workers from 1980-1982 and served from 1986-88 on the independent review of residential care, the Wagner Committee, which reported in *A Positive Choice* (HMSO, 1988).

Simon Cole

Simon Cole has worked at RSB Leatherhead since February 1983 as a Team Leader and since qualifying in 1985 as a Team Manager. In 1988 he completed post qualifying training as a counsellor and has since then pursued an interest in staff care and the use of counselling skills within a social work setting.

Etienne d'Aboville

Etienne d'Aboville broke his neck in a diving accident at the age of seventeen in 1974. After graduating from Liverpool University in 1980, he went on to obtain a postgraduate degree in Modern, Social and Cultural Studies at Chelsea College. He has worked for the Spinal Injuries Association since 1985 and is currently the Welfare Director.

Barrie Fiedler

Barrie Fiedler is Director, Living Options in Practice, a three-year DoH-funded project on behalf of The Prince of Wales' Advisory Group on Disability and the King's Fund Centre, working with health and local authorities to develop comprehensive services for severely disabled people. He previously carried out the Living Options action research project for The Prince of Wales' Advisory Group, and published *Living Options Lottery* in 1988. His background is in community housing association work: he has a BA from Columbia University (New York), 1965, and a post graduate diploma from the Architectural Association (London), 1978.

Paul Cornes

Paul Cornes is a Chartered Psychologist. He is Senior Research Fellow at the Disability Management Research Group, University of Edinburgh and Editor of the *International Journal of Rehabilitation Research*. His interest in vocational rehabilitation policy, practice and research has included several studies of the impact of new technology on training and employment for people with disabilities.

Philippa Russell

Philippa Russell is Principal Officer, Voluntary Council for Handicapped Children, National Children's Bureau. Part-time seconded to the Department of Health as an Associate Director of the National Development Team for People with a Mental Handicap. Author of a number of books and articles on disability issues, with a special interest in parent involvement and consumer advocacy. Publications include *The Wheelchair Child* (Souvenir Press) and the co-authorship of the *Handbook on Special Needs* for the Open University Course 'Caring for Children'.

Michael Hirst

Michael Hirst is a Research Fellow in the Social Policy Research Unit at the University of York. His main research interests are in disability, community care policies, and informal care. He is responsible for the national survey of young people with disabilities.

Gillian Parker

Gillian Parker is a Research Fellow in the Social Policy Research Unit at the University of York. Her main research interests are in informal care and caring, disability and employment, and community care policies. Recent publications include the second edition of *With Due Care and Attention: A Review of Research on Informal Care*.

Andrew Cozens

Andrew Cozens is a Deputy Divisional Director in North Yorkshire Social Services Department. He trained at the Department of Social and Administrative Studies, Oxford University, and has worked in a number of residential and fieldwork settings in both the voluntary and statutory sectors.

Paul Abberley

Paul Abberley was born in 1950. After contracting polio in 1955, he spend some eight months in hospital, and two years in physiotherapy. He is a member of the Avon Coalition of Disabled People, and works at Bristol Polytechnic, where he is a senior lecturer in Sociology. He has written several papers on disability.

The Contributors

Michael Oliver

Dr Michael Oliver is Reader in Disability Studies at Thames Polytechnic. He has written extensively on issues related to social work and disability, having previously lectured in social work at the University of Kent and worked as a development officer for Kent Social Services. He is active in the disability movement and a member of the Management Committee of the Spinal Injuries Association.

Vic Finkelstein

Vic Finkelstein came to Britain in 1968 after being imprisoned and banned from South Africa because of his opposition to apartheid. He worked as a Senior Clinical Psychologist in the NHS, trained as a teacher and is now Senior Lecturer at the Open University. He is actively involved in a number of organisations of disabled people, has written widely on disability issues and carried out consultancy work for the United Nations and World Rehabilitation Fund.

Bob Sapey

Bob Sapey worked as a social worker in Cornwall, with disabled people since 1975, and since 1990 working as a training officer for Cornwall Social Services Department.

Nadia Hewitt

Nadia Hewitt worked as a generic social worker in Cornwall, with a special interest in work with disabled people since 1984 and is currently working as a planning officer in the Primary Care and Community Services Unit of Cornwall and Isles of Scilly Health Authority.

Patrick Phelan

Patrick Phelan has been Assistant Director: Social Work at RSB Leatherhead since 1985. Previously he worked in a variety of social work agencies since qualifying in 1962. He was Chair of the British Association of Social Workers from 1980-1982 and served from 1986-88 on the independent review of residential care, the Wagner Committee, which reported in *A Positive Choice* (HMSO, 1988).

Simon Cole

Simon Cole has worked at RSB Leatherhead since February 1983 as a Team Leader and since qualifying in 1985 as a Team Manager. In 1988 he completed post qualifying training as a counsellor and has since then pursued an interest in staff care and the use of counselling skills within a social work setting.

Etienne d'Aboville

Etienne d'Aboville broke his neck in a diving accident at the age of seventeen in 1974. After graduating from Liverpool University in 1980, he went on to obtain a postgraduate degree in Modern, Social and Cultural Studies at Chelsea College. He has worked for the Spinal Injuries Association since 1985 and is currently the Welfare Director.

Barrie Fiedler

Barrie Fiedler is Director, Living Options in Practice, a three-year DoH-funded project on behalf of The Prince of Wales' Advisory Group on Disability and the King's Fund Centre, working with health and local authorities to develop comprehensive services for severely disabled people. He previously

RESEARCH HIGHLIGHTS IN SOCIAL WORK 21

Social Work

Disabled People and Disabling Environments

Edited by Michael Oliver
Foreword by Tom Clarke, CBE, MP

Jessica Kingsley Publishers
London and Philadelphia

Editor: Michael Oliver
Secretary: Anne Forbes
Editorial Advisory Committee:

Professor G. Rochford	University of Aberdeen
Professor J. Cheetham	University of Stirling
Ms I. Freeman	Strathclyde Region Social Work Department
Dr J. Lishman	Robert Gordon's Institute of Technology
Dr A. Robertson	University of Edinburgh
Dr P. Seed	University of Dundee
Mr J. Tibbitt	Social Work Services Group, Scottish Office

University of Aberdeen
Department of Social Work
King's College
Aberdeen

First published in the United Kingdom in 1991 by
Jessica Kingsley Publishers Ltd
116 Pentonville Road
London N1 9JB

Second impression 1993
First published in paperback 1993

British Library Cataloguing in Publication Data
Social work : disabled people and disabling environments. -
    (Research highlights in social work : 21)
    1. Great Britain. Physically handicapped persons social
    aspects
    I. Oliver, Michael II. Series
    362.40941

    ISBN 1-85302-042-7 hb
    ISBN 1-85302-178-X pb
    ISSN 0955-7970

Printed and Bound in Great Britain by
Biddles Ltd., Guildford and King's Lynn

Gerry Zarb

Gerry Zarb was formerly a Research Fellow at St. George's Medical School, University of London, and is now a Senior Research Fellow at Thames Polytechnic. He has worked on several research projects on disability issues and consumer perspectives of health and social services, and is the author of the first major study on ageing with disability in the UK. He is currently working on further research on ageing and disability funded by the Joseph Rowntree Foundation, and a PhD on culture and biography.

Foreword

People with physical disabilities can and do live in our community but they desperately require appropriate support services which are adequately resourced by central and local government. By the end of the decade there will be almost 900,000 severely disabled adults alone living in the community, while the numbers of those who are impaired or appreciably handicapped will be far greater.

Since I introduced the 1986 Disabled Persons (Services, Consultation and Representation) Act I have had numerous discussions with groups and organisations representing the disabled, as well as meeting with many delegations of disabled people themselves. The central message was essentially the same: disabled people need to be empowered by policies which allow them to lead as full and as active lives as possible.

Unfortunately, this is not a message which the Government either understands or listens to. Its attitude is highlighted by the fact that it still refuses after more than four years to implement in full the Disabled Persons Act.

The National Health Service and Community Care Act this year has also proved very disappointing to those of us who had hoped that the Government would use it as an opportunity to introduce the key provisions of the Griffiths Report.

One of the critical themes of this book, which I wholeheartedly agree with, is that the planning and delivery of services must begin only after disabled people have been properly consulted. I believe that the social worker has a particularly vital role to play in this process.

Tom Clarke, CBE, MP

From Disabling to Supportive Environments

Michael Oliver

Anyone who has edited or written a book will know that the gestation period between conception and publication is measured in months if not years. In the usual course of events this does not matter, particularly in the consensual world of social welfare and social work where change is gradual, incremental and slow. However, in recent years this cosy, consensual world of welfare provision has been shattered. In particular, the relationship between community care, social work and the provision of services to, for and with disabled people has increasingly come under scrutiny.

Beginning with a damning report on community care from the Audit Commission (1986), the Griffiths Report (DHSS 1988) followed some two years later and, after much delay, this was incorporated into a white paper, 'Caring for People' (DHS 1990). After a very short consultation period the white paper was incorporated into the National Health Service Act (1990) and discussions about implementation began in earnest. No sooner had these discussions begun, however, than the Government announced that implementation had been delayed and would be phased in over a longer period. Whether this is likely with a general election intervening remains to be seen.

The point about this brief history is to point out this book is aimed at a moving target and in the nature of its production, various authors have written and submitted their contributions at different points in time. Hence the moving target has not always been in the same place and discussions in individual chapters reflect this. As editor, it would have been possible for me to have adjusted each contribution but between deciding to do it and actually completing the task, the target may well have moved again. So I opted to leave each contribution as the author wrote it and it will be for the reader to determine where the target was at that particular time. The moving target analogy can be overdone however, and there are themes and issues that have remained fairly constant over the last ten years or so.

The disabling environment has been a major theme since the Union of the Physically Impaired Against Segregation shifted the focus of discussions of disability away from the limitations of individual impairments and onto the consequences of social restrictions for disabled people (UPIAS 1975). This theme is picked up in various chapters; Finkelstein and Abberley both provide different critiques of models and definitions based upon the individualising of disability. Cornes shows how new technology can disable as much as it can enable and Fiedler shows just how disabling inadequate housing environments can be. Russell, Hirst and his colleagues and Zarb, in different ways show how both the legal context and the provision of services can be disabling and Sapey and Hewitt show that these factors can disable social workers as well as disabled people.

The new environment - disabling or supportive?

In the new environment, previous debates about the pros and cons of specialism versus genericism have been made irrelevant. Social work, of whatever kind and using whichever method, is no longer seen as being relevant to the needs of disabled people. Instead we have the case manager or the care manager as they have variously been called, who will be responsible for purchasing packages of care on behalf of disabled people within a mixed economy of welfare.

Case management is now seen as the way of cutting through the tangles created by agency boundaries and different professional perspectives to arrive at flexible packages of care organised around the needs of individual disabled people. While it is true that a few published studies indicate an improvement in services delivered for those disabled people in receipt of case management, it is by no means clear that it can resolve some of the structural and ideological problems of the disabling environment.[1] To put the matter simply[2]

'. . . if you believe that the Welfare State is basically sound and all that is needed is some fine tuning, then case management offers a way forward. If, on the other hand, you believe that major structural reforms are necessary, then case management is unlikely to provide the catalyst for major changes. If you are a policy maker or professional seeking to provide services for disabled people, then case management will offer the potential for improved service delivery and professional practice. If, however, you wish to provide services with disabled people, then I'm afraid you will have to look elsewhere for genuine solutions.'

But it is recognised that this new managerial strategy for providing services to disabled people is not enough in itself and is, therefore, to be supplemented by a market strategy which involves stimulating the private and voluntary sectors to act as providers of services and for the statutory authorities to act as enablers and purchasers of services rather than sole providers. Markets should be characterised, however, by a balance of power between buyers and sellers. Unfortunately, such a balance does not exist in the social welfare market, at least as far as disabled people are concerned.

This crucial issue could have been addressed by adopting what might be called 'an empowerment strategy', but the Government has explicitly turned away from this approach. By its lack of commitment to the implementation of the Disabled Persons (1986) Act, its consistent refusal to instigate anti-discrimination legislation and its chronic underfunding of organisations controlled by disabled people, it has clearly shown that while it may want a market in social welfare, it does not want a market where users (as they are now euphemistically being called) have any power.

But disabled people are empowering themselves anyway.[3] The crucial issue for social work is therefore what role it does wish to play in a process that has already begun, always assuming, of course, that disabled people will accord the profession any role at all. This book is based upon the belief that social work and social workers do have a role to play in this empowerment process but precisely what that might be is something for social workers and disabled people to determine jointly.

The structure of the book

In Chapter One, Finkelstein provides a historical overview of the development of disability services focusing on the way in which definitions of disability are linked to professional practice and the way in which the inter-relationship between the two produce different models of service delivery. He further argues that it is the administrative model of disability which confronts disabled people and professionals as the disabling environment. He goes on to argue that some local and national disability organisations have made a significant contribution to the demystification of disability and hence the provision of a range of more acceptable and appropriate services. For him, the challenge confronting professionals is how to reorganise both their cognitive and their service structures to facilitate these developments still further.

In the next chapter Sapey and Hewitt provide an insider view of the disabling environment as social workers employed in social services department. They show how the legal context in which they operate, the financial constraints which they are under and the social attitudes to disability all shape the kinds of services provided for disabled people. They suggest that the professionalism of social workers may help to counteract the effects of the disabling environment for social workers themselves but, at the end of the day, they are employed to do certain things in certain ways. Their contribution is an important one for, if the relationship between social workers and disabled people is to become more fruitful, then disabled people need to understand how social workers are disabled in their work environments, just as much as social workers need to understand the effects of disabling environments on impaired people.

The next two chapters further develop the theme of service delivery in environments which may or may not be disabling. Phelan and Cole describe some of the ways in which, in a traditional voluntary organisation, attempts are being made to introduce change from within. This has been done by identifying the disabling barriers to change and developing intervention strategies which enable residents to define and articulate their own needs.

This theme is pursued by d'Aboville and he makes it clear that disabled people are not only capable of defining their own needs but also of providing their own services. He describes and analyses the Welfare Service of the Spinal Injuries Association in some detail, stressing that the service is under the same constraints and subject to the same kinds of pressure as are statutory services; financial, legal, professional and so on. However, because these services are run on an open basis and are democratically controlled by disabled people themselves, the levels of satisfaction are high among users.

The following two chapters switch the focus to the physical environment. Fiedler shows just how important the right kind of housing environment and personal support actually is, but reports that very few disabled people get the kind of environment or support that they need. She reports on the few examples of good practice that she actually found, draws out some of their implications and suggests a number of ways in which social workers can begin to take action to improve the situation.

Cornes provides a balanced view of the impact of new technology on the lives of disabled people, considering views that it can be both enabling and disabling. His central point is that technology is not neutral; whether it becomes enabling or disabling depends on how we, as a society, decide to use it.

The final four chapters look at disability in the context of the life cycle. Russell undertakes a comprehensive review of the literature on disabled children and families and suggests that such families are vulnerable, but that if they are provided with a supportive environment, the quality of life for all concerned can be vastly improved. She then considers the Children's Act (1989), its implications for service providers and its possible effects on family life.

The next chapter by Hirst, Parker and Cozens suggests that disabled young people are often ill-prepared for adulthood because they are a product of previous disabling environments, notably the special school and/or the over-protective family. They then discuss the range of services that disabled young people may receive including social work intervention and describe some of their own work, where disabled young people are asked to comment on the social work support that they receive. They conclude by suggesting that the social work role will have to change over the next few years, but that without adequate resources it will be no more effective than it has been up to now.

The next chapter by Abberley reviews the evidence on disabled adults produced by the recent OPCS studies. He begins by providing an important critique of the assumptions and methodology underpinning these studies and then goes on to abstract such data as might be useful to social workers. He concludes by suggesting that the significance of the OPCS surveys lies not in that data they contain but in the fact that they offer, both to social workers and disabled people, the opportunity to put disability squarely on the agendas of politicians, policy makers and service providers.

The final chapter by Zarb draws attention to a hitherto neglected group: people who grow old with a disability, as distinct from old people who become disabled as a result of the ageing process. He points out that this is likely to be a growing problem in the coming years, not least because even the piecemeal services that do exist are likely to be unavailable to this group, either because they do not meet the criteria for eligibility, or because, having struggled for many years to live as they chose, they are not prepared to exchange their autonomy for meagre services. Based upon their own views of what services should be like, Zarb draws up a model of service provision called the supportive environment, which he then discusses in detail.

This is an appropriate point for the book to end, for the supportive environment model, drawn out of many years of distilled experience of disabling environments, offers a platform on which to base services for all disabled people, not just those nearing the end of their lives. We would all, given the choice, prefer to live in a supportive rather than a disabling environment. This book is based upon the belief that it is possible to build just such an environment for all concerned and it will, we hope, be a contribution to its construction.

References

1. Hunter, D. (1988) (Ed.). *Bridging the Gap: Case Management and Advocacy for People with Physical Handicaps*. King's Fund, London.

2. Oliver, M. (1989). 'Bridging the Gap: a Review' *Disability, Handicap and Society*. 4, 1.

3. Oliver, M. (1990). *The Politics of Disablement*. Macmillan, Basingstoke.

Disability: An Administrative Challenge? (The Health and Welfare Heritage)

Vic Finkelstein

From action to words: segregation

Incarceration in residential homes has been practised long enough for it to be accepted as a perfectly legitimate way of 'caring' for 'the disabled'. Indeed the founders and supporters of such institutions have been showered with numerous awards from civic and voluntary authorities. Names of individuals[1] have become household words for helping the 'unfortunate disabled' and they are acclaimed in public by every sector of the media. There is a singular lack of awareness that there may be something profoundly undemocratic about able-bodied people supporting the systematic removal of disabled people from their communities, that it is only able-bodied people who write glowingly about each other for having done this to disabled people and that it is able-bodied people who give themselves awards for this contribution to the isolation of disabled people from the main-stream of life.

On the other side there is ample evidence in the writings of disabled people[2] that they have always regarded institutionalisation as a means of dealing with the problems that they face in the community with considerable misgivings; as a last resort to be resisted for as long as possible. When they have found themselves in a residential home they have not only complained about being there but have felt acutely aggrieved by the lack of control over their own lives in the day to day running of the institution. Residential homes, therefore, have been an active site for disabled people to struggle for basic citizenship rights. This has meant, firstly, a struggle for the right to control their own personal lifestyles and, secondly, the demand for the democratic right to have a say in the running of the community in which they live (the 'home').

In the event it was in the Le Court Cheshire Home that this struggle set in motion circumstances which were eventually to transform radically deeply-rooted views about disability - that is, to be disabled means to be unable to function socially as an independent citizen having the same rights and expectations as 'normal' people and that the management of disability demands life-long care and professional expertise.

It has been a characteristic of institutional care that this management was placed in the hands of respected able-bodied public figures who have substantial experience in the management and control of others in a variety of work and social situations. Since the social and physical environment has enabled the successful achievements of these individuals there has been little reason for them to think that the inability of disabled people to cope in the same environment is due to anything other than personal limitations. Removing those disabled people who are having difficulty coping with the able-bodied world is, therefore, seen as an act of kindness. In these circumstances pleas from residents for a greater say in the running of the homes was usually met with blank incomprehension. The idea of residents controlling the management of an institution in which they lived seemed to conflict with the very essence of why they were there in the first place - ie placed in 'care' because they cannot control their own lives and function independently in the community.

When residents in the Cheshire Le Court institution persisted in pointing out that they wanted

> 'to extend the range of control over (their) lives . . . to choose our own bedtimes, drink alcohol if we chose, freedom for the sexes to relate without interference, freedom to leave the building without having to notify the authorities, etc.'[3]

their wishes were stubbornly resisted by members of the able-bodied management. It was not only argued that management committee members had been given the responsibility by the charity to administer its funds in running the home but that residents were not qualified to do this. In the circumstances, the isolated and often poorly educated (as a result of interrupted education or attendance at special schools) residents found it difficult to sustain their arguments in the face of the experienced able-bodied public figures. To meet this challenge Paul Hunt, a resident in the Le Court Cheshire Home, and other disabled residents began a search for more factual evidence to back up the moral and logical case that they had been making for more power in the hands of a residents' committee.

Conflict between Le Court residents and the management committee following the appointment of a warden for the home encouraged the disabled residents to support an investigation into the nature and running of the home. Miller and Gwynne,[4] two social scientists from the Centre for Applied Social Research,

Tavistock Institute, were invited to carry out a research project on the running of the homes. They made a series of visits to a number of residential homes and suggested that

> 'by the very fact of committing people to institutions of this type, society is defining them as, in effect, *socially dead*, then the essential task to be carried out is to help the inmates make their transition from social death to physical death'[5] (my emphasis).

In their words, once a disabled person had entered an institution 'society has effectively washed its hands of the inmates as significant social beings.' Miller and Gwynne concluded that the function of the home was to manage the process from social death to actual death as effectively as possible. They identified two types of institutional residence, one operating a harsh and the other a more humane regime, looking after disabled people until death. Their recommendation was to encourage greater staff training and support so that care (social death) could be more efficiently managed in the homes.

As can be expected Le Court residents were appalled by the outcome of Miller and Gwynne's research.[6] They already knew from individual experiences, such as segregated education, unemployment, inability to use public transport, re-stricted access to sources of information and their placement in the home, that they were regarded as non-functioning beings. However, they could not accept this as an irreversible state, caused by a medical condition (being 'disabled', or what Miller and Gwynne refer to as being 'crippled'), to be managed or cared for until death. Their active engagement in struggles for control over the running of the institution provided living proof that they were perfectly capable of function-ing independently as responsible citizens.

Miller and Gwynne suggested that the boundary between the institution and wider society was also between the 'dead' and the living. However, in making this distinction they did not question the legitimacy of linking disability with social death but rather with effective ways and means of managing this in the institution. Persistence in encouraging administrators to manage residents as if they were socially dead, in the face of overwhelming and contradictory evidence from their active struggle for democratic rights, underlines the strength of popular assumptions that disability *must* mean intrinsic dysfunction and dependency on care. The only difference between the institution and wider society, then, is not between the living and dead but that breakdown of care in the community enables the link between 'social death' and 'disability' to become an *open* reality in an institution. In entering residential homes for disabled people to conduct their research Miller and Gwynne brought with them prevailing attitudes and allowed their prior ignorance of disability issues (freely acknowledged by them in their book) to colour their interpretation of what they were seeing.

In their research Miller and Gwynne's adoption of the widespread assumption that disability means inability to function independently, crystallised in what amounts to a social interpretation of the meaning of disability. From this point of view the social death of a disabled person can be interpreted as originating in the community, entry into an institution only marking a change in the practical arrangements of its management. What Miller and Gwynne had done was to make explicit an unspoken, but primary, 'social model of disability'. In this model disabled people are seen as socially dead, dependent upon others for a 'cure' or to provide permanent 'care'. Inadvertently, the struggles of residents in Le Court, and other institutional homes, for basic citizenship rights provided the spring-board for the clearest presentation of the outstanding social characterisation of disability. This construction or model can be called the 'social death model of disability'.

With Paul Hunt in a leading role the residents concluded that able-bodied social science could not be relied upon to carry out unbiased research - ie research which is not prejudiced by able-bodied presumptions about the social effects of medical conditions. Publication of Miller and Gwynne's conclusions did not encourage Paul Hunt and other disabled residents to welcome the better manage-ment of their social death! On the contrary, it added more clarity to the reasons behind public attitudes and focussed attention on the need for alternative strategies in interpreting disability and promoting non-segregated solutions.

An early fruitful source of information for discussion about integrated ap-proaches to educational and residential needs was obtained from Sweden. The Fokus[7] scheme provided a useful example of supported residential accommoda-tion for disabled people and Paul Hunt became an expert in writing and dissemi-nating information about this and other non-segregated approaches which enable disabled people to participate in their own communities.

Providing examples of alternatives to residential homes from other countries and criticising the interpretation of disability as an inability to function without able-bodied care and professional interventions in the education, health and welfare services, however, did not meet with much success in the UK. Disabled advocates of alternatives to residential homes found it increasingly necessary to support their case with more detailed criticisms of the British approach to disability. This meant looking more closely at what was wrong with current interpretations. Rejecting and then arguing *against* the dominant social construction of disability (as identified in Miller and Gwynne's model) provided a more rigorous theoretical challenge which, in the long run, prepared the ground for greater sensitivity amongst disabled people that 'disability' is indeed *created* by the existing structural organisation of our society.

The experience of disability: a reflexive pause

By the time Paul Hunt, Peter Wade and other residents managed to move into their own homes in the community they had become thoroughly convinced that the establishment and maintenance of residential homes was a powerful symptom of the predominant public attitude that disability means social death. They saw, therefore, the campaign to provide secure community based alternatives to residential homes as an essential component of regaining the citizenship rights of disabled people. To this end they became active participants in joining and creating organisations of disabled people which they felt could in some way further the integration of disabled people into the community.

An organisation which attracted much attention was the Disablement Income Group (DIG).[8] The stimulation for the creation of DIG came from two disabled women in 1965 and although it expressed wide concerns for social rights it maintained a central and dominant focus on the campaign for a disability allowance. It was argued that since disabled housewives did not contribute to national insurance they were not adequately provided for in the national benefits system. Male members and academics, however, very soon influenced the organisation and broadened its focus onto the campaign for a national disability income for *all* disabled people. The group attracted wide attention, spontaneously drawing in members who felt that a disability allowance would be a major contribution towards their integration into society. Perhaps, too, underneath this was an implicit faith in the ability of a money allowance (received 'as of right') to minimise the experience of social death.

The campaigning needs of DIG provided a base for disabled people to come together and discuss activities in support of the organisation. This created a very good forum for discussion at the grass roots level and there followed a period of vigorous debates about the potential of a disability allowance to facilitate integration. This was set against the established practice of providing segregated facilities. Concern about who was to receive any national disability income contributed to the debate by raising questions about the definition and meaning of disability.

At the narrow level, this discussion was anxious to avoid linking the provision of a statutory disability income with criteria concerned with 'the cause of disability'. DIG wanted to widen provision of an allowance beyond existing arrangements, such as compensation for disability following industrial injury. Here, the cause of disability was confused with site or origins of physical impairment and, as such, was considered irrelevant to the campaign.[9] On the other hand, it firmly maintained its focus on the 'single issue'[10] campaign for financial benefits as the route to integration. Paul Hunt, representing views arising out of residents' struggles against institutional segregation, felt that this approach was unlikely to succeed because it did not address the central issues of disability.

The demand for a disability allowance was presented by DIG as arising out of the need to 'compensate' for disability (meaning, the possession of a physical or mental impairment). But this demand, far from challenging the view that disability results in an inability to function socially, tends to reinforce this assumption (ie the social death model). This in turn encourages the dependency of disabled people on special provisions and the goodwill of able-bodied people for financial resources to facilitate their inclusion in society; and this dependency was precisely the situation that Paul Hunt and the residents had tried to change in Le Court.

Those who wanted DIG to promote less dependency amongst disabled people saw it as an organisation which opened up opportunities to engage in active work with its membership at the grass roots level. They therefore pressed DIG for more work within local groups. Those in DIG who were mainly concerned with putting pressure on government for a disability income felt that the paramount function of the organisation was to prepare careful and well-researched presentations to the authorities in the seats of power.

Paul Hunt saw this tension within DIG as repeating the same conflicts that had agitated the residents at Le Court. In the discussions that followed the publication of DIG's various incomes proposals he began to suggest that the time had come to work out a new, comprehensive strategy towards disability issues. He felt that the true condition of disability was consistently being misunderstood as a result of pressure on disabled people to develop single issue campaigns in response to separate statutory provisions in the areas of personal benefits, specialised vehicles, residential accommodation and special education, etc. He wanted an approach which could unite all these strands within a single philosophy (or theory) of disability which, in turn, could direct the development of a comprehensive support system in the community under the control of disabled people. He decided to pursue this idea by publishing a letter in a national newspaper inviting like-minded disabled people to contact him for discussions to see if a new organisation might be set up.[11]

There was an immediate and vigorous response from a wide range of active disabled people, many of whom had been members of DIG but who felt that its approach was inadequate for the changing situation. There followed a year of intense discussion through an internal circular. This resulted in the formation of a new organisation called the 'Union of the Physically Impaired Against Segregation' (UPIAS). In my view, publication of the UPIAS policy document marked a turning point in thinking about the meaning of disability in the UK because for the first time in this country a group of disabled people interpreted segregated facilities as a symptom of their oppression. In saying 'since the means for integration now undoubtedly exists, our confinement to segregated facilities is increasingly oppressive and dehumanising' the document recognised that social death was imposed upon them and that regaining citizenship rights involved resisting this oppression.[12] Clearly, UPIAS guidelines for action were based upon a 'social oppression theory of disability' and the model of disability inherent in their philosophy could be called a 'social barriers model of disability'.

The disabling experience: the administrative model

As members of UPIAS began presenting their alternative, new social approach to the integration of disabled people, they not only held their own in discussions with the experts but increasingly found themselves at the centre of innovative ideas about the future of community based services. Supporters of existing service approaches aimed at compensating for disability (and based on the 'social death model of disability'), however, have never managed to offer any alternative to their traditional demand for ever more money to be put into services, which they orchestrate, and which provide them with the main benefits in terms of careers and financial income.

At first, ideas from UPIAS attracted only the most active, but the view that disability is socially created steadily percolated into the disabled community. In this arena individuals from the Liberation Network of People with Disabilities (LNPD) (also set up in the early 1970s) asserted their own interpretation that disabled people were an oppressed social group and added momentum to the increasing drift away from DIG. On the other side of the internal DIG argument the advocates of more effective pressure on government for a disability income felt that a broader base than DIG was needed in order to make a more plausible case and they went on to set up the Disability Alliance. The formation of this organisation also significantly contributed to the weakening of DIG. DIG's failure to maintain the centre stage in presenting the basic concerns of disability, and differences between UPIAS and the Disability Alliance about appropriate ways to move forward, focused attention on the need for a clear presentation of the new concepts of disability and an indication of how these ideas could be more relevant to modern society.

In publishing their policy documents both UPIAS and the Disability Alliance recognised their differences as well as the importance of a unified approach to disability-related services and benefits. It was agreed, therefore, that a meeting should be held between the two associations in order to reach a common understanding about the fundamental meaning of disability and the appropriate way forward. No agreement was reached at the meeting but a report[13] was published highlighting the essential differences between the two groups.

In this document UPIAS expanded its policy statement by presenting for the first time a clearly articulated social definition of disability.[14] On this understanding it also argued that the problems faced by disabled people could only be effectively addressed when they were directly involved in decision-making to remove the barriers created by the way society organised exclusively for able-bodied living. The Disability Alliance, agreeing that disability should be defined in social terms, continued to maintain that poverty had to be tackled first, with a state disability allowance, before disabled people could take on the active role of participation in changing society for their integration. Their approach, therefore, maintains the popular assumption that reduction in social functioning is a result of individual possession of a disabling medical condition.

By accepting that disability is associated with poverty, and failing to question the origins of this connection, the Disability Alliance's solutions, like Miller and Gwynne's, were coloured by the simplistic assumption that to be permanently disabled means that the individual is *intrinsically* non-equal to their peers (ie without help, a non-being). While all those active in disability issues seem to agree that disabled people are, as a group, relatively impoverished, poorly housed, educated and serviced by public utilities compared to their peers (ie non-beings),[15] they do not agree about how this originates. On the one side this social deprivation is seen to be the result of personal inadequacy and on the other that it is due to social and environmental barriers. The former encourages campaigns for state handouts (or relief) and extra (or special) services to compensate for the alleged permanent inadequacy (disability). The latter view leads to searches for new ways to engage disabled people more actively in their own affairs to change or eliminate the barriers (which are seen as disabling).

From the point of view developed by UPIAS there is a mechanism in the way that society is organised for able-bodied living which brings about the social death of disabled people. There are then two intervention choices for those who do not question this process but who wish to help - either 'cure' the individual condition allegedly resulting in the deprivation, or provide an elaborate system of 'care'. Both forms of intervention assume that the problems of individual disabled people originate in their deprivation from essential standards of 'normality'. Both approaches, too, involve the imposition of able-bodied standards when defining appropriate actions on behalf of disabled people. As can be seen, the common elements in the cure or care approaches are derived from the same basic model of disability - that disability means social death necessitating interventions by able-bodied professional and lay workers who then 'administer' the cure or care solutions.

In my view the administrative model of service provision dominates all services in the UK, whether these are provided by statutory agencies or voluntary charities, or demanded by pressure group organisations. Facilities for disabled people constructed on the foundation of the administrative model assume services can be delivered in the separate, but tightly linked, cure and care areas of intervention. Each of these forms of service provision are, of course, guided by their own sub-set of the administrative model. For disabled people these are the rehabilitation and personal care service models. Rehabilitation services are prescribed on the well-known medical model and personal care services on the imperfectly identified welfare model of disability. Both these models of disability should be regarded as sub-sets of the dominant social death model of disability.

What is often not recognised, however, is that as long as the administrative model for services used by disabled people remains dominant any reduction in the relative importance of one of its sub-sets in directing services will only strengthen the influence of its linked complementary approach. The relationship between the prevailing disability models and their counterparts in service provision can be illustrated as shown in Figure 1.

The medical interpretation of disability, of course, is widely experienced as dominating service provision models for disabled people. A consequence of this is that in day-to-day interactions the medical model appears to lend the only meaning to the experience of 'disability'. The spontaneous way of reducing this power, therefore, seems to require replacing it with a social model. In my view, however, the medical interpretation of disability does not provide the outstanding principles which govern the dominant understanding and servicing of disability. It is, rather, one of the sub-sets of the over-arching 'social death' model of

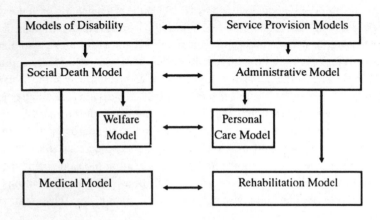

Figure 1

disability. Reducing the power of medicine in controlling the lives of disabled people while leaving the administrative approach to services intact, therefore, can only lead to the growing power of personal *care* approaches. In recent times we have already seen evidence of this in the growing concern about the needs of *carers* and the call for trained and professional service providers to administer more care in the community, while at the same time assumptions about the intrinsic dependency of disabled people remain unchallenged, if not actually reinforced.[16]

Interventions based on the medical model focus on the individual, and criticising this aspect of prevalent services, as Oliver[17,18] and Borsay[19] do, of course, also challenges one of the important links between the medical model and the various service models. As such polarising models of disability between the social and the individualised medical models undermines confidence in existing practice and opens the door to new approaches based upon different definitions of disability. However, in my view, space for the emergence of new support systems, enabling disabled people to develop their distinctive lifestyles in the community, will best be served by linking criticism of the individualised interpretation of disability with criticism of the dominant social model identifying disability with social death.

This is not the place to present a detailed account of how the social death of disabled people might have evolved within our social system. I have provided an outline[20] of such a possible process where further research might be fruitful, and

Oliver[21,22] and Borsay[23] have criticised and taken this suggestion further. For the purposes of this paper, however, the meaning of disability is regarded as a socio-economic construct originating in the way in which the industrial revolution set in motion processes which were to have a profound influence on the social status of disabled people.

In my view the introduction of machinery for factory production on a large scale meant employment, as a source of livelihood, became restricted to those of *normal* functional ability. The ability to integrate into an industrialised society not only required intact bodily functions in order to operate the machinery (ie varying degrees of finger dexterity, ambulation, sight and hearing, etc), but also the absence of various impairments to ensure access to public transport (designed to move *physically normal* workers between home and work), and an ability to read, write and listen so that the complicated skills for modern production could be acquired. Having a normal body was not only required in the area of production but also presumed for employment in the processes involving transportation of commodities from place of manufacture to site of sale and in the transactions across the counter with customers.

Since disabled people deviate from this 'norm' they are susceptible to progressive exclusion from an independent source of income with consequent isolation from mainstream life and their communities. The spread of industrialisation and the drive to increasingly efficient production seems to have operated progressively on disabled people by making them, as a social group, unemployable. Disabled people, therefore, suffered the more serious endless problem of unemployability rather than unemployment.

Disability itself has come to mean 'unable to work' and as non-earners disabled people are now fundamentally identified as incapable home makers and unsuitable love partners. In the formative years following the industrial revolution the modern concept of disability became associated with expectations for a life of dependency upon charity and beggary. When this became a major social problem disabled beggars were removed from the streets and placed in care. Ultimately, this led to the systematic isolation of disabled people from their peers and a thorough form of apartheid evolved which included special residential accommodation, sheltered employment, special transport, and special education geared for leisure rather than for careers in employment.

By the mid-twentieth century this process had succeeded to the point of making disabled people almost totally invisible in mainstream society. This social death of disabled people, however, as suggested by Miller and Gwynne's research, only gains its final material expression on entry into a residential home where all aspects of life are administered by able-bodied carers. Disabled people, of course, have always struggled for the right to life and as the modern meaning of disability evolved they spontaneously sought ways of countering this by defending their human dignity. In the early 1970s the struggle for greater power over their own lives provided the experience for challenging the prevailing understanding of disability and the development of their own interpretation of their situation. Not only was there agreement on the need to cultivate a new social theory of disability as a counter-balance to the prevailing models but it was argued that this should guide the development of future support services which they would control.

However the new model is defined[24] consensus is emerging that this should involve interpreting disability as a result of social and attitudinal barriers constructed by a world built for able-bodied living. This, I believe, can be called a 'social barriers' model of disability. Logically, this view leads to service approaches which focus on barrier removal.

The relationship between a barrier model of disability and related service provision approaches would also need to provide more acceptable boundaries between impairment and disability and their appropriate interventions, perhaps as follows:

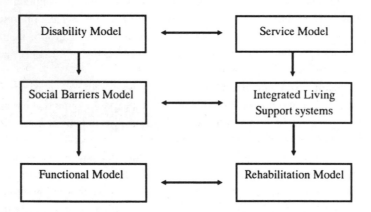

Figure 2

In this scheme the paramount control of disabled people over the support systems that they may use is ensured by structuring the medical 'Functional Model'[25] and its associated 'Rehabilitation Model' for services in the context and under the guidance of developing the higher order 'Social Barriers' and 'Integrated Living Models' respectively.

From words back to action: integration

It is clear that clarification of new ways of interpreting disability arose directly out of the experience of trying to influence attitudes of service providers about the appropriate control and delivery of support systems. Many disabled people involved in this debate were also engaged in expanding their experience by finding out and initiating practical alternatives for community based services. Ideas from internal discussions amongst disabled people in the UK, therefore, were seasoned with practical examples from other countries.

Paul Hunt, in particular, disseminated information about the FOKUS project in Sweden. This was seen as of particular relevance to residents who wanted to return to their own homes from their isolated institutions. FOKUS was seen as an approach which could enable disabled people to regain control over their lives and bring to an end their 'social death'. The project involved building a proportion of accessible flats within local housing schemes. These are evenly dispersed in an estate, to avoid ghettos, and linked to a central point where home help support staff can provide scheduled assistance and be on call for emergencies. Important elements of the scheme include the control exercised by disabled people over staff management and personal arrangements for home help and efforts to improve access to shops, employment and public transport.

Starting a FOKUS project in the UK, however, required convincing voluntary agencies already committed to residential homes and social services departments who were setting up Chronic Sick Units (later renamed the Younger Disabled Units). It was no surprise, therefore, that pleas to local, and central, government, for changes in residential arrangements for disabled people made no progress. Perhaps, too, the training of service providers has ingrained the social death model of disabled people to such an extent, reinforced by experiences of resigned and passive disabled people in the 'homes', that schemes for independent living in the community seem like far fetched experiments in risk taking.

Individual disabled people were driven to search for personal solutions which could establish the viability of living in their own homes under their own control. Amongst the most significant of the early projects started by disabled people was the Grove Road scheme set up by Ken Davis and Maggie Hines.[26] This was a modified version of the FOKUS approach. Both had experienced living in a residential hostel and they were determined to set up their own home despite consistent advice from professional workers that this was not a possibility. They began by negotiating a site to build accommodation consisting of a number of accessible ground floor flats with apartments for helpers on the first floor. The scheme involved subsidised rents for the able-bodied helpers and full management in the hands of all the residents in the building. This meant sharing decision-making between helpers and disabled people.

An important aspect of the scheme was the careful planning needed to organise the allocation of help that had to be built into the project. Based upon professional advice and their experience of 'care' in the hostel Ken Davis and Maggie Hines estimated the amount of paid time needed to facilitate security in their own home. This turned out to be a gross over-estimate and, in their view, illustrated both the limitations of professional expertise and the passivity generated by residence in institutions where all care and management is provided by able-bodied staff. The project was a tremendous confidence booster and a practical challenge to informed opinion about what services were appropriate for disabled people.

These messages spread rapidly through the disability grapevine, feeding the growing consensus that disability is manufactured by attitudinal and environmental barriers rather than functional limitations in the individual. Ideas about practical ways of enhancing the control of disabled people over their own lives were shared between individuals and organisations working in many areas, such as the Association of Disabled Professionals (ADP) and Association of Blind and Partially Sighted Teachers and Students (ABAPSTAS) who were promoting integrated education and the Spinal Injuries Association (SIA) encouraging greater self-management in daily life. This led to a more robust public profile and expansion of the self-help component of their aims. Local associations created with traditional charitable goals of providing leisure activities and putting pressure on local government for more able-bodied services came under increasing criticism for lack of 'consumer' representation and some were radically transformed. Many of the older organisations, such as the British Deaf Association (BDA) and National Federation of the Blind (NFB) became even more active in challenging the dependency assumed in the meaning of disability.

The growth in power and influence of these organisations highlighted the lack of knowledge amongst disabled people about achievements that were possible in the community. It became increasingly clear that limited information was itself an important barrier[27] hindering the development of new services planned, developed, set up and run by disabled people. The jealous control of knowledge exercised by able-bodied professional workers was attributed to their exclusive position in service delivery. As the sole administrators of services, only they required possession of the information and skills necessary for effecting the services. Paul Hunt, Ken Davis, Mike Oliver, Paddy Ladd, Anne Rae and the many others who agreed on the central role that disabled people should play in their own affairs made a point of stressing the importance of information networks and the need for self-education about new approaches to disability.

Ken Davis took the initiative and helped create a service run by disabled people to pass on information and advice. Disability Information and Advice Line (DIAL) local groups grew rapidly throughout the country and were very frequently managed and staffed by disabled people. DIAL not only contributed to the break-down in the knowledge monopoly held by professional disability experts but also gave disabled people a deeper sense of the increased choices possible for those wanting to live independently in their own homes in the community.

When this spread of knowledge was combined with the confidence and skills acquired in the new disability organisations, success in schemes like the Grove Road project and well rehearsed arguments that disability defined as functional inability could no longer be sustained, very many more disabled people added their voice for a controlling role in all aspects of their own lives. What can be called the social barriers model of disability intuitively appealed to active disabled people struggling for changes to the way they were being defined and they increasingly turned their attention to problems in removing barriers preventing their right to full citizenship.

A new round of organisations were created to bring different disability groups together. Most of these 'coalitions of disabled people' not only presented themselves as the democratic voice of disabled people at the local level but also as a vehicle for setting up new integrated (or independent) living services under the control of disabled people. The coalitions have also been joined by a rapid growth in arts groups. These have shifted their attention from the traditional focus of providing leisure activities for isolated disabled people and promoting access to able-bodied arts to the development and celebration of a disability culture.[28] The positive self-image emerging from these organisations directly contradicts the presentation of disabled people as inherently dependent on charity and functionally passive in the social death model which guides current services. The British Council of Organisations of Disabled People (BCODP) was founded in 1981 as the national body uniting all organisations controlled by disabled people. A common feature of these groups is that disability is not seen as a personal problem but as the social consequence of a disabling society. The focus is on removing the barriers which prevent the equal opportunities of disabled citizens.

The past five years have consolidated the ideas developed during the earlier period of struggles against segregation, mainly against residential institutions but also in opposition to special schools and sheltered employment. This has taken the form of struggles to implement practical projects in which disabled people could be directly involved. The organisations controlled by disabled people provided space for confidence building and the development of new skills. These experiences in turn paved the way for testing managerial and professional abilities in setting up and running community based services - the 'Centres for Integrated Living' (CILs). These are also often called Centres for Independent Living but not to be confused with independent living centres run by able-bodied professionals.

Integrated living: support systems

As is clear from the developments outlined above, a great deal of energy has been expended in this country to shift professional (local authority social services) and voluntary charities away from their acceptance of guiding principles based upon the assumed incapacity of disabled people to function independently of care in the community. This has not been successful despite recent marginal gains and consequently disabled people have established organisations, based upon a social barriers model of disability, to set up their own CIL services. CILs originated in the USA as a means of involving disabled people directly in community based services and were first adapted to the UK situation by Ken Davis in Derbyshire.[29]

CILs function in a number of ways, challenging disability stereotypes, providing examples of more relevant services concerned with advice, housing adaptations and ways of managing independence in the home. The CILs are also a focal point for disabled people to marshal their citizenship rights in campaigning for an accessible public environment, suitable housing, mass transport system, educational facilities, leisure opportunities and employment prospects. The fact that the centres and services they provide have been devised and delivered by disabled people also presents a positive and vigorous public image contradicting the general depiction of disabled people as a burden on the state and an appropriate focus for the attention of charity.

The emphasis is on changing the real world, removing real barriers to equality of opportunity, and not just modifying attitudes and changing the practice of service providers while maintaining dependency upon able-bodied people to 'administer' the solutions. From this point of view disabled people increasingly see themselves as oppressed, denied citizenship rights and disempowered. An important component of the changes wanted, therefore, is a 'Charter of Rights' and civil rights legislation which will facilitate more power in their own hands. Barrier removal is not only seen as involving the provision of ramps, information in braille and tape, signing on television, etc, to enable access to able-bodied facilities but also the right to develop a unique disabled peoples' perspective of the world and the opportunity to contribute to its future shape.

The administrative 'cure and care' approach to disability set service providers apart from those they wished to serve under the illusion that they were being 'objective'. We now see this 'professionalism' as having legitimised the imposition of able-bodied assumptions that to have a disability is to experience a form of social death. In this respect the promoters and defenders of existing services can themselves often be experienced as disabling barriers inhibiting the control of disabled people over their own lives.

The modern challenge is to provide alternatives to current practice so that workers and disabled people can share expertise in barrier identification and removal, both at the personal level (for the individual setting their own goals) and at the social level where public facilities need to be made truly public (and not just for able-bodied citizens). No doubt collaborating in this active way, agreeing to shift the focus from the disabled person as possessing the problem, will open up new experiences from which new and non-confrontational ideas can emerge. It was, after all, the actions of disabled people in just such a manner for the removal of barriers which prevented control over their own lives in the Cheshire Home that provided the springboard for a radical criticism of the administrative approach to service provision and the development of an exciting new interpretation of disability.

Shifting attention from the individual to the disabling barriers involves seeing disability as a consequence of the totality of the individual's relationships and provides an opportunity for sharing an objective discussion about the perspectives between the helper and disabled person. I feel sure that there is no more effective way of identifying and assessing this form of disability than with and through disabled people. This approach too, should help identify boundaries between appropriate models of disability and service approaches. Where an individual, for example, has recently sustained a permanent impairment, medical interventions involving rehabilitation to establish new skills in body management may well be appropriate.

However, as I suggested in the figure illustrating a social barriers model of disability, the medical model and its rehabilitation service approach should always be determined in the context of the social (barriers) model and not vice versa.[30] In effect, this means that the extent, duration and nature of medical interventions should be guided by an understanding and analysis of the barriers to be overcome, rather than on the functional limitations of the individual. Such an analysis, of course, cannot be provided wholly by the professional helper without falling into the administrative model trap. The shift from a functional assessment is, in my view, not only a radical transformation of accepted practice but a firm step in the direction of establishing a resource-based rehabilitation service. By this I mean workers in rehabilitation services should see themselves as a resource, to be tapped by disabled clients, rather than as professionals trained to make highly specialised assessments of what is appropriate for individual disabled people.

The 'social barriers model' of disability and its associated 'integrated living support systems' approach places disability related services logically in the same section of government concerned with barriers for able-bodied people - ie the Department of the Environment (rather than Health and Welfare) - and, of course, there would be a need for important new discipline developments in engineering and architecture. From this point of view, it seems perfectly appropriate for housing and adaptations officers working in local authorities to be disabled people and to be trained in the schools of architecture (or perhaps engineering).

Social workers are experienced in working with vulnerable and oppressed sectors of the community and would clearly have a major role in assisting disabled people attain and maintain their citizenship rights. Assistance with skills in managing personal support staff and liaising with CILs are other areas where the expertise of social workers could be very relevant. However, I believe that their main contribution could be as advocates in support and working with disabled people in identifying and helping to remove social and physical barriers in the local environment.

To summarise: a social barriers model of disability suggests at least the following fundamental changes:

(a) shifting the base for disability related service from 'health and welfare' to 'environment' based services,

(b) reformulated disability related services so that they are no longer service led but provided as a resource with clear access rights for disabled people,

(c) restructuring disability related services so that the integrated living support systems (CILs) provide the necessary central focus and guidance for all services used by disabled people including medical, educational, housing and transport services,

(d) redirecting the education and training of all service providers so that there are more fitting criteria for determining appropriate intervention (service) models, especially in relation to medical rehabilitation approaches, and improving the education and training of community based service providers so that their analytical and organisational skills are better focussed on barrier identification and removal with less emphasis on functional assessment, and

(e) enacting civil rights legislation as a framework for guiding the development of community based support systems for disabled people living in their own homes and ensuring equal opportunities in employment and equal access to education and medical services, housing, transport, leisure, the environment and information.

The adoption of a programme promoting aims along these lines will, I am sure, win the approval of disabled people who have pioneered a totally new perception of themselves and the services that they need. It will also bring to an end the long process triggered by the industrial revolution which led to the construction of disability as a form of permanent social death.

Notes

1. See for example Russell, W. *New Lives for Old: the Story of Cheshire Homes*. Victor Gollancz Ltd, London, 1980.

2. See especially copies of *Cheshire Smile* published in the late 1960s and early 1970s for a sample of critical writing from disabled residents.

3. Hunt, P. 'Settling Accounts with the Parasite People: a Critique of *A Life Apart* by E. J. Miller and G. V. Gwynne' *Disability Challenge*. 1, May 1981, 38. UPIAS.

4. Miller, E. J. and Gwynne, G. V. *A Life Apart*. Tavistock Publications, London, 1972.

5. Miller and Gwynne, 1972, p. 89.

6. See Hunt, P. , 1981, in particular, for a scathing critique of Miller and Gwynne.

7. Brattgard, S. O. 'Social and Psychological Aspects of the Situation of the Disabled.' Twelfth World Congress of Rehabilitation International, Sydney, Australia (Aug./Sept. 1972). Vol. 1, 1972. A number of pamphlets on the FOKUS scheme became available in the UK during the early 1970s which attracted a great deal of attention; articles by Dr. Brattgard were read and discussed by many activists.

8. See the editorial in *Disability Challenge* 1, May 1981, UPIAS, for a criticism of DIG; also Oliver, M. *The Politics of Disablement*. Macmillan Education Ltd, Basingstoke, Hampshire, 1990; also

Pagel, M. *On Our Own Behalf*. Greater Manchester Coalition of Disabled People Publications, 1988.

9. Mary Greaves, an active member of DIG, made clear her views that 'we all want integration, whatever the cause of disability', DIG Progress.

10. This was a point made both in Union of the Physically Impaired Against Segregation *Fundamental Principles of Disability*. UPIAS, 1976; and the editorial in *Disability Challenge*. 1, May 1981, UPIAS.

11. The letter was published in *The Guardian* on 20 September 1972 and subsequently in many of the 'disability' journals.

12. Union of the Physically Impaired Against Segregation. *Policy Statement*. UPIAS, 1976

13. Union of the Physically Impaired Against Segregation. *Fundamental Principles of Disability*. UPIAS, 1976.

14. For example, 'impairment [is defined] as lacking part of or all of a limb, or having a defective limb, organ or mechanism of the body; disability [is defined] as the disadvantage or restriction of activity caused by a contemporary social organisation which takes no or little account of people who have physical impairments and thus excludes them from participation in the mainstream of social activities. Physical disability is therefore a particular form of social oppression.' Union of the Physically Impaired Against Segregation. *Fundamental Principles of Disability*. UPIAS, 1976.

15. See, for example, the latest Office of Population Census and Statistics (OPCS) survey findings.
16. For example, *Care in the Community*. HMSO, 1989.

17. Oliver, M. *Social Work with Disabled People*. Macmillan, Basingstoke, 1983.

18. For example, '. . . functional definitions . . . focus on the problems of the disabled individual and do not attempt to develop research tools for measuring the disabling effects of the economic, social and physical environments.' Oliver, M. 'Social Policy and Disability: Some Theoretical Issues' *Disability, Handicap and Society*. 1, 1, 1986, 9.

19. '. . . the individualistic approach has a number of flaws. . . . impairment is assumed automatically to trigger off a single reaction which restricts functioning in all spheres . . . Most telling, however, is the omission of societal factors because without the socio-economic and political content provided by the 'public issue' or social perspective, we are ill-equipped to comprehend both the causes of disability and the social policies which it has provoked.' Borsay, A. 'Personal Trouble or Public Issue? Towards a Model of Policy for People with Physical and Mental Disabilities' *Disability, Handicap & Society*. 1, 2, 1986, 180.

20. Finkelstein, V. *Attitudes and Disabled People: Issues for Discussion*. World Rehabilitation Fund, New York, 1980.

21. In referring to my 1980 publication for the World Rehabilitation Fund, Oliver suggests that this publication offers '. . . the possibility of beginning to construct a social theory of disability . . .' He goes on to suggest that the model proposed '. . . over-simplifies, or over-romanticises . . . aspects of the historical process.' Oliver, M. 'Social Policy and Disability: Some Theoretical Issues' *Disability, Handicap & Society*. 1, 1, 1986, 14.

22. In referring to the 'role and potential of new technology' to provide directions for the future, Oliver suggests that the significance I attribute to developments in technology in triggering social transformations in the status of disabled people is too optimistic. He says, 'not all commentators see the issue as one of outdated attitudes, moulding technology in particular directions, but point to the fact that technology itself will not necessarily produce or equally distribute its benefits.' Oliver, M. *The Politics of Disablement*. Macmillan, Basingstoke, 1990, 125.

23. Borsay, A. 'Personal Trouble or Public Issue? Towards a Model of Policy for People with Physical and Mental Disabilities' *Disability, Handicap & Society*. 1, 2, 1986, 183.

24. The Disabled People's International (DPI) definitions, for example, refer to 'disability' and 'handicap' (in British terms 'impairment' and 'disability' respectively) as follows: 'Whereas disability has too long been viewed as a problem of the individual and not the relationship between an individual and his/her environment, it is necessary to distinguish between: (a) disability is the functional limitation within the individual caused by a physical, mental or sensory impairment, and (b) handicap is the loss or limitation of opportunities to take part in the normal life of the community on an equal level with others due to physical and social barriers.' DPI Constitution.

25. Functional models not only service medical interventions with rehabilitation goals but also all approaches which assume that poverty amongst disabled people directly results from individual disability. The Disablement Income Group, the Disability Alliance and the Office for Population Census and Statistics have assumed just such an individualistic functional (or medical) model. Their concern is to clarify eligibility for the allocation of financial benefits to compensate for disability and determine the administration of resources.

26. Davis, K. 'Grove Road' *Disability Challenge*. UPIAS, 1, May 1981.

27. Davis, K. and Woodward, J. 'DIAL UK: Development of the National Association of Disablement and Advice Services'. In Brechin, A. , Liddiard, P. and John Swain, J. *Handicap in a Social World*. Hodder and Stoughton, London, 1981.

28. Finkelstein, V. 'Disabled People and Our Cultural Development.' Paper presented to London Disability Arts Forum Conference, April 1987.

29. Davis, K. 'Consumer Participation in Service Design, Delivery and Control.' Derbyshire Coalition of Disabled People, Derbyshire, 1983.

30. The Disabled People's International (DPI) does not go this far, but is concerned with drawing boundaries between rehabilitation and community based services: 'Whereas rehabilitation is a process aimed at enabling a person to reach optimum physical, mental and/or social functioning level in order to provide that person with the tools to direct his/her own life, independent living and community services are not, and should not be, part of that process.' DPI Constitution.

The Changing Context
of Social Work Practice

Bob Sapey and Nadia Hewitt

Social workers are often, according to BASW,[1] at the interface between powerful organisations and relatively powerless applicants for service. This could justifiably be altered to say that social workers are at the interface of organisations that create disabling environments and disabled people. Environments, which can be physical, social, emotional and political, become disabling due to the lack of consideration of the needs of people with physical impairments. Barriers are either created or ignored and it is through this process that people are disabled. Disablement will arise from a number of factors, such as the lack of mobility, access and communication facilities; viewing disabled people as non-productive; the provision of segregated amenities and the placing of responsibility for disablement issues in the charitable sector. Social work agencies contribute to this process in a passive manner by their acceptance of medical models that see disability as an individual rather than a collective problem and in a more active way, by the procedures they have developed to limit people's access to resources under their control. While local authorities have powers and duties in legislation to deliver those services that parliament has felt likely to reduce the disabling environments, it is the experience of many social workers that their role is more akin to social control and the policing of disability than it is to the aspirations of legislators and their clients.

Social workers have adopted an ideological position in which the self determination of their clients is paramount. The tasks of enabling and empowering people is seen by many as their main duties. However, the majority find themselves employed by agencies whose perception is somewhat different. Local authorities, faced with the task of delivering services to a wide range of people, find it necessary to ration those services due to competing demands on a limited budget. Several groups of people have only ever received a Cinderella service and disabled people have always been amongst them. Fiedler[2] describes support services for severely disabled people as scarce, patchily distributed and a low priority of service providers. Social workers have found themselves acting as gatekeepers, determining who is most deserving of the applicants for a service, rather than empowering self-determination.

Although the role of voluntary organisations in the field of social work and more particularly, social care, has been a large one with regard to disabled people, it is the role of local authorities as providers or funders of services that is dominant. Three pieces of legislation, the National Assistance Act 1948, the Chronically Sick and Disabled Persons Act 1970 and the National Health Services Act 1977 have given local authorities the responsibility to assess the needs of disabled people; to arrange the provision of institutional and community services; and to be responsible for the welfare of disabled people. With a few exceptions, government funding for services to disabled people is channeled through local authorities. Voluntary agencies have traditionally been dependent upon charitable sources or local authority finance for their activities. Although much of this moved to the Department of Social Security during the 1980s with the Supplementary Benefit and Income Support funding of residential care, it seems likely that this may be no more than a temporary aberration, as we await the full impact of the recent White Paper[3] on the reorganisation of community care. While the role of local authorities in the future may be reduced, as direct providers of services, their control of the finances for services looks likely to increase and as such, so will their importance to disabled people. It is social workers in those agencies who, faced with the consumerist challenges, will have a major part to play in dismantling disabling environments.

Social work operates at the interface of legislation, between the implementers of that legislation, attitudes of society and disabled people. The majority of social workers also work within budgetary restraints that make the fulfillment of their task impossible. During the 1970s and 1980s, the growth of the disabled people's movement has added a further dimension to the context of social work practice. Oliver,[4] in describing the impact of the social model of disability on social work, rightly attributes much of this to the work of disabled people and their organisations. The consumer demand for greater involvement in, and control over, the way in which services are arranged and delivered, has challenged the disablist nature of both social work and social work agencies. This may be somewhat reminiscent of the position of social work in the 1970s as regards other groups of people, when, with the growth of Claimants' Unions and Tenants' Associations as part of a larger development of civil rights organisations, the validity and purpose of social casework was questioned and challenged. Disabled people seemed to have been excluded, or exempted from the theoretical battles of radical social work at that time, perhaps being felt to be a special case for kindness rather than political solutions and also perhaps because of the dominance of the medical model and personal tragedy theory. Such disablist attitudes have only delayed the debate, but may have provided some assistance by allowing others to test the methods of gaining power over their lives. There is a need to learn from the struggles of other groups to gain control, to acknowledge their mistakes and to be wary of some of the outcomes.

Legislative context

As statutory agencies, local authorities can only act within a legislative framework. The audit of local authority finances insists that all expenditure and income is within the powers and duties laid down in law. The wording of legislation concerning disabled people is such that broad interpretations are possible. In the National Assistance Act 1948, which permits expenditure on residential and day care facilities, there is also a general duty towards the 'welfare' of the recipients of those services. The concept of what welfare is changes with societal attitudes and political thinking. In this way the role of local authorities can be affected, sometimes quite dramatically as with the shift away from institutional care of people with learning difficulties.

The scope for interpretation also exists within the Chronically Sick and Disabled Persons Act 1970, section 2(1) of which requires that local authorities arrange the provision of a range of community care services in order to meet the 'needs' of disabled people. 'Need', however, remains undefined and is expected to be interpreted by professional assessment. We shall argue that this assessment should be undertaken in a way that empowers the self definition of need by disabled people, but it is worth giving some consideration to the concept of needs. Local authorities have failed to agree to any national criteria for services provided under section 2(1) with the exception of telephones and, therefore, have failed to define needs. Although most authorities have procedures for the provision of services, by leaving it to social workers and other to assess the needs of individuals, there is scope for these assessments to be as broad as the social work imagination will permit. Social workers can, if they assess properly, ensure that people are entitled to services for reasons not necessarily defined by agency procedures. If we see disabled people as people in need, rather than as people whose rights to resources are being denied or rationed, then the concept of need can also become disabling. While it is necessary to review the language of legislation, it is more important to ensure that it is interpreted in a manner that will afford disabled people their rights.

The role of social work agencies is primarily with individuals in each of these Acts, although the 1970 Act in particular was aimed at creating social policies which would remove many of the barriers to integration that create the disabling environment. In themselves the provisions are simple and are concerned with access and participation, collectively and individually, in institutions of society that able bodied people can take for granted. It is the closest that parliament has come to providing a charter for disabled people, but it is limited in its effectiveness by the ambiguity of the Money Order Resolution that was supposed to give it government financial support.[5]

The delivery of services to individuals is the responsibility of local authorities. That they may have seen their role, as implementing a charter of rights, is doubtful and as Topliss[6] points out, the position of disabled people, relative to able bodied people, has remained broadly unchanged since the '1970 watershed'. It would seem from the patchy implementation of the 1970 Act and despite attempts to force them to do so,[7] that local authorities have seen this act as increasing their own power and have fought to control or limit the demands of disabled people in order to preserve their position. As with gender and race issues, the maintenance of power by able bodied people is central to disablist attitudes. Judy Heumann[8] described the provision of services, irrespective of which part of the world you are in, as having certain factors in common - disabled people feeling they are not receiving appropriate services; that they are outcast from the community; that services are frequently provided in a custodial 'do unto us' fashion and that disabled people have little say in their methods of delivery.

Such viewpoints find favour amongst clients of social service departments as reflecting their experience of the attitudes with which services are provided. The ineffectiveness with which local authorities have implemented the 1970 Act, was given formal recognition by parliament when it passed the Disabled Persons (Services, Consultation and Representation) Act 1986. This Act aims to improve the effectiveness of the provision of services by involving disabled people in the assessment of their own needs and by giving them greater representational rights. Both the government and local authorities have failed, however, to implement it fully due to their fear of the increased cost of doing so. In fact all such costs would be attributable to earlier legislation, in particular the 1970 Act, as the 1986 Act does not in itself provide any new services, additional to previous welfare enactments. What it does, though, is to provide a framework of good practice for the manner in which earlier Acts are implemented by local authorities. In particular it says that disabled people should be informed of assessments and that their views should be considered. What central and local government hope to retain is their ability to control their expenditure by not giving disabled people the information needed to challenge them over their failure to implement the 1970 Act.

While the 1986 Act is awaiting full implementation by the Secretary of State, the government has produced its own White Paper which serves a similar purpose, though in some very different ways. Both express the aim of improving the effectiveness of community services to disabled people and others who require help from the welfare enactments. The 1986 Act, which was passed by parliament in the face of government reservations, aspires to improve the effectiveness of community care by involving disabled people in the assessment of their needs; by giving them the right to representation in the process of assessment; by giving fuller information of services available; by improving the liaison between agencies; by reducing the exploitation of relatives as carers; and by giving organisations that are controlled by disabled people the right to be consulted over who should represent their interests. The whole tenor of the Act is that by involving disabled people themselves in the processes that lead to the delivery of statutory services, they will become more effective. The key sections, however, that allow for representation and involvement, remain unimplemented.

The White Paper approaches the problems of community care from a different political perspective. It aims, by separating the roles of assessing needs and financing services from that of providing the services, to exert greater fiscal control in an area of expenditure that is seen by the government as being both out of control and unmanaged. The government proposes to transfer money from the Department of Social Security to local authorities. It is intended that this is used flexibly but primarily in the independent sector of welfare provision. The flexibility is welcome, but the movement of budgets to local authorities will mean that they will be cash limited and that the status of claimant, with its rights, will be lost. It is intended that the local authorities will have the lead role in assessing needs and in managing budgets, but disabled people are not given any additional control over their own lives.

This conflict between government and parliament is not new, as it existed also while Alf Morris was piloting the 1970 Act through the legislative process, but it is likely that the government will prevail as it controls the funding for all legislation. For disabled people it will be a further frustration to be excluded from control over their own lives and for social workers it will mean a continuing conflict between social policy and social work ethics. However, it is worth noting that as the 1986 Act is essentially concerned with the process of assessment, rather than the provision of additional services, there is no reason why local authorities cannot implement it as a policy of good practice without awaiting the permission of the Secretary of State.

Professionalism and meeting needs

The conflict between the roles of service provision and social control that seems to exist for local authorities, extends to their employees, in particular to social workers. Although many social workers recognise the extent to which they act as agents of social control, it is probably fair to say that few would have come into the work with that in mind. In fact social work tends to attract people whose ideology is opposed to the control of individuals by institutions; people who, for political or Christian reasons wish to enable powerless individuals and groups to maximise their access to resources. However, in the process of social work education and employment, such ideologies are exchanged for models of practice that, unwittingly, become an ally to social control.

There are two factors that bring this about. First, social work education is dominated by casework theories that have relied largely upon medical and psychosocial models of intervention with individuals. Bailey and Brake[9] said that, in the teaching of casework, there was no examination of the way in which men define the world of women, heterosexuals define the world of homosexuals, whites the world of blacks. It is necessary to add to such criticisms that there is no examination of the way in which able bodied people define the world of disabled people. In effect there is little or no examination of the disabling environment. The ensuing disablist nature of social work intervention is rightly criticised by such writers as Oliver,[10] who describes the 'individual model of disability' that he claims dominates social work practice, as processing people through the world defined by able bodied people and as lacking credibility in not concurring with the experience of disabled people. Social work theories ignore the disabling environment and concentrate on individual impairments and inadequacies as the causes of disability. This is reflected by the lack of attention given to issues of disability in social work training.

Second, social work as a profession has rejected any role in income maintenance, arguing that people should be claimants not applicants for welfare benefits. The 1987 changes in the social security system brought these arguments clearly to the fore with the creation of the Social Fund. When social workers thought that they might have been involved in determining people's eligibility for grants and loans from the Fund, their organisations, such as BASW and NALGO, were clear and precise in rejecting such a role. Determined advocacy was the method by which social workers were to act, which implied that they would not judge whether or not a person's application was justified or of higher priority than another, but would advocate for payment on the basis that the claimant had defined the need.

In the provision of services, disabled people should be accorded the status of claimant for services as opposed to the status of applicant as with the Social Fund. Such services are in effect a form of income maintenance as they are necessities to life for the recipients. Social workers do not reject their role of assessing eligibility for these services as they have done with the Social Fund. This apparent conflict is overcome by relating these services to casework criteria, so that they become resources of intervention rather than services of right. In this way social workers use a whole range of criteria which tends to reflect whether a person is deserving of a service or whether it is necessary in relation to agency function, rather than providing them on the basis of self defined need. The nationally agreed criteria for telephones clearly reflects this in that disabled people are not eligible for their own needs but in order to enable them to contact medical staff in emergencies.

Social workers unwittingly collude with local authorities to ensure that disabled people are not empowered to receive services as of right and in so doing help to limit the extent to which disabled people are assisted to overcome disabling environments. Claimants for practical help are forced to become clients of casework and are encouraged to conform to the individual model of disability which ignores disabling environments. The alternative approach is for social workers to question many of the assumptions made about professionalism and to develop an integrity of intervention that acknowledges that disabled people develop their own models of disability and should be empowered to define their own needs.

Professionalism need not be in conflict with providing a professional service if the emphasis is on ensuring that disabled people receive a certain standard of service rather than on promoting the status of the service provider. The primary task of social workers, in legal terms, is to assess the needs of disabled people. This task conflicts with the idea that people should be empowered to define their own needs. While it would take a major change of social policy to fully empower self definition of need and control of services, it is feasible for social workers to go some way in empowering people, within the constraints of existing policies.

It is necessary to adopt a position of determined advocacy within social work agencies. Changes are needed in the way social workers conceptualise the task of assessment, so that it concentrates on the way in which services are provided, rather than on whether they should be provided or not.

Change also involves questioning the assumption that certain services can only be provided in a certain manner, so as to avoid the institutionalisation that is so often imposed by local authorities upon groups and individuals. Most social workers will be familiar with the circumstances when it is assessed that the care needs of a person can only be met within a residential home. Social workers collude with such assessments and assist with the incarceration of disabled people into segregated communities. Budgets, policies and tradition combine to ensure the process takes place and managers fail to provide alternatives, as they believe them to be impossible.

If assessment is based on the individual inadequacy model, it will fail to change anything. If, however, it concentrates on the way in which services are provided, it is possible to bring about change. Each task that is performed for any individual need not be limited to particular buildings. Even complex medical tasks such as dialysis can be performed at home if the resources are available. Individually, each task can be performed outside of institutions but there is a need to arrange for their coordination and funding. In this way the packages of care that are organised with disabled people can be responsive to their preferred choice of integration, rather than segregation. People only need institutional care because of the failure of agencies to provide appropriate services rather than because of their individual inadequacies.

Self assessment is dependent upon information and the ability to make use of it. Social workers have a responsibility to provide people with information and should ensure that this is done in a manner that will enable them to make choices and to understand how their needs can be met. The responsibility to provide information, which is derived from the 1970 and 1986 Acts is not undertaken seriously and as such leaves people in a powerless position. When presented with information, people may need advice and sometimes counselling, in order to make use of it. A tradition of institutionalising people means that they may never have been given permission to make decisions on their own behalf. There is clearly a role for social work skills to be used to help people to assert their own choices and move to a less dependent role. The evidence of Miller and Gwynne[11] shows that this is possible, but that the onus is upon changing environments rather than upon diminishing individual impairments.

It is possible to draw an analogy between the social work tasks of service provision and that of retail trades such as car salesmen. In both settings the consumer is faced with major decisions, one involving spending large sums of money on machinery that is not understood and could go very wrong; the other on planning essential help in order to lead a fuller life. Both require that information and advice is given in an honest manner but that the decision rests with the consumer. It is the lack of integrity in the retail trades that has given rise to the somewhat suspect reputation of the 'used car salesman'. It is necessary however to consider the extent to which the failure of local authorities to provide information and choice, with the collusion of social work methods that blame individuals for their disability while ignoring the environmental factors, will give rise to the analogy of the 'used car salesman'. In other words 'would you buy a package of care from this social worker?'

Financial context

To seriously consider disabled people acquiring the services they need, in whatever environment they choose to live, the financial context of service delivery must be considered. Historically, local authorities have planned budgets on the basis of bureaucratic and political assumptions with little or no consultation with service recipients. Assessments have to be carried out by people who, if they are not budget controllers themselves, have an awareness of the limits set by others. Budgets are committed to resources which are largely personnel or buildings and therefore remain a commitment of the authority for years ahead. What planning that does take place is unlikely to reflect individual needs or actual trends. Neither will it allow for the type of flexibility that disabled people need.

The effect of this style of financial management is that assessments are likely to be resource led rather than needs led. Assessments are carried out by people who have access only to part of the resources, and those people may lack sufficient knowledge to make use of more appropriate services. It is also likely that those who have responsibility for budgets will provide only what they feel can be afforded and justify that position by tailoring the assessment to the budgetary limitations. While much training goes into this problem, the basic conflict of giving social workers a role, not unlike the social fund officer, is ignored.

The changes proposed by the government in the 1989 community care White Paper will extend this role and increase the conflict. Central to the White Paper's proposals is the case manager. This is a role that the government envisage being undertaken by a range of professional workers from both health and local authorities, though primarily the latter. The roles of the case manager are described as: identification of people in need, including systems for referral; assessment of care needs; planning and securing the delivery of care; monitoring the quality of care provided; and review of client needs.[12] Although the provision of services is expected to be contracted out, case management will increase the extent to which individual workers are given responsibility for assessing needs and for rationing services. The British Association of Social Workers have proposed[13] that although they see the role of case manager as appropriately lying with social workers, the funding of services should lie with disabled people themselves through the payment of a Disability Allowance. In this way the case manager's role would become advisory and enabling, rather than having control over the provision of services.

Inadequate or inappropriately committed budgets give rise to the inability to provide services that will meet people's needs. Social workers find themselves in the position of having to decide whether to compensate for this or not. If the 1986 Act is ever fully implemented, it will mean that disabled people will have to be told of such failures to provide services, but currently there is a tendency to suggest that counselling will provide an alternative. The individual inadequacy model is of great assistance here to help justify such a view. However, just as it was never adequate to counsel people to help them live with poverty, so it is not adequate to view counselling as an alternative to services for disabled people.

Budgets affect the appropriateness of services according to whom they belong. While many services are provided by local authorities, responsibility for certain services lies elsewhere. Housing, except in metropolitan areas, lies with a different local authority and there is unlikely to be any cooperation or joint planning. Many services overlap with those of the health authority and the Department of Social Security is responsible for funding others. The problem that this creates is not simply one of bad planning, but as Tony Newton said to the Social Services Select Committee in 1985, '. . . too often we have a situation in which the one interest of every party is to pass the whole bill to someone else'. The effect of this is seen most clearly with inappropriate admissions to residential homes. People are admitted for reasons such as the lack of night home care services or the unavailability of mobility housing. Yet the availability of residential care is not scarce due to the fact that it has been funded by Income Support.

In this way many people have been segregated on the basis of convenience for the provision of services, at times when their needs should have been met in simpler and more appropriate ways. It is the lack of a single budget that causes this and will continue to do so after the reorganisation of community care. Only part of the problem is being addressed, that between the Department of Social Security and local authorities. What is not considered is that it is the control of budgets by able bodied people who fail to consult with disabled people that has led to inappropriate resource development. It is not simply a case of local authority bureaucracy being inefficient and the independent sector being able to provide solutions.

Over the ten years from 1979 to 1989 there was an eighty-fold increase in the DSS expenditure on residential and nursing home care in the independent sector. In the same period the expenditure on domicilliary services increased by slightly less than three times.[14] Does the increase in the residential care option reflect consumer choice or consumer lack of choice? Kenneth Clarke in his statement to the House in July 1989 described this as an incentive to local authorities to rely upon DSS funded residential care. The clear implication of that is that people are being denied choice in care. Sir Roy Griffiths referred to the Audit Commission's description of this in his report, *Agenda for Action*, as a perverse incentive.

Arguments that the growth in residential care, through adequate funding, has served to meet needs, is a fallacy, as no real alternatives have been provided to test the assumption. The demand for alternatives that would meet the deficits continues to grow, but they are largely ignored due to the lack of planning, either jointly between authorities or with disabled people. Social workers are themselves handicapped in the task of enabling choice by the restrictions of such lack of planning. The government response to the Griffiths report is likely to achieve little in this respect, given that the report praises local authorities for their ability to plan flexibly for local needs and recommends an expansion of their responsibility. The idea that a local authority will carry a budget which remains uncommitted until the needs of an individual are known, runs contrary to the history and tradition of local government finance and means that services will not be tailored to meet individual needs.

Social attitudes and social work

Social work operates within a context of society and along with other professions it faces the dilemma of whether to be responsive to the society it serves, or to establish an independent position. Throughout the 1970s and 1980s there has been growing criticism of the police for their tendency towards a separatist position. It is felt by many people that they are unable to represent the wishes of society or to be part of the communities that they serve, and it has become necessary to implement special experiments in community policing to counteract the tendency. As social work has increased its social control role, it is tempting to establish its independence by means of professionalism. The emphasis of social work becomes one of intervening in the disfunction of the lives of individuals and families where people are thought to be at risk, rather than one of acting as a resource to communities so that risks are minimised.

As with the police, the focus moves clearly to the concept of offenders and victims, with the social work agency acting in a detached and purportedly independent manner, but as with the police this will lead to a loss of confidence on the part of the community. However, if social work were to be responsive to society, it is necessary to consider the position of social work clients within that system. Generally it is a position of powerlessness that leads people to become clients and for disabled people it is a position that has been defined by able bodied people. It is difficult to see how, in an age of consumerism dominated by monetary policies, relatively powerless people can hope to compete with those who are in power. The result will be that the social work task will not be concerned with assisting disabled people as the ones directly affected by disablement, but will primarily be a means of ensuring that they will not be an inconvenience to able bodied people. Sufficient help is offered to ensure that society feels free of any further responsibility but empowerment is discouraged as threatening to those in power. This policing of disability, as with any other form of policing, is a means of containing offenders and safeguarding victims. As with other aspects of society, it is those who have most power who will determine who the offenders and victims are.

Social workers reflect the prevailing attitudes of society in respect of the notion of citizenship and the status of disabled people within it. The necessity for special legislation reflects a different status for disabled people. The subsequent failure to implement the legislation indicates that able bodied people are granted a higher status. This is reinforced by local authorities, voluntary agencies and the social workers within them, who have collectively ensured that the bulk of monies available to assist disabled people has been spent on ensuring their segregation and their registration. The creation of segregated institutions and the identification of individuals results from the dominance of the individual model of disability. The motives that led to the development of isolated care may have been benevolent, such as to move people out of the pollution of city life or to protect them from exploitation, but the exploitation by the institution is still largely ignored. Segregation ensures that society does not have to change itself, rather that disabled people have to adapt to society if they wish to leave those parts that have been allocated to them.

Although modern care planners have put a facade of integration on both residential and community care institutions, the attitude of unequal citizenship prevails. This is most vividly illustrated by the attitude of professions and employers towards friendships that develop between care givers and care receivers. The social work profession and their employers maintain a position, in common with other groups in the paramedical field, that personal relationships between workers and clients may constitute an abuse of power. This position rightly recognises the powerlessness of disabled people, but it fails to recognise that that position is caused by external factors, including the policies of social work agencies, rather than as resulting from personal inadequacies. This professional posturing reinforces the lesser status of citizenship afforded to disabled people.

Equally, the argument is put that personal friendships might lead to workers acting favourably towards some people and therefore doing a disservice to others. This argument fails to recognise that the concept of favouritism only occurs in an environment of insufficient resources and where others are appointed to ration them. Disabled people are seen as people with individual inadequacies who are vying for the attention of social workers rather than as people who are asserting their rights. What is clear is that social workers and their agencies remain committed to ensuring that vulnerable people are protected from personal exploitation, but fail to see that the label of vulnerability itself is part of the institutional exploitation and that it is disabling.

Attitudes are also reflected in the role of case conferences, which gather together large numbers of people, often excluding the subject of the conference, in order to discuss that person's inadequacies. Many social workers have tried to involve their clients in case conferences and have attempted to concentrate the discussion on the person's abilities rather than disabilities, but such attempts can constitute a denial of the purpose of the conference. First, the discussion of a person's inabilities is quite likely to take place informally, elsewhere. Second, the main purpose for social work involvement with a disabled person is to provide services to meet the needs that arise out of their disability, so ignoring it becomes facile. What social attitudes do not allow for, is the possibility of turning the whole process on its head, so as to join with disabled people in case conferences that examine the effectiveness of social workers and agencies in meeting their needs. In this way we could move away from the individual focus and begin to assess the adequacy of service provision.

Conclusions

Much of the social work tasks with disabled people in the 1990s will be governed by the existing legislation and that which will follow from the 1989 White Paper, *Caring for People*. It is clear that although the 1948 Act and its provision of segregated services was intended to be superseded by the 1970 Act, the failure of local authorities to implement the latter has meant that people remain disabled. Parliament has seen fit to pass the 1986 Act, which was drafted in consultation with disabled people. This Act lays the blame for inadequate implementation of the 1970 Act on the failure of local authorities to involve disabled people in the assessment of their own needs. This Act has profound implications for social workers, their agencies and for social work practice. However, it remains only partially implemented and the government has put before parliament an alternative strategy in *Caring for People*, which supports the record of local authorities. It ensures that their budgetary structures offer no security to the services for disabled people and appoints able bodied people to manage their care. The only diminution of the role of local authorities will be in the handing over of services to the independent sector, whose record in the 1980s has been mainly one of tremendous growth of segregated resources. [15]

The position of disabled people relative to able bodied people is unlikely to improve significantly. Although the structure for change exists within the 1970 and 1986 Acts, it would take a determined shift of social policy and a willingness of able bodied people to relinquish power for change to take place. Social work practice is commonly referred to as intervention. Social workers intervene in the lives of others for the purpose of meeting their welfare needs. At present social work intervention into the lives of disabled people occurs because of the power that social workers represent regarding access to resources. Social workers need to recognise this and then return to their code of ethics to question the way in which they carry out their task - whether they are colluding with social control or are empowering disabled people.

References

1. BASW. *Code of Ethics*. BASW, 1975, 2.

2. Fiedler, B. *Living Options Lottery*. Prince of Wales Advisory Group on Disability, 1988, 69.

3. *Caring for People*. HMSO, 1989.

4. Oliver, M. 'The Social Model of Disability: Current Reflections'. In Jeffs, T., Smith, P. et al. *Social Work and Social Welfare Yearbook*. Open University Press, 1989.

5. Topliss, E. and Gould, B. *A Charter for the Disabled*. Blackwell and Robertson, 1981, 136-138.

6. Topliss, E. *Social Responses to Handicap*. Longman, 1982, 108.

7. Cook, J. and Mitchell, P. *Putting Teeth into the Act*. RADAR, 1982.

8. Shearer, A. *Centers for Independant Living in the US and UK - American Viewpoint*. King's Fund Centre, 1984, 1.

9. Bailey, R. and Brake, M. *Radical Social Work*. E. Arnold, 1975, 8-9.

10. Oliver, M. *Social Work with Disabled People*. Macmillan, 1983, 15-18.

11. Miller, E.J. and Gwynne, G.V. *A Life Apart*. Tavistock, 1972, 212-214.

12. *Caring for People*. HMSO, 1989, 21-22.

13. BASW. *Whose Choice*. BASW, 1989.

14. *Caring for People*. HMSO, 1989, 99.

15. Sir Roy Griffiths. *Community Care - Agenda for Action*. HMSO, 1988, 7.

Social Work in a Traditional Setting

Patrick Phelan and Simon Cole

RSB Leatherhead, originally St George's School at Blackfriars in London, owes its beginnings to four gentlemen who in 1799 formed the charity which remains today the basis of the organisation. In 1905 the present building in Leatherhead was completed and in 1911 the charity was granted the title 'Royal' by King George V who at the same time became patron. In the Annual Report of 1929 we read of the place as

> . . . a little world of its own with its workshops and sales room, its clerical offices, its chapel, gymnasium, laundry, dormitories, hospital and dental surgery, its power house and extensive grounds and kitchen gardens. Its situation amid the wealthy Surrey countryside makes it an ideal residence for the blind who are usually so delicate.

Deference to this delicacy may have been the reason for excluding from the list of amenities mention of the mortuary.

During the early part of this century RSB Leatherhead enjoyed a reputation as one of the foremost in Europe among training establishments for blind people. It provided training in crafts and trades to young adults who went on to employment elsewhere. In the late 1940s the charity's function began to change under the influence of social trends and it embarked on the provision of permanent residential accommodation for multi-handicapped visually impaired people.

Implications of this change of function appear not to have been considered and the practice of the past, which suited a craft and trade training establishment, seems to have been assumed appropriate for the provision of permanent residential accommodation. Two major implications which went unconsidered in this way were the rise in the average age of the resident population and the unsuitability of the building for its new function.

By the late 1960s the establishment had become a mausoleum of nineteenth century ideas and ideals. The mainly middle-aged residents were still referred to as 'the boys and girls', men and women were segregated, unless in groups under supervision, and it was necessary for a couple to obtain permission from the chaplain to 'walk out together'. If granted the dispensation would be notified in writing to the parents of the adults concerned. Attendance at chapel was compulsory and meals were taken in a communal dining room where at breakfast porridge was served from a galvanised bucket. Delicate dispositions were protected from the harshness of this by not being able to see the vessel in question.

In 1976 RSB Leatherhead was described as

> . . . an imposing red brick edifice, secluded in attractive grounds; long echoing corridors; almost equally long draughty wards, antique plumbing and other services and a seemingly total lack of privacy. A traditional relationship prevailed between certain staff and the 'boys and girls' . . . which did not encourage them to be independent.

This was a 1976 view of a 1901 establishment which by all accounts had remained untouched by the changes and chances of three quarters of a century.

When commenting on the values and styles of our forbears in social care we do well to temper our hindsight with humility. What we ourselves plan and provide today may itself tomorrow appear harsh or haphazard, ramshackle or roughshod. The warning is well put in the words of Christopher Fry: 'There may yet be another reality to make fiction of the truth we have already arrived at.' It remains that in the mid 1970s RSB Leatherhead had become fossilised in an existence where adults acted as knowing what was best for other adults with no thought of discussion or consultation with them. Answers were prescribed without questions ever being put, the aforementioned traditional relationship between staff and residents.

In 1977 a quiet riot began. Under the influence of the newly appointed Director the words 'rights', 'dignity', 'choice' became the order of the day in order to restore to people what should never have been removed from them in the first place. This was a process of rehabilitation which recognised the enormity of the circumstances it was setting out to rectify. The original meaning of rehabilitation was the restoration of honours to a person from whom they had been formally stripped on account of a crime or misdemeanour. The modern application of the term, in restoring dignities and opportunities to guiltless people, carries a sinister implication which requires scrutiny. It denotes an unequal relationship between superior and inferior where no inequality has been proven.

The first stage of the development programme, the quiet riot, was the renovation of the building. The imposing red brick edifice is a listed building, protected by statute from change. The long echoing corridors within and the almost equally long draughty wards did not enjoy such privilege and became the object of architectural re-design and re-building activity, what by the 1980s became all the rage as refurbishment. The antique plumbing went while the attractive grounds were retained but the seclusion they represented was dispelled by the very removal of the iron gates to the world outside. The mausoleum was on the way to becoming a living community. The standard presupposed answers given by staff, 'This is what you do', gave way to individual and debatable questions asked by residents, 'Shall I?' or 'Shan't I?', with corollaries such as 'I might or then I might not'. Dormitories for twenty-four people with half private, and therefore half public, cubicles gave way to flats for ten people, each with a single room and sharing domestic amenities and areas. A few of the staff survived the riot; most departed under its impact, a particular couple uttering to the Director the subsequently time honoured paradox, ' If you carry on like this you'll soon have the residents running the place.' Never has one person's aspiration been so unlovingly enshrined in another's denunciation.

By 1985, after seven years of upheaval characterised by the noise and dust of building works, the second part of the development programme was ready for initiation. The architect and the builders, by means of blueprints and bulldozers, had transformed the building. The riot was now extended to the practice inside the building. Bulldozers were exchanged for social workers and the blueprint of maximum independence for each individual was adopted as the basis of the operation. The quiet riot turned its attention from bricks to mortals and the traditional relationship between staff and residents was confronted and confounded.

The building as it had been had offered scant scope for ordinary living. There were limits on possessions, there were limits to arrangements for eating and drinking, there were limits on the clothes which could be worn and limits on how time could be spent. To redress all this limitation on living the social care policy of maximum independence was devised, maximum independence being ordinary living.

The residents had been involved in the development programme from its beginning by means of the Director listening to them as he encouraged them to express for themselves their own aspirations. This listening came into even greater prominence with the introduction of the policy and practice of maximum independence.

At RSB Leatherhead social work is listening, with the objective of upholding individual rights and responsibilities, respecting human dignity and enabling personal choice, which are the three elements of maximum independence. Listening requires time and leads to having to take trouble. Daily at RSB Leatherhead we are learning why institutions, even if nowadays comparatively small in size, remain popular with service providers; they are easy to run, with a place for everyone and everyone in his or her place, all planned and decided by the providers, who consider they know best for the recipients without reference to them. Our commitment to listening springs from our conviction that the process of institutionalising people takes very little time. Once personal freedom of choice has been denied and personal privacy removed the slippery slope towards feeling undervalued and uncared for becomes a fast and furious downward spiral towards despondency, desperation and depression and, finally and most sadly, acceptance.

Reversing these effects, we have discovered, involves a long and often difficult journey because the restoration of privacy and the right to make choices is in itself insufficient. These features of ordinary living provide only an opportunity for action which is the lesser element in the complex equation of positive choice and maximum independence. It is awakening the freedom of spirit which will bring life to opportunity for action which makes the social work task of overcoming the effects of institutional living time and energy consuming. Giving to the people who live at RSB Leatherhead keys to their own rooms was easy. The architect created sufficient single rooms and the locksmith fitted each with a lock and the social workers distributed the keys. That having been done it would be easy to assume that privacy reigned supreme and that the journey on the road to maximum independence was under way. Keys, however, are only tokens; in their own right they have little value. Turning the token into an item of worth is what in fact puts people on to the right road. It is an inescapable truth that most of us living ordinary lives have to arrange to be at home in order to let in the plumber we have asked to repair the dripping tap. At RSB Leatherhead the plumber is not let in with that undeniable sign of the institution, the Master Key, but is let in to do the necessary work by the resident who requested the visit in the first place. Even when the door happens to have been left unlocked staff do not fling it open with the words, 'It's only me!' but knock and wait to be invited in and, if there is no reply, go away.

Through every contact which we have with residents we endeavour to provide choices whether it be for example in compiling shopping lists, choosing what to do and where to go for a leisure activity or deciding what response to make to the suggestion of medical treatment. We have developed skills in helping through listening out of a commitment to responding to the challenge of offering choice to people whose expectation born out of experience is that they have none. We have confronted and overcome the paralysis which pervades when choice is first offered, the initial hankering to return to the golden age when all decisions were made by the houseparents. We have worked alongside the fearfulness which accompanies the opportunity to choose. We have grown with the residents as they have discovered that hand in hand with choice comes responsibility and we have weathered the eventual disbelief and anger which is inevitable in the emotions of adults who begin to exercise rights and responsibilities previously denied by other adults. 'Why didn't they tell us we could do all this before? What right had they to treat us all like children? I know it's better late than never but they should never have been allowed to treat us like they did.'

Now in his late fifties George was making a cup of tea for himself for the first time in his life when his satisfaction with the achievement turned to disbelief and anger as he recognised what he had been denied all his life. Helping George to acquire the practical skills of making a cup of tea had been straightforward, using the standard techniques of rehabilitation work, but it had taken weeks of patient listening and gentle persuasion to enable him even to consider that 'they' might have been wrong when they had told him that he could not do such a thing.

The provision of a service of residential care for adults has, at all times, to put the consumer first. The method of working which we have been developing since 1986 at RSB Leatherhead is essentially a way of translating the truth into action. A number of challenges present themselves when you provide a service in the face of a long established order. Traditionally, RSB Leatherhead had operated from the point of view of the staff. This is not unusual in residential establishments for adults, where a casual observer might gain the impression that the staff are the focus of the place and that others are there by grace and favour. At RSB Leatherhead we are endeavouring to maintain as our fundamental emphasis the point of view of the people who live in the place. This mode of operation is neither magical nor mystical and is, in fact, straightforward and simple. Like any cultural development it is an evolving and fluid process, ordinary life, as opposed to a strict code of rules and regulations, institutional existence. It is a process and way of being which enables residents and staff alike to value each other as people and to appreciate the contribution which each makes in the pursuit of agreed objectives and towards the fulfilment of shared tasks.

Viewing a different culture for the first time may be perplexing and at odds with received ideas and RSB Leatherhead is no exception to this general rule and we are accustomed to causing eyebrows to be raised in professional circles. Interaction between residents and staff has a quality which characterises the work of the organisation as being truly committed to the spirit of consumer first. As well as their competence, staff are required to possess the ability to adopt the spirit of never knowing better without asking the resident first. In ordinary life this is common courtesy; in social care it is rare to the extent of requiring us to invent a descriptive phrase. Within this simple method there are, we find, infinite complexities to be invented by those without our simplicity. Administrative convenience is the arch enemy; if a policy, a practice or a procedure is described as administratively convenient it is likely to be at odds with the principle of consumer first with its emphasis on serving the person before suiting the system.

Crucial to this style of working is the selection of staff. Our service is to adults and they have the right to be involved as realistically as possible in the process of staff selection. We achieve this involvement by means of the opportunities which we have created within the selection process which enable residents and applicants to spend time together. Applicants are shortlisted by senior managers by considering application forms in close detail and the benefit of any doubt is given to the applicant. We believe it is better to have interviewed and rejected than not to have interviewed at all.

The selection day begins with coffee and then a visit to the flat where the staff vacancy exists in order to meet the people who live there. This is an opportunity for residents to form an opinion of the applicant and for staff involved in the selection process to gauge the quality of interaction between applicant and clients. The ability of the applicant sensitively to initiate and to conclude conversations is a skill we value and this can be assessed in a short space of time. Next the applicant has lunch with the residents and staff. Sharing meals is a very important element of residential life and a meal together provides another opportunity to form opinions of a person's potential as a worker.

After lunch the formal interview takes place with two or three senior staff and increasingly we are able to persuade two residents to participate in the process. (Two, because they feel that there is safety in numbers.) It goes without saying that as adults they have the entitlement to be involved fully in the formal selection. Unfortunately it is often the case that matters which go without saying in social care also go without being done. Generally speaking if you take care over the courtesies the complexities fall into insignificance. In our experience at RSB Leatherhead this maxim applies soundly to the inclusion of residents in the process of staff selection.

The questions posed during the formal interview focus on personal qualities and life experiences and we are proud of our ability to put even the most anxious applicant at ease. We recommend opening with, 'Thank you for your application form and thank you very much for coming today.' With experienced workers we look for an element of excitement about their work and about what they have seen of what we are offering. We ask how they might change the style of working at their present place of employment and look for answers which reflect a wish to improve the quality of life for consumers in a creative and imaginative way. After the formal interview comments are sought from all residents and staff who have participated in the selection process and then a final decision is made for notification to the applicant. It is extremely rare for the decision to be less than unanimous, rare to the extent that it has so far happened only once in five years and on that occasion the residents' opposition to an appointment was overruled. The appointment proved to be a failure. Where there is doubt among staff we use as a key question to ourselves, 'Would I feel comfortable with this person reading a private letter to me?' This is a frequent task in work with people with visual impairment and its performance can be an acid test of sensitivity, honesty and respect for the individual. Tasks of similar intimacy are undertaken in other provisions of social care and they equally lend themselves to this application in assessing an applicant's suitability.

In due course the newly appointed member of staff takes up his or her post. This is one of the most exciting periods of our work. The new worker shares shifts with an experienced colleague and is encouraged to watch, listen, join in and question. At the same time some simple guidelines are taught in order to convey a cultural awareness of RSB Leatherhead's principles, aims and objectives.

We consider the guidelines simple, but again, the simple, the obvious is often the overlooked or disregarded. A first rule for a worker is that if you find yourself doing anything alone, ask yourself why you are alone. Are you denying the person or people for whom you are doing it the choice to participate and the opportunity to develop? Another rule is that if you hear being used such phrases as, 'We've always done it that way' or, 'We've tried that before and it didn't work', whether said by residents or staff, you should challenge them. The Golden Rule for beginning workers is, 'If you don't know, ask a resident.' Invariably residents either know the answer or know who will.

We value workers who recognise when they need to ask and who do so, as opposed to blundering on, pretending a knowledge or skill and doing nobody any service at all. This applies, of course, in the human, listening work we do. It applies equally in the practicalities of domesticity, which at RSB Leatherhead are shared by residents and staff. It is important for a worker to have some ability to carve a joint of meat before undertaking the responsibility of keeping Sunday lunch on an even keel for a group of eight visually impaired people. It is a context in which behaving as if you can and hoping for the best does not produce acceptable results. Even so mistakes are upheld as opportunities to learn. We regard risk as a means of promoting growth and forming identity and through a staff supervision structure staff development is monitored and assessed.

In the first few months a new member of staff encounters a range of challenges. They vary from person to person but possess some common characteristics. The challenge of work recognition is one such characteristic and it is often to be found in staff who have previously worked in structured environments. At RSB Leatherhead the ability both to recognise and to create opportunity for work is of paramount importance and a skill which requires careful nurturing in the guidance. It is not invariably apparent as to how the principle of maximum independence may be applied in a particular circumstance but our experience has taught us that almost always there is a way. To this end staff initiative is encouraged and valued within a framework of collaborative team working, which is in itself supportive of both residents and staff. An excess of individual initiative leads to an incoherent and reactionary style of working whilst an insufficiency is the cause of uninspired and uncreative practice. In social care obtaining and retaining a balance between the two is crucial.

The style of working employed at RSB Leatherhead is highly dependent on staff being valued and well supported. The workers are regarded as the consumers of an inner service, one which aims to provide them with the support they require in order to fulfil a difficult and demanding role. In this context supervision belongs to the worker and is primarily for the sake of the worker rather than of the organisation. It is designed to provide a structure of support for the worker and an opportunity for the consideration of work practices. Training is an integral part of staff development and we operate an in-house training programme, devised and run by our fully qualified Team Managers Group and aimed mainly at enhancing interpersonal skills such as careful listening and appropriate assertion.

Daily changeovers between staff provide a regular opportunity for peer discussion of challenges being faced as part of the working day. Much of the actual instruction in working practices is conveyed by experienced team members modelling good practice to the new worker and being prepared to answer questions and explain the purpose of procedures. Our principles are simple and may be said to be obvious. They are now widespread in practice and we find that in their apparent fragility they require constant demonstration in practice in order to be fully maintained. While we do not talk in terms of a therapeutic milieu, we do believe that every contact between worker and client can and should reflect our principles and aims in practice.

The social work management team of six are all qualified social workers. This heightens our concern at the very low number of formally trained staff working in residential social services. We are disturbingly aware that we ask a great deal of staff who are largely untrained and often with little experience. By endeavouring to provide a high standard of service to residents through untrained staff we do feel that the workers concerned gain experience which stands them in good stead for a career in any aspect of social care and provides a reliable stepping stone towards formal training. We actively encourage workers to involve themselves in the wider realms of social care through short courses, seminars and conferences since we have much still to learn as well as a range of valuable experience through practice to contribute.

At the end of the eighteenth century Jeremy Bentham, the founder of utilitarian philosophy, was formulating his ideas concerning the design and structure of establishments in which people could most humanely be kept under inspection. He envisaged such establishments as being, among other places, prisons, poor houses, work houses, mad houses and schools, and considered that there were principles of management common to them all. He published his first pamphlet proposing the panopticon in 1791 and in 1799 parliamentary approval was given for the erection of a prison according to his specification but nothing came of the plan. Also in 1799 the plan was created for a school for the indigent blind and it did come to fruition. It is in operation today as RSB Leatherhead and we like to think that the principles by which we work are in accordance with the humane aims of Bentham's utilitarian philosophy. Within the tradition of our setting our social work practice is today based on the principle of putting residents first in order that their choices may be given prime consideration. It may sound simple; it is not straightforward; it is inescapably right.

Social Work in an Organisation of Disabled People

Etienne d'Aboville

The last five years have seen a number of developments which are of significance both to social work and to the lives of disabled people. On the plus side we have seen the disabled people's movement move from strength to strength and the rise and consolidation of the carers' movement. On the minus side we have witnessed a time of economic constraint that has led to the erosion of many statutory services and to a harsh Social Security Act that even threatened the ability of some disabled people to continue living in the community. Parts of the Disabled Persons (Services, Consultation and Representation) Act 1986, which promised to improve the legal framework of local authorities' responsibilities, remain unimplemented four years after it reached the Statute Book.

Changes over the coming five years could be of still greater significance. In theory, the NHS and Community Care Act (1990) will radically alter the way social services departments respond to their clients' needs, forcing them to become service 'arrangers' rather than simply 'providers'. Whether the rhetoric of community care will be backed by sufficient resources to do the job properly remains extremely doubtful. The delay in implementation of the Act until 1993 only emphasises the fragility of the relationship between policy and practice. But even if adequate resources are made available, there is no guarantee that the new legislation will be translated into services and attitudes that reflect disabled people's own desire for genuine choice and autonomy. Doubts remain, not only about resources, but about assessment, consultation, training and the role of so-called 'care managers'. Further delays and confusion over the timescale of implementation seem inevitable.

What is certain is that an attitude change *is* required. Traditional social work can itself disable people if it does not recognise that services must reflect the choices and needs expressed by disabled people themselves. This view will be argued below in the context of an alternative model of social work as represented by the Welfare Service of an organisation controlled by disabled people.

Spinal cord injury

Prior to the Second World War most people with a spinal cord injury rarely survived beyond the first few weeks or months after injury as pressure sores and infections took their toll. Largely through the pioneering work of Sir Ludwig Guttmann at Stoke Mandeville Hospital and Donald Munro in the United States, techniques were developed which now mean that even those with high spinal cord injury (SCI) lesions can expect to live long and, with some care, comparatively healthy lives.

Nevertheless, experiencing a spinal cord injury is likely to have a significant impact on a person's life and will, at the very least, have far-reaching implications regarding the practical details of their everyday life. Most, though by no means all, injuries are incurred traumatically and the physical consequences may include substantial paralysis, loss of sensation, loss of voluntary bladder and bowel control, changed sexual function and disruption to the automatic nervous system (which controls sweating and blood pressure). Naturally, immediate and acute medical intervention is necessary, first to save the person's life and then to stabilise the injury so that the rehabilitation programme can begin. Doctors, nurses, physiotherapists, occupational therapists and social workers are only some of the professionals involved in this process, which may take anything between four to twelve months depending on the neurological level of the spinal cord lesion and the extent of other injuries.

While considerable progress has been made in the treatment of the medical complications of SCI, and indeed the standard of medical care in the specialist regional spinal injury units (SIU) remains very high, the potential long term practical and emotional problems of living as a paraplegic or tetraplegic have not received the same attention. (Paraplegia involves paralysis of the trunk and lower limbs, while tetraplegia (or quadriplegia) also affects the arms and hands).

Some SIUs are at last beginning to address seriously the potential psychological implications of SCI, for instance by employing the services of a clinical psychologist or by using group work involving experienced SCI people. However, in general, the potential for peer counselling and peer support as a way of mitigating psychological distress remains largely unexplored in this country. While it is wrong to assume that emotional and psychological problems are an *inevitable* consequence of SCI, the experience has nevertheless been, for many people, one of extreme emotional distress and isolation (Oliver, Zarb, Silver, Moore and Salisbury[1]). This has been the case even more, perhaps, for women who may be less likely to respond to the 'stiff upper lip', 'sink or swim' philosophy which has historically dominated the rehabilitation process in the majority of SIUs (Morris[2]).

The comparative neglect of psychological issues has been accompanied by the lack of a sound theoretical basis for understanding psychological reactions after SCI. Traditional theories have relied almost exclusively on the 'personal tragedy' model, an interpretation challenged by many authors including Trieschmann[3] and Oliver.[4] The true complexities of immediate and longer term individual reactions to SCI are better represented by the notion of the 'disability career' (see Carver,[5] Oliver[1]). The concept of the disability career is an attempt to acknowledge the multidimensional nature of the question of social adjustment to disability. This process of adjustment is better represented by a complex series of interactions between individuals and their physical and social environments, and is mediated by the meanings these interactions have for the individuals and their families, than by a single unitary process with stages which follow each other in a specific order:

> However, . . . the relationship between satisfaction with disability (social adjustment) and time is not a simple one but is related to a whole range of other factors, material and social. Whether it is possible to return to work; how suitable housing is and how long it takes to obtain it; levels of income, which may change over time; the delays in compensation settlements; and so on: these are all factors which make time a crucial component of social adjustment. It is not a matter of 'time being a great healer', but of the speed (or lack of it) with which support services are mobilised, as well as changing perceptions and relationships that occur throughout the disability career. Each of these factors may be different for each individual, so social adjustment is not about following a fixed path through fixed stages but rather about negotiating a passage through the disability career.[1]

When it comes to confronting the range of difficulties faced by SCI people when they return to the community, the traditionally professionally organised and medically dominated spinal injury service and the community based social work services have generally been inadequate to the task. In their study of seventy-seven ex-Stoke Mandeville patients, Oliver et al. (page 89)[1] concluded:

> Everyone we interviewed had their own individual perceptions of what they required from the various services available. Such needs did not remain static; the kind of support required over the disability career is characterised by changing

combinations of medical, emotional, practical and social support. However, administrative fragmentation and service providers' narrow definitions of need often mean that services are too inflexible to respond to people's evolving requirements.

Delays in the supply of aids and equipment, inadequate accessible housing, arranging sufficient personal assistance support - these are just some of the problems which can face SCI people on discharge from hospital. Longer term issues such as employment, finance and the pursuit of leisure activities are further difficulties which have remained relatively untouched by traditional statutory services.

It was an awareness of issues such as these - which went beyond the short term problem of simply surviving the injury, but went on to question just what kind of quality of life could be expected in the long term - which led to the formation of the Spinal Injuries Association (SIA).

The Spinal Injuries Association

The SIA was set up in 1974 as a self-help group to provide information and support to people with spinal cord injuries and to articulate their needs in a way which the traditional spinal injury service could not. However, it was not set up in opposition to the medical and paramedical service, but as a complement to it.

Hasler and Oliver[6] have located the development of SIA within the historical context of the growth in self-help organisations as a whole, from the creation of working men's associations in the nineteenth century to their resurgence in the late 1960s and early 1970s. It is sufficient to say here that, along with other self-help groups in the area of health, SIA is different from traditional human service agencies in three major respects (Robinson and Henry[7]). First, all its members share a common experience - all Full Members (ie voting members) must have a spinal cord injury. Second, there is reciprocity of helping amongst these members, in this case through the sharing of information and advice. Finally, the group is self-managing. In SIA, this is effected through a democratically elected Management Committee which is composed of spinal cord injured people and which can co-opt non SCI people.

The Association rapidly developed from a small organisation, with a single paid General Secretary and 300 members, to its present state where there are twenty full-time and two part-time staff, plus a number of volunteers. There are currently over 5,000 members, of whom three quarters are Full (ie SCI) Members.

The philosophy of the Association has both individual and collective dimensions. It is individual in the sense that members are assisted in achieving their own goals themselves. Assistance may be provided in the form of information, advice and support, either from paid staff or from other members, but individuals are encouraged to solve their own problems rather than expecting to have them solved for them. It is collective in the sense that SIA seeks to identify members' needs, for example via questionnaires, and to articulate them to statutory and political bodies at both the local and national level.

The basic 'enabling' philosophy of the Association finds expression in SIA's main services. An Information Service provides information on aids and equipment as well as accessible holiday facilities; there are specialist holiday and legal services, and a quarterly Newsletter is packed with articles and ideas, *without* the usual pictures of cheques being gratefully received by ever-cheerful wheelchair users! SIA has published a number of books including one on employment and *So You're Paralysed* . . . - a basic guide to living with spinal cord injury for the newly-injured which has been translated into five languages.

The Welfare Service

There was, from the start, a recognition that many members required more than simply information to achieve their aims, but it was only when resources allowed, in 1980, that it was decided to set up, in addition, a specialist, professionally structured Welfare Service. No suitable model existed on which to base the new service and it was thus necessary to invent an appropriate one.

It was decided early on that a traditional casework service would not be appropriate. The reasons for this were threefold. First, as a national organisation the Association could not hope to resource the large number of staff required to cover such a large geographical area. Large amounts of resources would be wasted in travelling to and fro and it was doubted whether this approach could ever be effective without the service being organised on a regional basis. Second, the philosophy of the Association was one of self-help and a casework approach was seen as inappropriate in principle. Finally, we saw many of our members' problems as socially or culturally derived rather than as purely individual problems and we wanted this to be reflected in our approach.

It was also clear from our members' experiences that the traditional professional social work model had in most cases failed our members (see also Shearer[8]). This was not simply because the emphasis and resources devoted to physical disability in social services departments was (and is) minuscule in comparison, for instance, to that devoted to more politically sensitive client groups such as children or elderly people (Barclay,[9] SSI[10]). It is perhaps even more to do with the fundamental approach of traditional social work practice. Traditional methods of social work linking into rigid and inappropriate services have been regarded by disabled people as, at best, irrelevant to their needs and, at worst, a positive obstacle to the chosen lifestyle. Commenting on his own experience of trying to arrange a personal assistance scheme providing flexible, user-controlled care support, Ford[11] writes:

> The experience has been one of a frustrating battle, both personally and for others assisting me. The inability of my social worker within Staffordshire to secure any progress and the consequent professional intimidation that I understand was experienced when trying to progress my case, is one more example of the non-productive forces which come into play when collaboration fails to take place.
>
> I learnt the importance of peer support and experienced the very reassuring help of committed advocates. I was fortunate in having this commitment of others, their positive and effective collaboration highlighted its absence elsewhere.

It was this failure on the part of the professionals to collaborate, to help facilitate the choices and aspirations of the individual, that highlighted the need for a different approach based on self-help and an agenda set by disabled people themselves.

Hence, it was recognised that the approach adopted by some charities of simply raising money and disbursing grants to individuals in financial difficulties would only serve to perpetuate the existing power relationship between an oppressive society (and its concomitant stereotypes of disabled people as either heroes or victims[8]) and disabled people themselves.

What was needed was a way of empowering disabled people by providing the information and support they need to act for themselves. Central to this self-help philosophy is a social definition of disability.

The individual and social models of disability

Within the social model, as opposed to the medical or individual model, disability is seen as arising not as the direct result of an impairment, but out of the interaction between an impaired individual and an essentially hostile environment. Thus, the Union for the Physically Impaired Against Segregation (UPIAS) define disability as,

The disadvantage or restriction of activities caused by contemporary social organisation which takes little or no account of people with physical impairment and thus excludes them from participating in the mainstream of social activities.[12]

Put simply, the social model focuses on the steps, not the wheelchair. Disability is seen, therefore, as a particular form of social oppression, rather than an individual problem. This social concept of disability may not, on its own, have sufficient explanatory power to address the way disabled people actually behave and feel about disability as it does not explicitly include the range of meanings that disability can have for different individuals. It is nevertheless highly significant because it immediately raises the possibility of alternative social arrangements more suited to the requirements of disabled people, arrangements which would facilitate their participation in society and actively change the experience of disability.

Social work theories and practice which are based on the individual model of disability generally start from the position that impairment is itself the source of disabled people's problems. According to this model, people who become disabled must necessarily experience their disability as loss and must therefore experience the phases of shock, denial, anger and depression before they can 'come to terms' with their disability (Berger,[13] Weller and Miller[14]). Thus, as one social worker put it:

> Patients must be allowed to come to terms, they must grieve and mourn for their lost limbs, lost abilities or lost looks and be helped to adjust to their lost body-image. Personally, I doubt if anyone who has not experienced the onset of irreversible disability can fully understand the horror of the situation (Dickinson[15]).

Finkelstein[15] has argued that such personal tragedy theories impose value judgements on disabled people which are based on able-bodied assumptions about the experience of disability.

Like any dominant paradigm, until such a time as it is discredited completely, this individual model is self-perpetuating in the way it spawns theory, research and practice. For SCI people it has resulted in the primary focus of rehabilitation being first, the maximising of physical independence and second, the 'adjustment' to the newly disabled status. Valuable though these intentions may be, neither addresses the social reality of disability.

The lack of emphasis on disability issues in social services departments has already been noted. The origins of this may be traced in part back to the organisational restructuring which followed the Seebohm Report. Satyamurti[17] has referred to the interprofessional rivalries which occurred between child care specialists and welfare department social workers as one factor determining the low status of disability issues in the new departments.

But clearly there are immense organisational and bureaucratic constraints on social workers and, in fact, the entire nature of the relationship between social workers and disabled people and between needs and resources is hugely problematical.

Social workers have often found themselves in the uncomfortable position of rationing scarce resources in the face of increasingly competing demands. Services have been determined, not by reference to the expressed needs of disabled people, but by political and economic considerations as interpreted by predominantly able-bodied professionals and local authority committees. Although Section 15 of the Chronically Sick and Disabled Persons Act (1970) places a requirement on local authorities to appoint at least one disabled person on committees not restricted to officers and members alone, the extent to which this has been effected is almost non-existent (Topliss and Gould[18]).

We shall now return to the issue of independent living to explore first, why the problem exists; second, how SIA's Welfare Service helps its members; and finally, how social workers might work *with* rather than simply *for* disabled people.

Independent living and the right to self-determination

The provision of domiciliary care support services is one example of how little existing services meet the needs of some disabled people and yet consume considerable resources in the process.

In the past, disabled people who need personal assistance support in order to remain living in the community have faced considerable difficulties in obtaining the amount and type of support they need (Fiedler[19]). Many rely on relatives, usually women, to provide this help, sometimes supplemented by patchy and inflexible statutory services. But where the individual is either unable or unwilling to place such responsibilities on relatives, there are no easy solutions unless s/he has sufficient resources to pay for private personal assistance support. Indeed, where a substantial amount of help is required, existing statutory services may sometimes be reluctant to become involved at all.

Even where domiciliary services are available, it is almost impossible to maintain an everyday, active lifestyle when reliant on a combination of home help, district nurse, meals on wheels, local care attendant service, community transport service etc. The design and delivery of these services are predicated on the assumption that disabled people are passive, inactive and, by no means least important, always at home to be 'helped'! Brechin and Liddiard[20] have listed no less than twenty-three different professionals who may be involved in helping the disabled person (a list to which we can, no doubt, now add the 'care manager').

But while the potential sources of professional intervention may be bewildering in number, they do not add up to anything like a coherent system of support, still less to one over which the disabled person can expect to have any significant degree of control. Where existing services do not meet the actual needs of the disabled person, such help as they are able to offer may often be rejected as too disruptive of that person's lifestyle (Zarb, Oliver and Silver[21]). Indeed, a cynic might argue that these services are deliberately designed as inappropriate so as to avoid too great a demand on them!

Increasingly, therefore, severely disabled people, including many tetraplegic members of SIA, are beginning to demand more flexible support services under their own direct control, services which actually enable them to lead the lives they choose. Personal assistance support workers (see Brisenden[22] for a critique of the term 'care') providing anything up to twenty-four hour support with personal, domestic, social and even employment activities can liberate even very severely disabled people, allowing them to participate and contribute towards their community in a way which able-bodied people take for granted.

A growing number of people for whom it had long been assumed that residential care was the only realistic option have demonstrated their ability to lead active lives integrated within the community if provided with appropriate support. Thus, it can be argued that it is the professionals' response to what they see as the 'problem' of disability, a response which has manifested itself in residential care establishments and inappropriate domiciliary services, which itself *disables* people with personal assistance needs.

The scale of the achievement involved in making such a transition from residential care into the community is not be underestimated. John Evans, founder of Hampshire Centre for Independent Living (and now Chair of the BCODP) described it thus:

> After many long and laborious soul-searching years, what was once a latent perception and hope finally became a reality. Five long years of hard work and strife, excitement and adventure, saw the struggle for independence, and a chosen lifestyle once again returned to me. It was a fact beyond words, a kind of liberation that emanated from the fact that I was the centre of the operation and it all rotated

around me. I was in control. The door to the rest of my life had been opened. It was now up to me to make the most of it.[23]

Central to the concept of independent living is the notion that independence is not a measure of how much a person can do for him/herself *physically unaided*. Rather, it is defined by the quality of control that a person is able to exercise over the important decisions that affect his/her life.

> ... independent living is about control, choice, participation, the ability to decide and to choose what a person wants - where to live and how, what to do and how to set about doing it. The goals or decisions about a person's life and the freedom to participate fully in the community have been, and will continue to be, the essence of independent living.[24]

Brisenden is unequivocal about the role that society plays in disabling people with impairments:

> In fact, the medical definition or model has to a great extent contributed to placing us outside society, in special institutions and ghettos. We desire a place *in society*, participating as equal members with something to say and a life to lead; we are demanding the right to take the same risks and seek the same rewards. Society disabled us by taking away our right to take decisions on our own behalf, and therefore the equality we are demanding is rooted in the concept of control; it stems from our desire to be individuals who can choose for themselves. People with disabilities are increasingly beginning to fight against structures that deprive us of control of, and responsibility for, ourselves, and hence leave us with no real chance of participation in society. We are the victims of a vicious circle, for the control that is denied the disabled individual by the medical profession, social services, relatives, etc., conditions that individual to accept a dependent status in which their life only takes place by proxy, resulting in them being unable to visualise independent ways of living.[25]

Disabled people and their own organisations continue to develop these concepts through co-operation nationally and internationally. In 1989 a seminar on personal assistance attended by over seventy severely disabled people from fourteen countries was held at the European Parliament in Strasbourg. The result was the formation of an international network on independent living and a set of resolutions concerning the principles on which personal assistance support provision should be based.[26]

SIA's Welfare Service aims to support those seeking to exercise their right to self-determination in a number of ways. First, by arranging peer support - putting them in touch with others who have already fought similar battles. Second, by collating and disseminating information based on the experience and advice of other members. Third, by contributing to the wider debate within the disabled people's movement on independent living issues at local, national and international level. Fourth, by articulating these issues (and examples of good practice) to social workers and administrators within social services departments and to Central Government. Fifth, by acting as a payment intermediary for some members whose support packages are funded by the local authority. Sixth, by providing a source of short-term help through the Care Attendant Agency. Finally, by seeking legislative changes which facilitate realisation of members' aspirations.

In early 1990, this last function has been especially focussed around the NHS and Community Care Bill and, in particular, the need to secure the legal right for local authorities to make direct payments to disabled people so as to allow them to pay for and control their own personal assistance.

By and large, those who have managed to set up their own self-directed personal assistance schemes have done so despite, rather than because of, the help of social services professionals. Suffolk[27,28] has detailed how social workers could actively contribute towards disabled people's emancipation by adopting the social model of disability and *promoting* disabled people's self-determination. One way they can do this is at the collective level by assisting disabled people's own efforts to organise themselves. For instance, Centres for Independent/Integrated Living (CILs) are becoming more widely established within the UK as they have been since the 1960s in the USA. Run by disabled people, they can, for example, act as a centre of expertise in such matters as independent living, peer counselling, aids and equipment; they can provide a source of consultation to the local authority; and, ideally, they can participate more actively in actual service provision. In the UK, this last function has been most clearly developed by the Derbyshire Centre for Integrated Living (Crosby and Davis[29]).

At the individual level, social workers must begin to renegotiate their very relationships with disabled people. They must seek to become a resource, facilitating the individual's own goals and aspirations rather than rigidly prescribing the terms of the relationship. They must seek to foster self-determination and decision making in those who, for whatever reason, may be unused to exercising these rights. This need not be a passive activity for social workers but, on the contrary, should prove challenging, stimulating and ultimately rewarding.

A closer look at the welfare service

It might be assumed that there is potential for conflict between the individual and social dimensions of the Welfare Service's work. This can occasionally lead to difficulties when, for instance, it is necessary to co-operate with charities operating in the 'traditional' mode, particularly in raising money for aids and equipment not provided by statutory sources. Some, mainly new, members do sometimes expect SIA to operate within a conventional model. However, by and large, the role assumed by the Welfare Service is clearly recognised as one of facilitating members' own actions and assisting them in being more effective as their own advocates.

Early on, the Welfare Service set itself the following tasks:

(a) to provide an information and advisory service both to the membership and to all professionals concerned with the problems of those with spinal cord injury

(b) to develop the Link Scheme and to set up a peer counselling service

(c) to provide a casework service on a limited basis for a small number of members

(d) to liaise and co-operate with statutory and voluntary agencies including spinal units, general hospitals, social services departments and voluntary agencies

(e) to keep up to date on current developments in disability and promote any new developments as might seem appropriate.[30]

These aims have largely been achieved and continue to underpin the work of the service, although, as expected, the amount of casework which it has been possible to do is minimal.

Currently, the Welfare Service staff comprises the Welfare Officer (who is tetraplegic), Assistant Welfare Officer, Welfare Secretary, Counselling Development Officer, Care Attendant Agency Co-ordinator and three full time Care Attendants. A number of disabled volunteers also help out with specific tasks such as inputting computer information. The Welfare Officer is responsible for the Welfare Service as a whole and reports to the Management Committee. Professional supervision is provided by an appropriately qualified member of the Management Committee. The Welfare Officer is also a member of the Management Team which also includes three other senior staff members and manages the Association on a day to day basis.

Information and advice

In 1989, the total number of enquiries received by the service was 1,518. Table 1 shows a breakdown of the number of enquiries in each of twenty-four categories as a percentage of the total number of Welfare enquiries, averaged over a three-year period (1987-1989). While some of the queries received may have straightforward responses based on existing knowledge, others may require several hours or even days to research.

In some areas there is a danger of merely duplicating the work of other specialist organisations with more expertise of a given issue. In such cases, and highly complex benefit enquiries are one example, the enquirer may be referred on to the more appropriate organisation (such as the Disablement Income Group or the Disability Alliance). Factsheets on a number of key issues such as incontinence and parenthood are available and are distributed along with references to other sources of help and information.

The information given out comes from a variety of sources including local, national and international publications as well as scientific journals, Government departments and other voluntary agencies. However, much of it is based upon the vast practical everyday experience of SIA's members and this gives it a relevance and immediacy which it would otherwise be difficult to match.

It can be seen from Table 1 that financial issues have a high priority for SIA's members. Requests for financial help are regularly received for equipment which many people might expect to be available from statutory sources. New generation manual wheelchairs which are light and manoeuvrable; outdoor electric wheelchairs; car and van adaptations; even such basic equipment as hoists and essential household furnishings like carpets are all much in demand. Normally, SIA only makes grants to members or their families for certain specific reasons such as the Relatives Travel Fund (see below). However, other charitable trusts may be approached on a member's behalf if no other source of help is available.

Benefits for disabled people are widely perceived by those who request help as grossly inadequate to meet the many additional costs of living with a disability (see also DIG[31]). The benefits system as a whole is seen as excessively complicated, incoherent and inconsistent in its approach, and unnecessarily bureaucratic.

Incontinence is also a problem for many SCI people. However, it should be noted that the vast majority of queries on this issue are not to do with the physical

Table 1: Types of enquiry received by the Welfare Service (number averaged over three years (1987-1989) expressed as a percentage)

Type of query	% Total queries
1. Grants	10.0
2. Benefits & Finance	8.7
3. Incontinence	7.7
4. Link Scheme	7.4
5. Independent Living	6.6
6. Relatives Travel Fund	6.0
7. Housing	5.0
8. Medical	4.7
9. Aids & Equipment	2.9
10. Pain	2.9
11. Counselling & Depression	2.8
12. Sexuality	2.8
13. Parenthood	2.1
14. Women's Group	2.0
15. Employment	1.7
16. Research	1.6
17. Mobility	1.3
18. Legal	1.3
19. Residential Care	1.2
20. Leisure & Social	0.8
21. Carers	0.8
22. Education	0.6
23. Access	0.5
24. Other	18.6
Total	100.0

aspects of bladder and bowel management (which are, by and large, resolved before discharge from hospital), but because of problems with the supply and suitability of equipment such as drainage sheaths, leg bags, pads and pants etc.

Independent living features high on the list of priorities and has already been discussed. A more detailed analysis of enquiries on this topic in fact shows an increase from 4.4 per cent in 1987 to 8.6 per cent in 1989, illustrating how interest in (and, perhaps, expectations regarding) independent living have risen in recent years. The majority of those who are most concerned about the subject are, perhaps predictably, tetraplegics. However, with an increasingly ageing population of SCI people finding that they need greater levels of support as they grow older, this may change in the future.[21] At present, no statistics are kept on the age of those contacting the Welfare Service.

It should be noted that queries regarding aids and equipment, mobility and access are also routinely handled by the Information Service. Legal claims, advice and reports are also handled by another department. Thus, the relative prominence of these issues would appear greater if the statistics on these issues from all services were combined.

With queries regarding grants, benefits, personal support, housing, and aids and equipment all featuring highly in the list of most frequently raised issues, it is clear that the social and economic environment in which spinal cord injured people find themselves plays a significant part in determining the quality of their lives. Though important, issues such as counselling, depression and sexuality, which might be said to relate more to people's emotional needs, prompt far fewer enquiries. This might be said to run counter to the oft perceived view of spinal cord injured people as tragic victims whose prime task is to 'adjust to their disability'.

We shall now consider how specific services address some of the issues outlined above.

The Link Scheme

The Link Scheme is one of SIA's oldest services. It consists of a register of members (recently computerised) and numbering some 450 plus, who are willing to be contacted by others in order to provide practical and emotional support. Those requesting help are matched as closely as possible with the Link Scheme member, particularly on geographical location, level of lesion, age and sometimes sex depending on the issue. The Link Scheme member is asked if s/he feels able to help the person on that occasion and then the details are passed on to the caller - it is for them to take the initiative and telephone, write to, or arrange a visit with the Link Scheme member. Inevitably, this means that some Links do not come to fruition but it is felt that the principle of the individual taking steps to help him/herself is an important one. There is no formal procedure for vetting Link Scheme members - those found to be unsuitable are simply dropped from the scheme.

The kind of issues on which contacts are requested range from help in setting up an independent living scheme to advice on coping with pain. In each case the Link is followed up to establish if contact was made and to support the individual in the event of there being any difficulties with the Link. Thankfully, few problems have arisen, although some Link Scheme members do feel they would prefer a more structured scheme with more training and regular meetings etc. In one sense, these issues arise out of the success of the scheme - that is, because of the number of Link Scheme members, each one may be contacted only once or twice a year.

Relatives' Link Scheme

More recently, there has been a recognition that the needs of relatives and carers have not had the attention they deserve. While it had always been possible to arrange Links for carers through the 'regular' Link Scheme, it was decided that a separate scheme would be more easily able to address these issues. Following a mail-out of questionnaires through the SIA Newsletter, a separate database was set up and this now contains the names of over 200 relatives/carers who are willing to offer support to others, particularly at the time of injury when such help can be especially important.

This recognition of the needs of carers echoes a wider societal (and, to a lesser extent, political) acknowledgement of their role. During the last ten years, carers have themselves organised politically and now, as the Carers National Association, have a sound organisational basis for political lobbying, self-help and advocacy.

Relatives' Travel Fund

This Fund was originally set up as part of a campaign to urge the DHSS (as it then was) to make proper provision for the travelling expenses of those visiting relatives in hospital. This is an issue which particularly affects families of SCI people because of the wide geographical area covered by each spinal unit, because of the extended length of admission (on average around five or six months) and because of the psychological importance of frequent visits from relatives and friends.

Travelling grants are made to relatives on the basis of spinal unit Medical Social Workers' recommendations. These are commonly £100 - £200, although larger, or repeat grants can be made if the circumstances warrant it. There is no stringent means-test or intrusive questionnaire, simply a recognition of need.

Despite SIA's essentially non-grantmaking approach, the failure of the DHSS to give ground on the level of help available, meant that the Association felt that the Fund was too important to discontinue and it, therefore, continues to operate, currently with a budget of £12,000.

Care Attendant Agency

The Care Attendant Agency (CAA) is perhaps the best example of SIA's self-help philosophy in action. The need for it became clear as a result of a survey of the tetraplegic membership carried out in 1983. It was apparent that, where tetraplegic members were relying on relatives or paid carers for personal assistance to live their daily lives, any sudden interruption in the availability of that support had profound consequences for the individual, and usually meant that they ended up in hospital or in residential care. Statutory services were simply not flexible enough to take over a substantial amount of personal assistance support.

It was, therefore, decided to set up a service, initially with one full-time care attendant, but also using a pool of casual workers, to provide twenty-four hour support *in the member's home* to cover such crises, or indeed for planned periods of respite or for holidays.

Six years on the service is firmly established and now employs three full-time care attendants plus casual workers, providing more than 40,000 hours of cover during 1989/90. Care attendants do not, on the whole, have nursing qualifications or experience. They are, however, trained to act as the arms and legs of the disabled person and to work under his/her direction. Training is provided at the national office and in members' homes, a service for which members and their regular carers are paid.

The result is a service which actually responds directly to members' expressed needs and enables them to remain in the community with dignity and, most importantly, allows them to remain in control of their lives. A major boon has been the reassurance that the existence of this gives members. Many report feeling psychologically more secure knowing the service is there even though they may never have used it yet. The service is heavily subsidised by SIA as no one is refused help because they cannot afford to pay for it or contribute towards its cost. However, this does mean that there is a limit, currently two weeks per year, on the amount of cover available to each member.

Recent developments have included the making of a video to publicise the Agency, a drive to increase the number of placements funded by local authorities and some consultancy work with other voluntary organisations interested in setting up a similar service.

Current projects

The Welfare Service is continuing to develop its services in response to members' needs. In fact, at the time of writing, a further survey of the membership's views on the Association is being analysed and will, no doubt, play a part in determining future developments.

There are also three current welfare projects which are either actively being developed, or for which funding is being sought.

Telephone counselling service

Providing an effective, professional counselling service for SCI people on a national scale has always been a matter of some concern to SIA. However, the logistical problems of doing so have hitherto proved insurmountable. The Association organised a Counselling Conference in 1978 (followed by a workshop in 1981) and it has been widely acknowledged that there is a need for such a service to help people talk openly and in confidence about their feelings regarding their experience of disability. It is intended, therefore, to set up a telephone counselling service in order to address this issue and to test the actual level of demand. This will involve professionally trained SCI people providing telephone counselling from their own homes under the supervision of a recently appointed Counselling Development Officer.

SIA/Spinal unit joint working

The Welfare Service already organises and services regular meetings of the spinal unit medical social workers and, more recently, the clinical psychologists. Some of SIA's local Groups also have varying degrees of involvement with their regional spinal unit. However, it is felt that there is great potential in joint working on a more formal basis, perhaps by establishing joint posts which could address specific issues such as independent living. One such project, for which funding has recently been secured, aims to employ a SCI person in a spinal unit to provide independent living advocacy, ie helping to arrange personal assistance schemes, funding, training, information on interviewing and advertising, and arranging peer support. Additional roles will include co-ordinating group discussion sessions on matters of concern such as sexuality, family relationships, returning home etc., and arranging awareness study days for community professionals.

National Care Attendant Register

The Griffiths Report[32] and subsequent (some might say very subsequent!) NHS and Community Care Act 1990 have highlighted the need for disabled people to have the option to remain living in the community with appropriate care support. Whether the Act will indeed provide the framework to enable severely disabled people to exercise genuine choice and control over their care arrangements, and hence their lifestyle, remains to be seen.

However, as discussed earlier, many of SIA's members are among those members of the Independent Living Movement who have blazed the trail on independent living which others now seek to follow. They have shown by their own example, often against considerable professional opposition or apathy, that very severely disabled people can indeed live in the community and run their own lives without burdening relatives, provided that appropriate resources and/or services are available.

The new responsibilities which are placed upon local authorities under the act are likely to see a continued expansion in the private care agency sector, However, while many people do not wish to become involved in the administrative responsibilities of being their own direct employer of care, there are others who prefer the level of control that this offers.

One of the major problems, however, in employing one's own personal assistance support is recruiting suitable staff. The National Care Attendant Register would be specifically aimed to address this problem. It would provide an employment bureau which would put disabled people and potential personal assistants in touch with each other while leaving the responsibility for interviewing and taking up references etc. squarely with the disabled person. A further possibility would be a training section providing basic training on topics such as lifting techniques or incontinence management for care attendants, and administrative and managerial advice for disabled people.

Future developments

The Welfare Service may be at, or near, its maximum capacity in terms of what it is possible to do on a national basis. It may be that future developments will lie more in developing the potential of local SIA Groups than in expanding the activities of the national office. There are currently some fifteen or so established local Groups but so far none have paid staff. There are some definite advantages to working at a local rather than a national level, particularly in areas such as advocacy and assisting members in obtaining the best possible service from their local social services or housing departments. It will never be the aim to replace existing statutory services, but a more personal local involvement than is possible on a national scale would nevertheless be welcome and permit a more detailed level of contact.

Conclusions - the changing face of community care?

In giving responsibility for community care to local authorities, the present Government has handed them what some people see as a golden opportunity to improve services radically, while others see it as a poisoned chalice. During the passage of the Bill through Parliament, the Government successfully fought off intensive lobbying on a wide range of amendments from the ringfencing of funds transferred from Social Security, to the requirement to consult service users before drawing up plans. Without even such basic safeguards there remains a great deal of uncertainty about whether adequate resources will be made available to improve the quantity and quality of services, and whether the new options proposed will reflect disabled people's needs any better than did the old ones.

There are two great uncertainties. Whether the preferences of service users will be translated into genuine choices for clients rather than simply choices for care managers. And whether the economic forces brought to bear in a competitive market will result in services which are able to respond sensitively to individual need. The danger is that the most efficient and therefore viable services will be those that cater for the lowest common denominator. In an unregulated market, the tendency may be for these organisations to take over their less efficient competitors resulting in larger and less user-sensitive organisations. One unwieldy, inflexible bureaucracy will have been replaced by another. This tendency for a competitive market of service providers to lead ultimately to less rather than more choice for the user is already evident in some parts of the United States.[33]

During the past ten years disabled people's own organisations have continued to grow in number, in sophistication and in political astuteness. Their national umbrella organisation, the British Council of Organisations of Disabled People (BCODP) represents some one hundred and fifty thousand disabled people and is being increasingly recognised as the legitimate voice of disabled people in Great Britain. The BCODP is just one part of a network of disabled people's organisations which, via Disabled People's International, extends throughout

Europe and the world. The World Council of DPI has achieved Category 2 consultancy status at the United Nations.

There is little doubt that the expectations of individual disabled people have also risen during this period. These are not simply expectations of more or better resources and services, but expectations of a change in the nature of their very relationships with medical, rehabilitation and social services professionals. Unless disabled people are themselves involved in the design and, some would say, the delivery of services, the fundamental structure of service provision will remain flawed. There is evidence that some social workers are adapting to new ways of working with disabled people and that this can be a rewarding experience for both client and professional alike.[27,28] It is essential for the good of both disabled people and social workers themselves that this partnership approach become the norm rather than the exception in the years ahead. That is the challenge facing social work in the 1990s.

References

1. Oliver, M., Zarb, G., Silver, J., Moore, M. and Salisbury, V. (1988). *Walking Into Darkness: The Experience of Spinal Injury*. MacMillan, Basingstoke.

2. Morris. J. (1989). (Ed.) *Able Lives*. Women's Press, London.

3. Trieschmann, R. (1980). *Spinal Cord Injuries*. Pergamon, Oxford.

4. Oliver, M. (1981). 'Disability, Adjustment and Family Life: Some Theoretical Considerations'. In Brechin, A., Liddiard, P. and Swain, J. *Handicap in a Social World*. Hodder & Stoughton, Kent.

5. Carver, V. (1982). 'The Individual Behind the Statistics'. Unit 3 in *The Handicapped Person in the Community (Block 1)*. Open University Press, Milton Keynes, 90.

6. Hasler, F. and Oliver, M. (1987). 'Social Work in a Self-Help Group: A Case Study of the Spinal Injuries Association' *Disability, Handicap & Society*. 2, 2, 113-125.

7. Robinson, D. and Henry, S. (1977). *Self-help and Health*. Martin Robinson, Oxford.,

8. Shearer, A. (1983). *Living Independently*. CEH/King's Fund, London.

9. Barclay Committee (1982). *Social Workers, their Role and Tasks*. NCVO/NISW, London.

10. Social Services Inspectorate Report (1990). *Developing Services for Disabled People*. Department of Health.

11. Ford, C. (1986). 'Collaboration: a Personal Experience of Social Work in Application'. Paper presented at BASW/BCODP Conference - *Disabled People and Social Workers, Changing Philosophy, Changing Practice*.

12. UPIAS (1976). *Fundamental Principles of Disability*. Union of the Physically Impaired Against Segregation, London.,

13. Berger, R. (1988). 'Helping Clients Survive a Loss' *Social Work Today*. 19, 34.

14. Weller, D. J. and Miller, P. M. (1977). 'Emotional Reactions of Patient, Family, and Staff in Acute Care Period of Spinal Cord Injury: part 2' *Social Work in Health Care*. 3.

15. Dickinson, M. (1977). 'Rehabilitating the Traumatically Disabled Adult' *Social Work Today*. 8, 28.

16. Finkelstein, V. (1981). *Disability and Professional Attitudes*. NAIDEX Convention, Sevenoaks.

17. Satyamurti, C. (1981). *Occupational Survival*. Blackwell, Oxford, 20.

18. Topliss, E. and Gould, B. (1981). *A Charter for the Disabled*. Blackwell, Oxford, 132.

19. Fiedler, B. (1988). *Living Options Lottery*. The Prince of Wales Advisory Group on Disability, London.

20. Brechin, A. and Liddiard, P. (1981). *Look at it this Way: New Perspectives in Rehabilitation*. Hodder & Stoughton, London, 138.

21. Zarb, G. J., Oliver, M. J. and Silver, J. R.(1990). *Ageing with Spinal Cord Injury: The Right to a Supportive Environment?* Thames Polytechnic/Spinal Injuries Association, London, 12, 16-17.

22. Brisenden, S. (1988). *A Charter for Personal Care*. Southampton, Centre for Integrated Living.

23. Evans, J. (1985). 'An Ordinary Street with Ordinary People' *Spinal Injuries Newsletter*. Spinal Injuries Association, London, 34.

24. Evans, J. (1986). Quoted in Suffolk, V. *The Challenge of Demanding Autonomy*. University ofManchester: Extra Mural Department, Manchester, 9-10.

25. Brisenden, S. (1986). 'Independent Living and the Medical Model of Disability' *Disability, Handicap & Society*. 1, 2, 177-178.

26. *Resolutions* (1989). (issued by Independent Living Expert Seminar: Strasbourg 1989) Disabled Peoples International European Independent Living Sub-committee.

27. Suffolk, V. (1986). *The Challenge of Demanding Autonomy*. University of Manchester: Extra Mural Department, Manchester.

28. Suffolk, V. (1986). 'Collaboration: Practising the Social Model of disability' (Paper presented at BASW/BCODP Conference - *Disabled People and Social Workers: Changing Philosophy, Changing Practice*).

29. Crosby, N. and Davis, K. (1986). 'Future Trends: Centres for Integrated Living' (Background paper to BASW/BCODP Conference - *Disabled People and Social Workers: Changing Philosophy, Changing Practice*.

30. Hasler, F. and Oliver, M. (1983). *Social Work in a Self-Help Group: An Evaluation of One Such Service*. Spinal Injuries Association, London.

31. Thompson, P., Buckle, J. and Lavery, M. (1988). *Being Disabled Costs More Then They Said*. Disabled Income Group, London.

32. Griffiths, R. (1988). *Community Care: Agenda for Action*. HMSO, London.

33. Douglas, R. (1989). 'Lessons from an American Experience?' (Paper presented at United Kingdom Home Care Association Inaugural Conference). London.

Housing and Independence

Barrie Fiedler

In late 1988 the Living Options action research study of housing and support services for people with severe physical disabilities, undertaken through the Prince of Wales' Advisory Group on Disability, reported that provision was largely ineffective, uncoordinated and patchy and was meeting the needs of very few disabled individuals.[1] These findings came as no surprise to disabled people on the receiving end of such services, many of whom had been pointing to service shortfalls for the past decade and more. What was surprising - and appalling - was that so little had changed and that the messages about inadequate housing and personal support had made so little impact on statutory or voluntary service-planning and -providing agencies.

Behind the practical problems of inadequate housing and personal support lay a range of fundamental issues concerning participation, partnership and power. Increasingly, disabled people were rejecting the traditional attitudes and expectations that result in special, different and lesser living arrangements. They sought instead independent and ordinary lifestyles - including a home, a job and a family - not just for a particularly tenacious, extraordinary or privileged few, but for people with all kinds and degrees of disability. Disabled people wanted access to, and enablement for, the same range of opportunities and responsibilities as their able bodied peers.

One year following the report of the Living Options study, such issues are more commonly and publicly aired, but little has changed on the ground for disabled service users. The Living Options messages remain pertinent to social work practice.

The initiatives which led to the Living Options research and the publication of *Living Options Lottery* began in the early 1980s when some thirty voluntary organisations came together under the auspices of The Prince of Wales Advisory Group to share their concern about the low priority and lack of provision for severely disabled people. From this initial meeting grew the Living Options

Working Party which in 1985 produced the Living Options *Guidelines*[2] setting out the key principles that underpin all the subsequent Living Options activities:

- *choice* as to where to live and how to maintain independence
- *consultation* with disabled people on services as they are planned
- *information*, clearly presented and readily available to the most severely disabled consumers
- *participation* of disabled people in the life of local and national communities
- *recognition* that long-term disability is not synonymous with illness and that the medical model of care is usually inappropriate; and
- *autonomy*, or freedom to make decisions regarding the way of life best suited to an individual's circumstances.

These fundamental principles have been widely circulated, and widely applauded, and indeed have made their way into the policy documents of many social service and health authorities. Hoping to discover where these values were being realised in existing facilities, the Living Options Working Party obtained funding from the DHSS and the King Edward's Hospital Fund for London to carry out a two and a half year study of good practice in accommodation and care support services for people with severe physical disabilities.

The Living Options project

The focus of the work was to be those people aged 16-64 requiring help on a long term basis in order to carry out normal living tasks, who - falling between paediatric/education and geriatric services - were particularly poorly served. Although named a 'priority group' by the Government in 1981,[3] younger physically disabled people were not receiving the same focus of interest in and planning for 'community care' services as, for example, elderly people or those with mental handicaps; and their service needs were not being addressed to the same extent by health and local authorities.

The study aimed to investigate a broad range of supported housing options in order to identify the kinds of housing and personal assistance arrangements that enabled severely disabled people to live independently, in the way that they wished. This approach acknowledged the concept that 'independent living' did not mean the ability to manage daily living tasks, but the possibility of exercising control over the way in which help to carry out these activities was planned and delivered.

The Living Options project began with a trawl of directors of social services and housing, general managers of district health authorities, voluntary organisations and consumer groups, seeking information about effective, innovative schemes. This exercise uncovered a number of interesting initiatives, but also established that only about one quarter of social services departments even claimed to be offering good services; a slightly smaller proportion of health authorities, and only a fraction of housing authorities, put forward suggestions of effective provision.

This survey of good practice was followed up by visits to many of the services identified, including interviews with hundreds of service users and providers, in about fifty local and health authorities. Services were assessed in the light of the Living Options principles and in the context of a full and ordinary lifestyle for users.

While a number of effective schemes were found - and these are documented in *Living Options Lottery* - the project fieldwork generally confirmed the national picture of scarce, patchy and arbitrary services. Even the best services were helping only a few individuals, and service users and providers alike were keen to talk about obstacles to achieving good practice. Many were experimental 'pilots' where users were worried about future security; many depended on turning a blind eye to, or bending, established rules; others were concerned that publicity would create a demand that could not be met.

From the research experience, *Living Options Lottery* identified a number of conditions that characterise current disability services:

- Despite talk of care in the community, and the promise of the International Year of Disabled People, the only options for most severely disabled people are living in the community with little or no help, or living in traditional institutional facilities or hospital beds.

- Housing and support services are a lottery for people with physical disabilities - it's chance, not need, that determines the kind and level of services they receive.

- Personal support services are complicated, piecemeal, inflexible, and insecure. There is not enough appropriate, accessible housing; adaptations and equipment are hard to come by and often inappropriate when they are delivered. Housing and care support services are rarely coordinated, so disabled people may have to forego the offer of one because of lack of the other.

- There is no clear structure or funding mechanism that enables people with disabilities - or their families, advocates, or professionals - to find their way through the maze of information and services, or to achieve the kind of housing and personal support they need.

- Disabled people rarely participate in service planning, or exercise choice in or control of their own housing and support arrangements.

- There is not one model, or a few, of housing and personal assistance that is the right answer for everyone; a variety of options is needed from which people can choose depending on their life stage and circumstances.

Sensitively designed and equipped housing and flexible, dependable support enable even the most severely disabled person to live independently.

At age twenty-one, Ms J left the (over) protection of her family home and, after living in a succession of residential homes during the next few years, succeeded in moving into her own housing association flat. Ms J has twenty-four hour live-in assistance, shared between two care workers who live locally, whom she employs herself. The care assistants work alternate three and four day weeks, carrying out all the personal and housekeeping tasks necessary. Ms J's DHSS benefits - including domestic assistance allowance - are topped up by her local authority, which pays Ms J via the voluntary agency home from which she moved (Fiedler 1988, p. 40).[1]

Mr B left his family home to live in a substantially adapted council bungalow. Although severely disabled by muscular dystrophy, he is able to live without personal care support, with individually designed kitchen fittings and equipment, a special shower and toilet, and bed and bathroom hoists. A warden alarm link gives extra security but Mr B prefers to use his cordless telephone. The location of his home gives electric wheelchair access to local accessible transport (Fiedler 1988, p. 40).[1]

Ms G, aged twenty-four, suffered onset of multiple sclerosis several years ago, which has left her also blind and epileptic. She now lives in a self-contained flat which forms part of a registered hostel managed by a voluntary agency. When in remission, Ms G needs only night-time checks and help for epileptic seizures and is otherwise independent and active. During a multiple sclerosis attack, however, she is paralysed from the neck down and requires constant attention. Her needs are met by hostel staff - including some qualified nursing staff - in her own flat. The self-catering arrangements (food money is reserved from the hostel fees) allow Ms G to buy back a meal voucher when unable to prepare her own meals (Fiedler 1988, p.58).[1]

The failure to provide adequate, appropriate services, however, at best limits, and can have devastating consequences for individual disabled people.

Mr and Mrs D, in their thirties, both have cerebral palsy. They moved into their present registered bed-sitting flat because Mr D found work in the area, but are frustrated by the loss of independence. Although kitchens are provided, Mr and Mrs D do not self cater because the scheme requires that they pay for the three meals provided daily (ironically, residents' kitchens are not being put in a new scheme because they are not used by residents). Domestic cleaning is provided. There are washing machines available but Mrs D can't reach them and laundry is done for her. The bed hoist provided is not appropriate and so Mrs D cannot get in and out of bed unaided. Although there is a private outside door to their flat, she must use the common entrance in order to get staff help to transfer from her electric to indoor wheelchair. On the basis of their current arrangements, Mr and Mrs D have been refused an independent bungalow in the grounds of the scheme because they require too much attendant care (Fiedler 1988, p.16).[1]

Mrs P, in her late fifties, has a deteriorating spinal condition. The care demands on her husband caused the breakup of their marriage, following which the home care service was brought in to support her at home. Several years later Mrs P was reunited with her husband, but as a result her home care hours have been substantially reduced - although he has suffered a stroke in the meantime. Mr P provides the majority of his wife's personal support and she is now in her words 'more fixed to bed' ((Fiedler 1988, p.18).[1]

Mr N, in his mid-forties, has multiple sclerosis. He continues to live on his own at home with the help of care attendants provided by a voluntary scheme. As his condition deteriorates, however, the attendants' time is taken up increasingly with physical care support tasks allowing little time to accompany him out socially, etc. But the scheme organisers are unable to provide additional attendant care hours unless, as they say, another client should die. Mr N anticipates a future of increasing isolation, with an ever-present threat of residential care (Fiedler 1988, p.19).[1]

The Living Options findings build on and are confirmed by a growing body of literature. The difference that appropriate housing and enabling services make to the lives of severely disabled people was described by A. Shearer, *Living Independently*.[4] Disabled people have documented their own experiences of moving into independent living (for example, Hampshire Centre for Independent

Living's Project 81 - *One Step On*.[5] A series of Government-commissioned reports (by the Audit Commission, 1986; Sir Roy Griffiths, 1988; Lady Wagner, 1988) raised awareness of community service needs but said little about the particular issues pertaining to people with physical disabilities.[6,7,8] A research report produced in 1988 by the King's Fund Institute confirmed the national picture of chaotic and fragmented community physical disability services.[9] And a 1988 Shelter briefing paper showed the disadvantage faced by disabled people due to their housing requirements.[10]

Starting points for change

In order to build on the research findings, *Living Options Lottery* outlined a number of 'starting points for change'. While recognising that central government has a responsibility to create a climate of change by setting fair and consistent standards - for personal, domestic and social care support, for housing, and for funding - these recommendations targeted social workers, and their colleagues in other agencies, who have the power and resources to create change.

Individual needs

People with even the most severe physical disabilities can and do live in the community if appropriate support is available. Such support includes ensuring that people who have multiple disabilities, and may be less able to articulate their needs, or lack advocates, have equal access to services.

Few authorities participating in the Living Options research claimed to know either the numbers of the needs of the disabled citizens for whom they have a responsibility to provide services. Few have any systems for finding out what their disabled citizens would prefer, if options were available - especially those people living without support in the community who become known to social services only at times of crisis when family support networks break down and an apparent demand for residential care is created.

Personal 'care packages' (known by a variety of names) are increasingly seen as the best path to appropriate, individually tailored services. But there is a danger that the views of the client can be swamped by the array of professionals whose input is required, and the role of the social worker as 'enabler' must be stressed.

Professional responsibility

Responsibility for service provision must be accepted by those in control of resources, and standards set for services and staff. Quality services demand that professionals stop just talking about services, and start producing them. Under the provisions of the new community care White Paper[11] responsibility for ensuring the delivery of community services will be firmly in the court of social services departments.

Authorities working with the Living Options project often confess that they have never met their colleagues in other agencies who deal with services for disabled people, and joint planning and provision is scarce. Health and social services authorities usually have separate policies (if they have them at all) for providing disability services. Housing authorities generally have a low profile in disability services, but their equal partnership with social work and other departments is essential to coordinate the delivery of appropriate housing and support.

Disabled consumers, informal carers and professionals are often confused by the fragmentation of services delivered by various agencies - social workers, occupational/physio/speech therapists, district nurses, health visitors, care attendants and volunteers. Coordination of roles within social services also needs to be addressed: overlaps between the tasks of social workers, home helps/carers and occupational therapists are rife.

Help in negotiating this service maze is essential for many people. The concepts of case/care management, service brokerage and advocacy, and the key worker need to be explored by social workers, with attention to the possible conflict between an independent, neutral role, versus access to services through the control of resources. Organisations of disabled people may be able to provide these functions most successfully.

Sources of funding for housing and support services are of course critical. Lack of money is often cited as the obstacle to producing appropriate services, but coordination of budgets between agencies, and shifting of resources between, say, residential placements and domiciliary services, can go a long way toward good practice.

Disabled people are increasingly looking for direct funding to employ their own personal assistants. The Independent Living Fund is helping a number of individuals but availability and take-up appears to be uneven. Other options for achieving direct funding need to be explored.

Consumer control

Planning and delivery of services must begin with consumer consultation. This means acknowledging that people with severe physical disabilities are the experts, who will have the best knowledge of what they need and how it should be delivered. It means involving users *before* decisions are made about facilities or services for them, as well as in specific design and day to day management matters.

Consumer consultation also means enabling people with disabilities to participate. Assertion training, skills training, and experience in committee procedures may be needed. Practical issues like accessible venues and reliable transport also need addressing. As a result of institutionalisation, over-protection or negative experiences, many individuals have low expectations of their own abilities, of the responsiveness of service providers, and of the benefits of the political process. Others who are less articulate, are speech impaired, or have a learning difficulty, need particular help in order to participate.

Some disabled people will prefer training, support and advice provided by other disabled people, and user organisations can be resourced and encouraged to provide such support. The importance of employing disabled people as social workers and therapists in social work departments will be obvious.

Housing and support services

The provision of sufficient and appropriate accommodation and home-based personal assistance, properly coordinated by the various authorities concerned, is fundamental to disabled people's independence.

People with severe physical disabilities require a range of housing options to suit their life stage, sensitively designed and appropriately equipped - that is, ordinary housing, built to generous space standards, that can be tailored to suit individual requirements. And in order to take up such options, severely disabled people need to be able to choose from a range of flexible, dependable, financially secure personal assistance services, available at home, offering help with personal, domestic and social tasks.

Some disabled people choose to live in a residential facility, but the Living Options research confirms that - given real options - most prefer more ordinary lifestyles in the community. Personal satisfaction levels are higher when individuals have more control over their own lives. Statutory authorities and voluntary organisations are therefore asked to ensure that no additional residential facilities are built unless it is clear that potential residents would prefer them, and that such a preference is not based on the lack of other options. Training may be needed to enable people to understand the possibilities for, and to achieve, independent living; transitional arrangements may be helpful to give individuals a chance to experiment with independence.

Living Options Lottery describes some thirty supported housing schemes, as examples of the variety of approaches that can offer an effective 'living option' for particular individuals. These include client-managed set ups where disabled people employ and direct their own support staff; care attendant services run by statutory or voluntary bodies; 'paid volunteer' schemes in which volunteers on short term placements live with disabled people; core and cluster schemes where centrally based staff support clients living in their own homes nearby; and residential projects operating in non-institutional ways.

A framework for comprehensive services

A place to live, with the support necessary to live there, is the starting point for independence for disabled people. But quality of life will only be achieved if housing and support services are provided in the context of a comprehensive service system enabling a full life in the community. From the strengths and gaps of current services documented in *Living Options Lottery*, a picture of what constitutes a comprehensive service, based on users' needs, begins to emerge. The elements of such a system would include:

A method for identifying potential service users' requirements

The Living Options study showed that few authorities are aware of the requirements of the physically disabled people, in the community or in institutions, to whom they have a responsibility to provide services. Registers quickly become outdated and inaccurate. Authorities need to establish a simple strategy for getting to know who and where disabled citizens are, and for determining and updating their service requirements.

A unified entry point to services

Disabled people, their families and advocates, and professionals need to know what services are on offer and how to access them. A single local response-point for information and advice is essential. For clients who wish, help with the process of obtaining services - through case management/service brokerage, for example - should be made available from this response point.

Access to ordinary housing and community services

Disabled people wish to choose from the same range of ordinary community services as their non-disabled peers, including education, employment, transportation, leisure and health care services, as well as a range of housing options.

Enablement services

Some severely disabled individuals require assistance in order to use ordinary community facilities. This may include the help of other people to carry out daily living activities, and/or alterations and equipment in the home and in public and work places. Enablement services need to be flexible to provide back-up and emergency cover for those whose needs vary or whose day-to-day arrangements break down.

Opportunities for personal development

Many people with severe disabilities will be aiming toward independence from a protected family or institutional environment. Confidence training, skills training, and counselling may be needed to enable individuals to aspire to and reach their full potential and to use the services on offer. Clients may prefer training and counselling offered by disabled people.

This framework for a comprehensive service is being developed by the latest Living Options initiative. The Living Options in Practice project[12] will be working with statutory and voluntary agencies, consumers and their organisations to develop effective, user-led services for people with severe physical and sensory disabilities. The project is also identifying the strategies - based on a commitment to fundamental values; an acceptance of responsibility for ensuring good services; and the involvement of users at all stages - that seem to be essential to achieving such a comprehensive service system. This work continues to be coordinated through The Prince of Wales' Advisory Group on Disability together with the King's Fund Centre, and is funded for three years by the Department of Health and the King's Fund Centre.

Social work challenges

A number of issues arising from the Living Options work impinge on social work practice. Social work professionals at all levels could consider the following messages:

Think again

Traditional attitudes and values, and assumptions about disabled people's abilities, continue to work against best practice. Meeting and listening to disabled service users is an essential first step. An about face from thinking 'special' to thinking 'ordinary' may be called for, and the implications of putting declarations of principle into practice locally need to be considered. Statements of intent, and charters of rights, could be explored. Training in awareness, as well as in new ways of working, will almost certainly be required.

Empower users

Disabled people need to be enabled and empowered to play their full and legitimate role in every stage of planning, designing, implementing and monitoring the services they use. Lip service is commonly paid to 'consumer consultation' but ways need to be found to genuinely include disabled people in the planning and decision-making process. The new 'enabling' role for local authorities anticipated in the community care White Paper provides incentives for exploring new ways to devolve responsibility and resources to users.

Talk to strangers

Lack of coordination of services between and within agencies means service gaps, overlaps and confusion. Ways of working with colleagues across departmental and professional boundaries need to be explored. Collaboration on joint planning, joint budgets, joint information and advice and on joint services is essential to ensure continuity and efficacy of provision. The White Paper may provide incentives for new kinds of contract partnerships.

Be creative

Social workers need to adopt a 'can do' approach, and investigate new ways of using existing resources - physical, manpower, and financial. Many of the best practice services identified by *Living Options Lottery* were the result of generous interpretations of rules and regulations, and the creative use of budgets earmarked for, say, residential placements. Networking - of problems as well as successes - between local authorities can bring new ideas and examples of good practice. Social workers can look positively at the opportunities presented by change - new roles, new jobs, new ways of working - and help other staff who are frightened of or resistant to change. And finally,

Start now

There's been an unspoken pressure to wait - for the 1986 Disabled Persons Act; for Griffiths; for the disability income review; for the community care White Paper. All of the barriers to good practice identified in the Living Options research (confirmed by evidence from many other sources) remain, and all the essential elements of an effective service system for people with physical disabilities will be required, no matter what new laws and management structures are devised.

There is a real danger that basic principles and service goals will be lost in the systems changes that are imminently expected. Many of the positive features enshrined in the 1986 Act and the Griffiths report can be implemented in advance of legislation and without new monies.

Planners and practitioners can proceed posthaste on many other fronts - toward ownership of values, understanding of consumers' needs and preferences, building partnerships with other agencies, and exploring with users various options for supported housing and home-based services.

The Living Options study offers widespread evidence that people with severe physical disabilities can live full lives in their communities - if they are enabled to do so. The challenge to social workers is to create the environment in which disabled people can live independently in ordinary homes with appropriate personal, domestic and social support.

References

1. Fiedler, B. *Living Options Lottery: Housing and Support Services for People with Severe Physical Disabilities*. The Prince of Wales' Advisory Group on Disability, London, 1988.

2. The Prince of Wales' Advisory Group on Disability. *Living Options: Guidelines for Those Planning Services for People with Severe Physical Disabilities*. London, 1988.

3. DHSS. *Care in Action*. HMSO, London, 1981.

4. Shearer, A. *Living Independently*. Centre on Environment for the Handicapped/King's Fund, London, 1982.

5. Hampshire Centre for Independent Living. Project 81 - *One Step On. Consumer Directed Housing and Care for Disabled People*. Petersfield, 1986.

6. Audit Commission. *Making a Reality of Community Care*. HMSO, London, 1986.

7. Griffiths, R. *Community Care: Agenda for Action*. A report to the Secretary of State for Social Services. HMSO, London, 1988.

8. Wagner, G. *Residential Care: A Positive Choice*. Report of the Independent Review of Residential Care. National Institute of Social Work/HMSO, London, 1988.

9. Beardshaw, V. *Last on the List: Community Services for People with Physical Disabilities*. The King's Fund Institute, London, 1988.

10. Morris, J. *Freedom to Lose: Housing Policy and People with Disabilities*. Shelter, London, 1988.

11. Department of Health. *Caring for People*. HMSO, London, 1989.

12. For further information about the Living Options In Practice project contact the project directors, c/o King's Fund Centre, 126 Albert Street, London NW1 7NF

Impairment, Disability, Handicap and New Technology

Paul Cornes

The products of modern science-based industries and the new technologies which underpin their operation are now too much in evidence for their potential to improve the independence and quality of life of people with disabilities to be overlooked. It is therefore not at all surprising that, in the decade since the International Year of Disabled Persons (1981), 'new technology' has been an increasingly popular topic for research, conferences, and scientific and technical publications.

During this period, people with disabilities have been able to make increasing use of the ever-widening range of new technology-based products - from personal computers to communication aids, from everyday household and telecommunications equipment to sophisticated, personalised environmental control and interactive robotic systems - to enhance independence and broaden opportunities at home, at leisure, in education and training, and in employment. At the same time, politicians, policy makers and rehabilitation engineers, amongst others, have also turned their attention to the perceived promise of new technology in this field. Nicholas Scott, British Minister for Social Security and Disabled People, is just one example. When, in early 1990, at the launch of a new database on residential care facilities, he informed his audience that advances in technology offered people with disabilities 'unlimited prospects for the future',[1] he was expressing a point of view that is gaining wider currency.

Undoubtedly, there is some justification for such optimism. However, people with disabilities themselves remain cautious. More clearly than most of their fellow citizens, they recognise that more is entailed than the production and availability of new equipment. Other obstacles need to be negotiated if they are to afford, gain and maintain widespread access to, use, enjoy and profit from the various products of new technology and the impending 'Information Age'.

Few crusaders for the 'new technology' cause are as optimistic about future developments as Frank Bowe, the disability community leader whose early work[2] was so instrumental in bringing disability issues into the mainstream of American political debate and who is one of the 'architects' of the far-reaching reforms embodied in the *Americans with Disabilities Act*, 1989. He now envisages a world in which technology can eliminate disabilities - with machines which 'see' for persons without sight, 'listen' for those who cannot hear and 'speak' for those who lack speech - and in which developments in telecommunications enable others to surmount architectural and transportation barriers or to 'leapfrog' distances which otherwise could not be travelled.[3]

In Bowe's vision, alongside other efforts to design a world that is accessible to as many people as possible and in which specific adaptations are necessary only for a small minority with very special needs, such applications of new technology are means toward the attainment of longer-term policy goals of integration and normalisation. Although he recognises many potential applications of new technology in the achievement of these goals - and also the crucial importance of gaining wider social and political consensus for their realisation - Bowe regards vocational applications as providing the main thrust for future development. Strongly opposed to greater social security buttressing, he expects increased take-up of new technology to enable more and more people with disabilities to enter employment or self-employment, thereby relinquishing their dependence on such sources of income. It follows that the litmus test of his 'model' for future development will be the success that people with disabilities achieve in securing such employment opportunities and the extent to which that success attracts wider support, both for the extension of this process and the attainment of the longer-term policy goals he has identified.

Frank Bowe's vision is inspired and sustained by a rapidly growing number of examples of technological innovation and individual achievement making use of its many practical applications. In an age when almost every office and a significant proportion of private homes are equipped with computers - not to mention other 'hi-tech' gadgets - the scale and scope of progress in recent years are often taken for granted. Yet it was only in the mid-1960s that the first, elementary environmental control systems were installed in the homes of a handful of people with severe disabilities and, even ten years ago, schools, training establishments and workplaces with computing equipment were the exception rather than the rule. Two examples may serve to underline the truly phenomenal nature and extent of the changes which have occurred in the past decade. One is the compilation for in-house use by IBM Corporation staff of a densely packed, telephone directory-sized manual devoted solely to specifications for the adaptation of computer equipment for use by people with disabilities. The other is the proliferation of extensive databases, like the EEC's HANDYNET system, cataloguing an ever-expanding field of information on currently available technical aids, adaptations, items of equipment and services for people with disabilities.

These databases, while very expensive to set up and maintain, have helped to keep people with disabilities and/or rehabilitation services personnel in touch with new developments. It is, however, a moot point whether there will be a continuing requirement for them. Consumers are quick to point out numerous instances of deficiencies in the design and operation of specialised items of equipment which could have been avoided if manufacturers had consulted prospective users at the design stage or enabled them to have hands-on experience with prototypes before going into production. They are also concerned that many other products could be more user-friendly. In this respect, Geoff Busby and his colleagues working on the British Computer Society's IT Support for Disabled People project are pressing manufacturers to go further by designing computer hardware which is immediately accessible to disabled people. They contend that such products would tap a large, new market, not only of people with disabilities but also others because

> . . . any system which is friendly enough to be used by disabled people must naturally be much easier for an able-bodied user to operate. So, by considering the needs of disabled people, computer manufacturers will be producing products which are more attractive in their total markets.[4]

Bowe[3] makes an equally valid, though more widely ranging case in maintaining that housing, public buildings, public areas and transport systems which are accessible to elderly and disabled persons almost certainly would make everyday living more convenient and congenial for everyone else.

All of these considerations suggest that a review which concentrates on new technology products or case studies to illustrate good practice in their utilisation would skirt around, if not evade, the main issues of concern. These have little to do with particular products or applications - although, clearly, there is scope for much more sympathetic design to reduce dependence on adaptations or specialised equipment. As commentators like Daniel Bell[5] remind us, it is invalid to regard technology as occupying a stand-alone position, isolated from and uninfluenced by other social, economic, political and cultural dimensions of society. The principal issues of concern to people with disabilities - access to new technology, opportunity to use its various products and the handicap or disadvantage associated with restricted access or limited opportunity - inevitably reflect the ever-changing interactions between technology and these other aspects of modern society.

A single chapter does not permit more than the most superficial reference to such complex interactions. Nevertheless, it may be possible to indicate how they impinge on the everyday lives of people with disabilities by examining how new technology is opening up new possibilities for the medical treatment of illness or injury, the restoration or substitution of function and the achievement of independent lifestyles. That is the more modest objective of this chapter. Taking the World Health Organisation's (WHO) classification of impairments, disabilities and handicaps[6] as a frame of reference, it aims briefly

(a) to review the extent to which applications of new technology at each level are enabling people with disabilities to become more independent and enhance their quality of life and

(b) to identify some of the obstacles to more widespread take-up and utilisation of the new opportunities they offer.

Impairment

The WHO classification defines an impairment as 'any loss or abnormality of psychological, physiological or anatomical structure or function'. The focal point for considering new technology at this level therefore concerns its application to the diagnosis and medical treatment of illness, injury or other disorders and, of increasing significance in an age of health promotion, the identification of risk factors and other aspects of prevention.

In this context, no visitor to a modern hospital, where most but by no means all new developments in this sphere tend to be based, could fail to be impressed by the vast and ever-widening array of new technology-based techniques, products and items of specialised equipment. These items, too numerous to list and whose purchase represents a significant proportion of the mounting cost of health care, are to be found in almost every area of the hospital - accident and emergency units and the specially equipped vehicles used to ferry patients from home or the scene of accidents or other emergencies, operating theatres, intensive care units and other wards, and such support services as radiology, radiography, medical physics, pathology and pharmacology. They utilise many varieties of new technology from microelectronics to information technology, from lasers and optical fibres to biotechnology and robotics.

The availability and skilled use of new technology-based techniques of diagnosis, investigation, monitoring and treatment; technical and pharmaceutical products and highly specialised instruments and equipment have been - and will continue to be - associated with both refinement of existing practices and procedures and development of new ones. While its role has been to supplement rather than supplant the ever-present need for basic, 'low-tech' medical and nursing care, new technology has undoubtedly enhanced the treatment of patients with a wide range of illnesses or injuries. Its impact and potential, however, are most evident in life-threatening, emergency circumstances in which patients require resuscitation, life support and intensive care. Reduced acute mortality rates, for example, for persons who have suffered heart attacks or serious brain or spinal cord injury, are all in considerable measure attributable to technological advances in the treatment of such conditions, particularly at the earliest stages of recovery. As Oliver[7] has pointed out in relation to spinal cord injury, the major issue for persons with such injuries is no longer *life expectancy* but *expectation of life*, concern with the quality of life to which survivors of such injuries are entitled. Current medical research is also looking beyond life-saving to morbidity, to the part that new technology-based procedures can play in reducing disablement, by assisting the earlier detection and treatment of secondary conditions and other potential complications associated with serious illnesses and injuries.

The earliest applications of new technology yielded or utilised equipment whose use was restricted to such fixed locations as operating theatres or intensive care units. However, further progress in this field resulted in miniaturisation and increased portability, enabling equipment to be used not only in different locations in a hospital but also in ambulances or at the scene of accidents or emergencies. Portability of equipment, in turn, has facilitated other developments in health screening and early detection of medical risk factors. At present, such initiatives are mainly confined to mobile clinics which, for example, screen for breast cancer or commercial services which specialise in more general health screening of work forces. Typically, services of this kind operate on a stand-alone basis. However, it is quite conceivable that future developments, incorporating yet more sophisticated screening and investigative facilities, may be used in a variety of mobile and static settings - including work places, local health centres and doctors' surgeries - with on-line links to centralised units with specialised facilities for data processing and analysis, making preventive check-ups much more generally available. As current investigation of the possibility of using robotic procedures in surgery and medical applications of biotechnology also demonstrate, the potential of new technologies to enhance the diagnosis, investigation and medical treatment of a wide range of impairments is only just beginning to be realised.

Disability

According to the WHO classification, a disability is 'any restriction or lack (resulting from an impairment) of ability to perform an activity in the manner or within the range considered normal for a human being.' The role of new technology in this context therefore is to be considered from the perspective of its contributions to therapeutic procedures to restore sensory, physical or mental functioning or technical aids to augment, compensate or substitute for reduced or lost functions. In this case also, as examination of any one of the databases holding information on technical aids and adaptations would quickly confirm, development and marketing of new technology-based equipment for these purposes has grown exponentially during recent years, with far too many different products to permit here an exhaustive listing of the wide range of items now available. In any case, given the rapidly increasing availability of new products and the ever-decreasing 'shelf-life' of existing ones, there is little to be gained from a one-off snapshot. A more helpful approach might be to consider, with reference to a smaller number of illustrative examples, progress made to date toward realisation of Bowe's vision of a world in which technology can eliminate disabilities. Disabilities of sight, hearing, speech, locomotion and upper limb function can all be considered from this perspective.

Enabling blind persons to 'see'

Guide dogs, personal readers, Braille print, Perkins machines and tape recorders have all contributed significantly to the enhanced mobility, independence and quality of life of men and women who are blind or have severely restricted vision - and, for many, remain indispensable. In recent years, these aids to everyday living, at home and at work, have been supplemented by a range of new equipment. Examples include miniature cameras which read printed material and reproduce it in magnified form on visual display units, Braille terminals for personal computers which can be operated on a stand-alone basis or linked as workstations to larger systems, and speech synthesizers. With the availability of equipment of this kind, therefore, assistance with 'reading', if not 'seeing', is already available. Workstations incorporating such equipment have enabled many persons who lack sight or who are partially sighted to gain employment in a variety of secretarial, word processing, clerical, data processing, administrative and professional capacities. But, while others have been equally successful in computer programming and systems analysis, they have recently found that new technology may also have 'down sides'. The technical aids currently available are not able to handle new developments in programming languages which incorporate graphics, and a solution to this problem has yet to be found. However, factory-based applications of new technology are now also in the pipeline, the latest development enabling persons who are blind or partially sighted to program and operate computer-numerically-controlled (CNC) machine tools.

Enabling persons who are deaf to 'hear'

Recent advances in medical treatment of hearing loss, involving the insertion of cochlear implants, literally have restored hearing to a small number of persons with that disability. Regrettably, however, the proportion of profoundly deaf individuals who might benefit from this surgery is expected to remain small. Most therefore will remain dependent on hearing aids, lip reading and signing skills, at least for the foreseeable future. Nevertheless, new technology is assisting such persons in other ways. Examples include special computer programs to improve their speech, a range of equipment which amplifies telephone receivers and the availability of closed captioning technology. The latter has been made possible by the development of very cheap microchips which can be installed in television receivers and which decode additional signals accompanying normal programme transmissions and display speech as subtitles. This revolutionary technology has many other potential applications - remedial education and language learning are just two examples - but, for people with hearing disabilities, it represents a major breakthrough in access to the spoken word.

Enabling persons without speech to 'talk'

Communication aids for persons without speech represent one of the major focal points for research and development work on technical aids for people with disabilities. As a result, many different aids, with varying degrees of technological sophistication, are now available. They range from simple machines ... es linked to telephones, containing pre-coded messages - everyday ... and calls for assistance - to more sophisticated systems which trai... an use to create unique messages. Susini and Tronconi[8] have re... ribed an example of the latter kind, based on Bliss symbols, a graph... communication originally devised to facilitate communication bet... kers of different languages. Developments in information technology and telecommunications have enabled the Bliss symbol system to be adapted for use by persons who are unable to speak. Trained users can now use graphics programs to create symbols, other software to assemble symbols into messages and commercially available computer hardware (suitably adapted, if necessary) to transmit messages to their immediate vicinity or, using the BLISSCII code (the ASCII code of Bliss symbols), wherever telecommunication links permit. Messages can be received as Bliss symbols or decoded from text to speech by a synthesizer. The availability of this kind therefore have made it possible for those without speech to 'talk', and other developments, using Bliss workstations, are now enabling persons without speech to pursue education, training and employment in integrated settings.

Enabling persons with paraplegia to 'walk'

The tragic experience of PC Philip Olds, who was paralysed by gunshot wounds, was associated with a wave of publicity about the potential of functional electrical stimulation (FES) to enable persons with spinal cord injury to walk. Creasey's[9] recent review of scientific literature on this subject for the Medical Research Council, however, suggests that it may be some time before this particular goal is achieved. Meanwhile, other therapeutic and functional applications of the technique could yield earlier dividends.

FES aims to restore useful movement or sensation by electrical stimulation of excitable tissue, normally muscles, in patients whose neural pathways have been disrupted or damaged. Since the potential of this technique was first recognised many years ago, doctors have used electrical stimulation in a variety of ways for diagnostic, therapeutic and functional purposes. One of the most widely used applications is the cardiac pacemaker, first implanted less than thirty years ago. Technical developments now permit nervous tissue to be safely and reliably stimulated for many years by implanted neural prostheses with a potential to restore useful movement or sensation. Applications of the technique now include restoration of function to paralysed diaphragms enabling long-term respiration in small numbers of severely disabled people and restoration of continence, reliable micturation and some sexual function in selected patients. Therapeutic applications of FES include its use in pain relief; to assist the correction of spinal deformity (Scoliosis); and the exercise and strengthening of atrophied muscle tissue.

The use of FES as a means of enabling patients with paraplegia to walk was first proposed in the early 1960s. Early demonstrations of the technique's potential to assist such persons to stand for periods of up to two hours paved the way for further work on its potential to assist walking. To date, progress in this field has been restricted to limited success under laboratory conditions. Creasey's report for the Medical Research Council concluded that the restoration of walking to patients with complete paraplegia is an ambitious goal that will require considerable further progress over a decade or more to reach clinical usefulness. In the shorter term, the improvement of gait in patients with incomplete paralysis, and the ability to stand up or sit down with the assistance of stimulation are more obtainable goals, as is a combination of electrical stimulation and orthoses to achieve some mobility.

'Hands' for persons with tetraplegia and other upper limb disabilities

While the dream of persons with paraplegia to walk is some way from fulfilment, Creasey's review holds out more hope for the restoration of upper limb function in patients with tetraplegia or hemiplegia. Although much less research and publicity have been devoted to this aspect of FES, work to date has indicated that electrical stimulation of paralysed upper limbs, used in conjunction with tendon transfer surgery, can help patients to grasp and release objects, and also to maintain grip over short intervals. This enables them to undertake a range of simple activities of daily living - for example, eating or drinking - for which they would otherwise be dependent on others. It may also enhance self-esteem. Because loss of upper limb and hand function causes much greater dependence than loss of lower limb function, and because tetraplegia is now more prevalent than paraplegia, there may be a strong case for more investment in this particular aspect of FES. Certainly, in Creasey's judgment, further developments in this sphere are both feasible and of greater potential practical significance.

Alongside the interest in FES, other work is under way to explore and evaluate the potential of interactive robotic aids to substitute for loss of upper limb function. A recent state-of-the-art review of work in this field[10] describes several different approaches, generally at the prototype stage, and outlines various problems which rehabilitation engineers are having to solve. These are not just concerned with robotic technology and the creation of effective and acceptable user-machine interfaces but also with questions of safety, complexity and cost. Some work is directed to development of high cost, customised, multi-function robots while other projects are exploring simpler, lower cost, less technically sophisticated versions which could be made more widely available. In all cases, however, the primary objective is to increase users' independence by enabling them to 'perform' simple manipulations required, for example, for drinking, feeding or controlling their immediate environment at home or at work. While individuals are benefiting from prototypes, all of this work is clearly at an early stage of development. Like FES, therefore, it would appear that there is still a considerable way to go before interactive robotic technology is more generally available. Even then, because potential users' acceptance of this technology is far from guaranteed, its applications may be limited.

The preceding examples only sample a much wider field of new technology-based products and related research and development work, and do not embrace all of the disabilities in relation to which such work is currently under way. They indicate that, while a range of relatively simple and comparatively inexpensive technical aids and adaptations have been produced and have helped many users to overcome disabilities and become more independent in performance of a range of activities of daily living, solutions to more complex problems, like those associated with upper and lower limb function, have yet to be found. Thus, while considerable progress has been made, realisation of Bowe's vision of a world in which technology can eliminate disability is still some way off.

Handicap

In the WHO classification, handicap - in orientation, communication, physical independence, mobility, social integration, occupation or economic self-sufficiency - is described as 'a *disadvantage* for a given individual, resulting from an impairment or a disability, that limits or prevents fulfilment of a role that is normal (depending on age, sex and social and cultural factors) for that individual' (author's italics). While handicap may follow from impairment or disability, it is important to note that it is not inevitably associated with either. An individual may have impairments and/or disabilities but not necessarily be handicapped by them, although there is some support for the view that some impairments and more severe disablement are more likely to be associated with disadvantage. Consideration of new technology in relation to handicap therefore raises questions about the extent to which access to and utilisation of its products and processes help to reduce or eliminate disadvantage.

Previous examples have already illustrated how developments in new technology are helping some individuals with disabilities to lessen handicapping consequences of disablement and have indicated how future developments may also contribute to this objective. However, the crucial question of cost has not been addressed. All too frequently, serious illness or injuries are associated with loss of employment, and there are few people with disabilities who are of independent means. If people with disabilities will not be able to rely upon the state for assistance with the purchase of aids and equipment, funding - as Bowe envisages - will need to be found from wages or salaries. As the most significant key to reducing handicap in other dimensions is expected to be the achievement of economic self-sufficiency through employment, discussion here is restricted to these pivotal dimensions.

No one can doubt that new technologies - especially information technology - and the emergence of new science-based industries have dramatically transformed the labour markets of modern societies.[11] This is apparent from recent and ongoing changes in where people work, the sectoral shifts from primary and manufacturing industries to service industries. It is also evident in related changes in what people do, the shifts which have taken place in the distribution of occupations, with decreased demand for unskilled and semi-skilled labour and increased demand for highly qualified technical, scientific and professional staff. To a less marked, but possibly equally significant, extent it is also apparent in changes in working conditions, the organisation of work and - some would say - in attitudes to work.

Even before these developments took place, there was evidence that people with disabilities in all industrial societies were much more vulnerable than their non-disabled peers to discrimination in the labour market and, hence, that they were much more likely to experience the social and economic disadvantages with long-term unemployment. Certainly, no country could claim that policies or special employment measures designed to help them secure greater equality of opportunity or achievement have attained these objectives. New technologies, however, have been widely heralded as an opportunity to break with the past, paving the way for a significant expansion in the number and range of jobs that properly trained and equipped people with disabilities could undertake.

There were three main reasons for adopting this more optimistic point of view. First, technological developments included a range of new technical aids, adaptations and ergonomic applications that would help overcome the handicap associated with some major physical and sensory disabilities. Second, many of the new jobs generated by new technologies make use of electronic skill, strength or precision rather than the physical strength of human operators, and such jobs should be particularly suited to the residual skills and abilities of persons with disabilities. Thirdly, progress in telecommunications is enabling some persons to work 'remotely' in their homes, a pattern of employment that is clearly appropriate for many people who previously have been handicapped by restricted mobility or inaccessible work sites.[12,13]

Recent studies have confirmed the feasibility of employing people with severe sensory and physical disabilities in a range of different new technology-based occupations, either in conventional work places or working from home.[14] While there is comparatively little information about the number of persons benefiting from such arrangements, there is some evidence that the number employed is increasing, even though progress has been slower than anticipated. The reasons for this appear to be much less associated with technology than with employers' attitudes, practices and procedures. This has certainly been the experience of the creative and well resourced Swedish TUFFA project which set out to demonstrate the art-of-the-possible in innovative, new technology-based, employment creation for people with severe disabilities.[15] Its progress has been impeded not by technology-related problems, to which a series of highly inventive, practical solutions have been found, but by employers' reluctance to accept more employees with such disabilities. Similar difficulties were identified in a series of case studies of individuals with severe sensory and physical disabilities who had succeeded in gaining employment in new technology related occupations.[16] These investigations - which embraced their experience of education and training, involvement in recruitment and selection procedures, requirements for technical aids and other work place 'accommodations', job satisfaction and career development - also found that procedural and attitudinal factors were much more significant than those of a technological nature.

For example, while many had tried to find employment in open competition with other job seekers, few had been successful in this sphere. In most cases, jobs had been obtained as a result of interventions made on their behalf by vocational rehabilitation services' personnel and other persons or because they were able to take advantage of various special measures to assist the employment of people with disabilities. Certainly, subjects' reports suggested that they experienced considerable difficulty in overcoming obstacles imposed by routine personnel selection decision making practices and procedures. Given that such cases were studied because they were considered to be examples of success in obtaining and retaining employment, there is no telling how many others may have been put off by the experience of discrimination.

Another dimension of this problem was apparent in the cases of some younger people with physical disabilities resulting from illness or injury experienced after leaving school. In such cases, it was not uncommon for long periods of medical rehabilitation and vocational training in order to learn a new occupation to be followed by appointment in temporary or entry-level jobs which made little or no use of their skills and potential. It would seem that employers were imposing additional hurdles, requiring them to demonstrate acceptable records of timekeeping, attendance and safety, or to prove themselves in other ways, before contemplating offers of more permanent employment in capacities that made better use of their skills and expertise.

There was a clear indication that generally employers remain resistant to the employment of people with disabilities, about whom many stereotyped perceptions and inappropriate expectations persist. Such attitudes may be modified a little by experience or by employers' involvement in successful cases. Indeed, some stated that, given their experience with the persons involved in the case studies, they would now be much more willing to consider employing suitably trained and qualified people with disabilities, and one or two were actively taking steps to do so. If more people are to benefit, however, it will be necessary to ensure that many other employers are persuaded to follow their example.

In the past, the problem of employment of persons with severe disabilities has been mainly perceived as a technical or technological problem. In the EEC, for example, the HANDYNET system has been much more generously supported than any other aspect of the Commission's vocational rehabilitation programme. The evidence from studies such as those reviewed here, however, suggests that it may be desirable to achieve a much better balance between measures of this kind and others which deal more directly with financial and social dimensions of employment handicap, for example, by providing more generous funding for technical aids and adaptations and by tackling discrimination in personnel selection, appointment and career development practices and procedures. Dissemination of 'good practice' is one approach to be tried, but it may need to be reinforced by appropriate anti-discrimination legislation or other similar measures.

Conclusions

This chapter has reviewed the impact of new technology on the lives of people with disabilities at the levels of impairment, disability and handicap, as defined by the World Health Organisation. Whilst it is apparent that some progress has been made at each level, applications of new technology are most widespread, well established and securely funded at the level of impairment. At this level, new technology is already making significant contributions to saving life, improving diagnostic technique, investigation and treatment of a wide range of illnesses and injuries, and health screening - with a clear promise of more to follow in such areas as prevention and health promotion.

At the level of disability, applications of new technology are much less widespread, less well developed and less securely financed, being more tied to research and development rather than service budgets. Nevertheless, as the examples of progress in different areas demonstrated, an increasingly wide range of new technology-based products are helping to restore, augment, compensate or substitute for many different sensory and physical functional deficits. There is a considerable way to go before technology eliminates disability, as Frank Bowe envisages it will. However, it is already enabling a small but gradually increasing number of people with disabilities to be more independent, to engage more fully in various activities of daily living and to achieve and enjoy a better quality of life. And, in this case also, there are good prospects of further progress, especially if prospective purchasers are able to afford new products, or other ways are found to make them available to a larger number of potential beneficiaries, and if consumers are permitted a greater say in the design of new equipment.

It is at the level of handicap that least progress has been made, with the sticking points possibly having much less to do with new technology itself than with access to, and opportunities to utilise, its various products. There is therefore still a wide gap to be bridged between the perceived benefits of new technology and the prevailing generally low levels of take-up by people with disabilities. The existence of this gap highlights the extent to which changes in technology pose wider questions of a social, economic, political and cultural nature, as illustrated by the example of employment handicap.

It is only quite recently that serious consideration has been given to redesigning jobs and adapting workplaces to match the residual capabilities of employees with disabilities. The willingness of employers to consider implementing such 'accommodations' is therefore one favourable sign for the future. Also new jobs and new opportunities to organise and locate work on an entirely different basis using new technologies are increasingly perceived as offering even more grounds for optimism. But there may be several reasons why such optimism should be qualified. One is the fact that some people with disabilities may lack the educational attainment or training potential needed to make a career in this field. Another, suggested by Croxen,[17] is the possibility that the skills associated with new technologies, with emphases on jobs in designing, engineering, programming and administering automated systems, could put individuals with disabilities at a disadvantage. As she maintains, the planning, communication and teamwork skills necessary for such jobs all require personal qualities, like confidence and independence, which are rarely enhanced by their life experience. Schworles,[18] who conducted a survey of access to new technology, is also pessimistic. While

acknowledging that people with disabilities are benefiting from personal computer technology, he expressed concern that they were falling behind other
members of society in their mastery of this new technology owing to problems
of access, mobility, finance and discriminatory attitudes. If he is correct in
identifying an emerging 'culture gap' of this kind, there are undoubtedly grounds
for disappointment over the persistence of problems of a kind to which new
technology was expected to contribute some more positive and effective solutions.

Recent developments confirm that new technology has enabled some people
with disabilities to take advantage of new opportunities for employment or
self-employment. But it is questionable whether their achievements have increased employment opportunities or merely enabled them to hold on to a
previously low share of jobs in a changing labour market. Certainly, if labour
market participation rates are a litmus test of Bowe's vision, it has to be concluded
that new technology has not been a panacea. People with disabilities are still a
long way from achieving a fair share of job opportunities: survey evidence[19,20]
indicates that few societies can boast that more than a third of citizens with
disabilities who are of working age are in employment, less than half of the labour
market participation rates of their non-disabled counterparts. Increased participation would appear to depend on such other factors as funding and access to
appropriate education, rehabilitation and training to equip them with the qualifications, technical skills and personal competence to enable them to secure a fairer
share of employment opportunities.

Schworles' reference to discriminatory attitudes is a reminder that changes in
education, rehabilitation and training provision, however essential and valuable,
may not be the whole answer. People with disabilities undoubtedly will continue
to be reliant on all the expertise and resourcefulness that professional services
and parents have always provided. But future needs may call for much more. For
example, there are clear indications that, in the past, well intentioned parental
protectiveness and a correspondingly well meant paternalism of professions did
not equip people with disabilities with the social and emotional maturity needed
to cope ably with the world of work. Personal competence and independence,
however, will be just as important to success in tomorrow's world as they are
today, possibly more so. New initiatives in education, rehabilitation, training and
employment therefore should also seek to facilitate their independence and
empowerment. In part, this may entail legislation, for it is evident that it is in
those countries which have implemented anti-discrimination and related civil
rights legislation that more progress is being made toward the achievement of

equality of opportunity for people with disabilities. However, to exploit fully the opportunities created by legislation, it may be equally important to ensure that people with disabilities feel empowered to act in the same way that those who have participated in the independent living movement[21] were able to act. This will require a markedly different, 'enabling' response from parents, professions, services and society at large.

People with disabilities recognise this. The plea made at the First World Congress of Disabled Peoples' International was for 'a voice of our own'.[22] Their fuller participation in all spheres of life - social, economic, political and cultural - will depend greatly on the extent to which they and their supporters or 'enablers' can lay claim to and exercise that right during the transition from school to work and throughout their lifetimes. In this respect, access to new technology is an issue to be considered and bargained for alongside such other issues as income, housing, transportation and employment, with which organisations of people with disabilities are already concerned.

References

1. *Therapy Weekly*. 25 January 1990, 20.

2. Bowe, F. G. *Rehabilitating America: Toward Independence for Disabled and Elderly People*. Harper & Rowe, New York, 1980.

3. Bowe, F. G. 'Disabled and Elderly People in the First, Second and Third Worlds' *International Journal of Rehabilitation Research*. 13, 1990, 1-14.

4. *Technology Support*. Summer 1990, 6.

5. Bell, D. *The Coming of Post-Industrial Society: A Venture in Social Forecasting*. Heinemann, London, 1974.

6. World Health Organisation. *International Classification of Impairments, Disabilities and Handicaps*. WHO, Geneva, 1980.

7. Oliver, M., Zarb, G., Silver, J., Moore, M. and Salisbury, V. *Walking into Darkness: The Experience of Spinal Cord Injury*. MacMillan, Basingstoke, 1988.

8. Susini, C. and Tronconi, A. 'Italian Research on Computers and the Physically Handicapped' *International Journal of Rehabilitation Research*. 13, 1990, 215-223.

9. Creasey, G. H. *Functional Electrical Stimulation: A Review*. Unpublished report for the Medical Research Council, 1988.

10. Foulds, R. (Ed.) *Interactive Robotic Aids - One Option for Independent Living: An International Perspective*. World Rehabilitation Fund, New York, 1986.

11. Cornes, P. *The Future of Work for People with Disabilities: A View from Great Britain*. World Rehabilitation Fund, New York, 1984.

12. Department of Trade and Industry. *Remote Work Units Project for Disabled People: Evaluation Study*. DTI, London, 1985.

13. National Rehabilitation Board and Work Research Centre. *Teleworking Applications and Potential: A Feasibility Study of Home-based and Centre-based Telework for People with Physical Disabilities*. NRB and WRC, Dublin, 1989.

14. Rehabilitation International. *The Impact of New Technology on the Employment of Persons with Disabilities*. Unpublished report for the International Labour Office. Rehabilitation International, New York, 1988.

15. Breding, J. and Keijer, U. *An Overview of the TUFFA Project*. Swedish Labour Market Board, Stockholm, 1990.

16. Cornes, P. *Effect of New Technology on Employment of Young People with Severe Sensory or Physical Disabilities: Selected Case Studies from Ireland, Scotland and Sweden*. Unpublished report for the Centre for Educational Research and Innovation, OECD, 1989.

17. Croxen, M. *Employment and disability: Choosing a Way of Life*. Unpublished report for the European Economic Community, 1982.

18. Schworles, T. R. 'The Person with Disability and the Benefits of the Microcomputer Revolution' *Rehabilitation Literature*. 44, 1983, 322-330.

19. Bowe, F. G. *Demography and Disability: A Chartbook for Rehabilitation*. Rehabilitation Research and Training Center, University of Arkansas, Arkansas, 1983.

20. Martin, J., White, A. and Meltzer, H. *Disabled Adults: Services, Transport and Employment*. OPCS Surveys of Disability in Great Britain, Report 4. HMSO, London, 1989.

21. DeJong, G. *Environmental Accessibility and Independent Living Outcomes: Directions for Disability Policy and Research*. University Center for International Rehabilitation, East Lansing, MI, 1981.

22. Miller, K. (Ed.) *A Voice of Our Own*. Disabled People's International and University Center for International Rehabilitation, East Lansing, MI, 1982.

Working with Children with Physical Disabilities and Their Families - The Social Work Role

Philippa Russell

CHILDREN AND YOUNG PEOPLE AND THEIR PARENTS SHOULD ALL BE CONSIDERED AS INDIVIDUALS WITH PARTICULAR NEEDS AND POTENTIALITIES.

Whilst clear policies and guidelines are necessary and helpful, standardised routine decisions or rigid across-the-board policies do not lead to acceptable practice. All regulations, policies, guidance and procedures should take into account the wide diversity of ages, needs, ethnic origins, cultures and circumstances that lies behind general categories such as 'foster children', 'children in care' or 'children in need' (*The Care of Children: Principles and Practice in Regulations and Guidance*. HMSO, 1990).

Developing a philosophy of family support

A number of studies have endeavoured to assess the levels of stress experienced by families with disabled children with a view to developing effective programmes for family support. Glendinning;[4] Brimblecombe and Russell;[8] Cunningham and Davis[1] and Pahl and Quine[9] all identify a range of stress-related problems in such families. In general research - not surprisingly - identifies a greater degree of stress and psychological and physical problems in families with disabled children. However, the above studies do not suggest that a 'handicapped child is a handicapped family' (Younghusband[9]), but rather that disability is a major and *potentially* damaging life event which is amenable to intervention and which is compatible with good quality family life. The Honeylands' assessment of stress using the Rutter Malaise Inventory[8] replicated other findings but also clearly indicated the need to avoid making sweeping generalisations about family experiences and life-styles. Not all the Honeylands user families experienced abnormal stress levels but stress - when it existed - appeared to be frequently linked to severe restrictions on social and family life, on poor physical health, marital and economic difficulties as much as upon the disability of the child.

A study by Chetwynd[10] of families in New Zealand, using the same Rutter Malaise Inventory, also found stress levels and stress factors very similar to the Honeylands study. Stress factors in the Chetwynd study were not specifically linked to the severity of the child's disability but seemed to be higher according to the impact of a particular disability within the family structure. Thus parents who perceived their social life as severely restricted or their health adversely affected were more likely to be depressed and anxious. The Honeylands study, like Chetwynd's, indicated that existing personality and other problems could affect adaptation and acceptance. Bradshaw and Lawton[11] also used the Malaise Inventory and found that the impact of disability needed to be put in the broader context of 'internal' factors such as the personality and health of the parents as well as on the severity of the disability. The Honeylands evaluation found, importantly, that stress levels were not static and that parents using services could actually become *more* stressed because of changing family circumstances than actually coming to terms with the fact that their child had a long-term disability or difficulty. The Honeylands conclusion was that 'one-off' snap-shot pictures of family stress should be avoided and that support services should be continually reassessed in the light of individual family needs. All the above studies clearly indicate that acknowledgement of stress is essential in order to ensure take up of existing services. The Pahl and Quine research showed some families to be so stressed that they were incapable of negotiating personal support.

The impact of the *initial* diagnosis of a disability on future family expectations of both child and professionals has been well documented. Cliff Cunningham[1] found that fifty-eight per cent of parents of Down Syndrome babies in the Manchester area were dissatisfied with the initial diagnosis. Pahl and Quine[9] found sixty per cent of parents of a wide range of disabled children similarly disenchanted with how the bad news was broken. The Manchester study led to revised procedures which produced *high* degrees of parental satisfaction. Parents were told together, were given a 'follow-up' visit for clarification and further discussion and were immediately offered access to community services and a developmental programme for the child. Recent research by both Cunningham and Davis[2] has additionally shown the importance of *counselling* as an integral part of early intervention in order to enhance parental confidence, competence and use of services. Both studies indicated a consequent improved take-up of services and positive attitudes to young disabled children.

A key factor in creating a supportive environment for families with disabled children appears to be the availability of a 'named person' or designated worker for families using services. Dr Hilton Davies[2] has developed the concept of a 'parent adviser' in a child development team working in Tower Hamlets. He saw the role of a parent adviser as liaison with other professionals and agencies; monitoring the child's and families' progress, acting as communicator and counsellor and providing personal and emotional support. Dr Davis, like the Honeylands evaluation study, emphasised the importance of developing trusting relationships with families, of demonstrating respect for the family (with a recognition of social, ethnic or other variables) and recognising the real difficulties experienced by many parents. One role for the 'named person' may be resolving the different views and interests of the child and the wider family network. A Report on the Carraigfole Paediatric Support Unit in Northern Ireland (Barnardos Irish Division[12]) observes that:

> The importance of family networks was important in the course of our work. The extended family often shared in the care of the child and provided emotional support. *But* sometimes this also brought emotional complications. While giving that emotional support, all parties were under strain as they (the extended family) lacked the necessary information to be able to help adequately.

Other networks may also be important. Hatch and Hinton,[13] evaluating the parent self-help group 'Contact a Family' found that membership of a voluntary or community group had direct benefits. User families were more likely to make good use of existing professional services. Families had higher expectations for their disabled children and families felt less isolated and better supported. An unpublished review looking at mothers' use of 'social networks' for child care advice in the USA,[14] found that some parents much preferred using social to family networks for some kinds of advice and that 'providing the context for interaction amongst parents' should be a positive part of professional services.

Social networks may be particularly important for disadvantaged families. Negative feelings in some families with disabled children may occur where the parents concerned already had low self-image and saw their child as part of a cumulative disadvantage of poor performance at school, poor self image, difficult marriages and relationships and general inability to cope. Where disability formed part of a cluster of 'bad things' happening to particular families, family therapy and specific support for the parents' existing problems might be a prerequisite for effective use of other services. Membership of therapeutic self-help groups could have major benefits in terms of heightening expectations and encouraging parents to feel they could cope.

Parents as co-workers

Since the 1970s major shifts of opinion have led to parents being recognised as 'partners' and having not only a voice but direct skills to utilise in meeting their child's special needs. But although the majority of service providers for families of disabled children acknowledge the need to encourage active partnership with parents, such partnership cannot be assumed to be present simply because professionals are working with parents. The increasing popularity of the Portage home teaching scheme for parents of pre-school disabled children has demonstrated the importance of a known, trained and supported home visitor making regular visits to a family in order to monitor the child's progress and to identify goals and structure simple teaching programmes. Portage[15] is becoming a major source of skill training (and skill sharing) for professionals as well as for parents. Health visitors, community nurses, social workers, home liaison teachers and psychologists have learned through Portage how to work as a team, how to share ideas and skills directly with parents and the importance of mutual support in selecting *appropriate* goals and teaching techniques for children with a wide range of special needs. Many parents do not know how to utilise their unique knowledge of their child in a meaningful way and do not understand the principles behind the practice of treatment and early intervention programmes. Portage is an important example of involving all consumers in a programme which teaches success, which is sensitive to social, personal and cultural variables, and which can be utilised in a wide range of care settings. Such partnership is not, however, a cheap resource and an alternative to the full range of support services such as respite care, aids and equipment and appropriate housing. Cunningham and Davis[1] note the need to put any family support in the context of available and accessible resources; accurate and comprehensive information and continuity rather than one-off interventions. Many parents still feel marginalised by procedures which they do not fully understand and where they are uncertain how to express their views. The 1981 Education Act does, however, offer a framework for shared assessment of individual children and for consumer participation. Using this legislation to plan for children (and ensuring that local authority social services departments support care workers or other staff working with separated children) is one way forward in making better use of resources and in giving parents and carers a genuine sense of partnership and ownership in decision-making about their children. Home-based learning programmes like Portage are also still under-used in a social work context. Historically they were developed as part of a USA federal programme to provide early support for disadvantaged families. Portage in this context can be used to develop mothering skills and to encourage developmental play and other activities.

Respite care: opportunities for shared care

Respite or short-term care for families with a disabled child has developed historically as an emergency service - frequently providing short-term care within a long-stay hospital or other institution in order to meet a family crisis. Traditionally respite care was offered in 'block' bookings for summer holidays or similar periods and was usually distant from the family home and local services. However, in the last decade there has been a general commitment to flexible family support services, which include respite care as one of a range of options for individual families and children. This shift in thinking towards seeing respite care as part of an *integrated* service and not a special one-off intervention was based upon Maureen Oswin's principle that 'short term care should be regarded as a very specialist service needing clearly defined aims based on principles of child care practice and requiring continuous monitoring of standards with an emphasis on how it might be affecting individual *children*'. Maureen Oswin's research[16] stressed the need to think of *children* first and identified an inherent tension in respite care which is frequently directed to supposed parent relief and not necessarily treated as part of a coherent local authority child care policy for all children.

   In the past decade there has been growing concern to provide flexible short-term care which offers:

a) A local service, where the child can continue to attend school as if he or she were living at home.

b) Good quality child care which ensures that the child is not treated as a sick patient, but as any child who happens to have a disability.

c) Availability on *demand*. Research into different models of respite care has clearly indicated the importance of *parents* choosing patterns of use and being able to use a service flexibly. There is good evidence that many families prefer to use respite care services for short periods of time (sometimes during the day only) rather than in longer-term block bookings.

d) A service which meets the needs of all children. Concern has been expressed about the lack of respite care for children with emotional and behaviour difficulties or complex medical problems.

e) Age-appropriate care - so that young children and adolescents are given relevant care and occupation.

f) An integrated programme of family support which sees respite care as part of a wider range of professional support services to meet family needs. Maureen Oswin[16] in a research study of different models of respite care, identified concerns about escalating use of respite care indicating a need for preventive services to prevent some children slipping into long-term care.

Respite or short-term care is available in a number of forms. Some children still receive such care in long-stay *mental handicap* hospitals. The most recent DHSS statistics show over 11,000 annual *short-stay* admissions to long stay mental handicap hospitals. This group of hospital users represent the multiple physical and severe behaviour difficulties which many local authorities are currently unable to place. Some respite care is provided in local authority children's homes, together with a number of voluntary organisations' small residential units or staffed holiday homes.

A particular problem in some respite care schemes has been apparent under-use, despite parental appreciation of the availability of such a service. The Honeylands evaluation[8] and the DHSS Social Work Inspectorate study of respite fostering in Norfolk and Oxfordshire[17] both identified a number of families who emphasised the importance of guaranteed availability of respite care in enabling them to maintain severely handicapped children at home. Two families in the Honeylands study (Brimblecombe and Russell[24]) actually claimed they had used emergency short-term care when in fact they had never done so. But so real was their perception of the service offered that they felt secure enough to feel that they had used it and found it a critical factor in continuing family care.

The non-take-up of precious and expensive beds (or substitute families) can be a problematic issue for service providers and planners. The National Development Team (1985) in its annual report noted that:

> anxieties about occupancy rates and the cost of the establishment deter management from being willing to risk places being unused for a time. The need to book short-term care as much as a year in advance discourages parents from requesting help and a vicious circle develops of cutting places because demand appears low.

Studies of short-term care in the Preston Skreens Family Support Unit in Kent (Pahl[9]), Honeylands (Brimblecombe and Russell[24]) and Avon (Robinson[18]) have all found very varied patterns of use amongst families if services are used in ways and at times appropriate to individual family needs. The Preston Skreens study, for example, found that out of twenty-one families using the unit for respite care, thirty-eight at one end of the scale had only once stayed overnight (day-time respite care becoming an increasingly popular option for many parents) whilst three children had made over fifty visits respectively. The majority of families using both Preston Skreens and Honeylands were light users, with respite care complementing a range of other services. The Avon research[18] emphasises the fallacy of assuming that respite care is a universal panacea for all family problems. This study found that

> many of the *user* families had unmet needs as did many of the *non*-user families
> . . . in both groups there was a call for more home-based services such as sitters,
> helpers to assist mothers etc. It is evident that the respite care service alone cannot
> meet the needs of all families with a handicapped child . . . it is important to
> provide a range of services for these families.

Evidence about the ability of short-term respite care to alleviate family stress is inevitably subjective. The Honeylands evaluation suggests that many families may in fact need relief, but will still only use respite services on an incremental basis. Hence family relief may not be instantaneous and, indeed, measurements of stress levels in families in the Honeylands studies suggested that some families were actually *more* stressed at the start of using a service than before they did so. Overall stress levels were clearly significantly reduced after a period of time. But the stresses associated with letting a child go to another family or unit for the *first* time are frequently under-estimated. The DHSS Inspectorate Report[17] in Oxfordshire made a similar point, noting the stages through which parents needed to go in becoming positive utilisers of respite services. This study identified three hurdles for potential users to overcome, namely using the service chosen for the first time; leaving the child overnight; and placing a child for a longer period while the parents went away on their own.

It is also clear from a number of studies that parents with children with special health care needs or difficult behaviour may feel safer with a small residential unit rather than a substitute family.

Although there has been no comparative research into parental satisfaction with different models of respite care, it seems that parents are more likely to be satisfied if a service is clearly linked to a voluntary organisation, school or a wider service like Honeylands or Preston Skreens in order to put the service in context and to ensure that respite care is a rewarding experience for the child.

Children living away from home

Children with disabilities will live away from home for all the reasons that affect their non-disabled peers. The OPCS Reports[19] looking at a sample of 1,000 children with disabilities living away from home found that:

- 33% lived away because their parents or foster families could not cope with specific behaviour or health problems
- 33% had unsuitable family homes
- 25% had 'problems at home'
- 15% had experienced sexual or physical abuse.

The figures suggest that some children *might* have remained at home if support services had been more specific. but they also indicate that child *protection* is also a factor to be considered and that child abuse should be acknowledged as a risk factor affecting all children.

Decisions about the type of placement will undoubtedly be more complex when the child has a disability. But as *The Care of Children: Principles and Practice in Regulations and Guidance* (1990) notes,

a child's age, health, personality, race, culture and life experiences are all relevant to any consideration of needs and vulnerability and have to be taken account of when planning and providing help.

The same guidance emphasises the importance of participative decision making by parents *and* children, based upon informed choice and with serious consideration being given to the feelings and perceptions of the *child*.

Lessons undoubtedly need to be learned from the experiences of children's services working in wider residential and foster care programmes. Berridge and Cleaver[20] found that breakdown was most likely if 'profound social, emotional, geographical, educational and economic changes' occurred simultaneously. The same study underlined the consequences of ignoring significant person relationships in children's lives and the importance of permanence and security. Sonia Jackson[22] has also shown the often disastrous long-term effects of frequent educational disruption and lack of planning in the lives of children living in the care of the local authority.

As Ann Leonnard[21] commented, 'in a society as complex as this one, . . . there are no standardised households or lives against which the households and personal autonomy, dignity and risk, an ordinary home life may all be interpreted differently within different communities.' However, *Out of Hospital* provides some invaluable insights into the process of achieving strategic change. It is also a rare study of the everyday lives of children and young people with severe disabilities.

The Leonnard research identified certain key factors in providing good residential services for this group of children who have generally failed to find support within mainstream children's services. First, attitudes were crucial (in particular the support for staff of 'life-minded management'). Second, planning and involvement of everybody concerned at an early stage was essential for later success. Third, the actual housing was 'unexceptionally homely, comfortable, without being ostentatious, ordinary family houses in ordinary streets'. In effect severely disabled children can live well in non-purpose built accommodation like the rest of us.

There has been little substantive research into the lives of disabled children living in local authority or voluntary residential homes (although Barnardos has evaluated and published findings on a number of its residential projects). There is, however, growing concern amongst both health and local authorities at the consequences of wider changes in provision for *all* children living away from home. A number of local authorities are closing residential provision in favour of a shift to fostering. Although the outcomes from the National Children's Bureau evaluation of the Warwickshire plan of closure is not yet available, formal reports from other local authorities where there has been a reduction in residential provision give cause for concern.

There appears to be a growing number of disabled children attending residential *schools* (usually in the independent sector) primarily for residential care. A growing number of schools in the independent sector are already catering for fifty-two weeks a year provision. Whilst an *educational* focus in care is important, there are concerns about the quality of child care practice and an 'ordinary life' philosophy in schools which extend their terms to cover the whole year. There has been no recent research into the lives of disabled children *living* at their school (or perhaps going from school to a succession of short-stay placements when on holiday). Children living away from home for *educational* reasons do not necessarily have a care order and the transition back to their place of origin when leaving school will cause major problems without adequate pre-planning. An important area for future research would, therefore, seem to be some evaluation of the quality of life and personal experiences of pupils at residential special schools, in particular where there is no regular home contact, and an exploration of the reasons why such children do not remain in their own local communities at day schools but with foster-care or other support. There are no national figures for the numbers of children and young people with disabilities who are living in voluntary or private residential homes or schools. Where the latter provide education of a kind on the premises there are again doubts (but no firm data) about the quality of provision offered to children and the alternatives in the local community.

The Children Act 1989 will give social workers clear duties with regard to children and the residential sector (including health and education). Local authorities *must* be informed by health and education authorities, residential care, nursing or mental nursing homes of any child who spends *at least three months* in their provision. Social Services Departments now have new duties to ensure the welfare of children in such establishments and have right to inspect as required.

As part of this new provision, health and education authorities must also inform the social services department for the area in which a child or young person proposes to live, if a child has reached sixteen and leaves accommodation which has been provided for at least three months. In theory this should encourage more effective implementation of procedures under the 1986 Disabled Persons Act and the forthcoming NHS and Community Care Act, which will require social services departments to make new arrangements for the care and support of people with special needs in the community.

Because of significant concern about child protection in independent schools (highlighted in the 'That's Life' programme about Crookham Court) the Act gives new duties with regard to all children accommodated in independent schools. An independent school is defined as 'any school at which full-time education is provided for five or more pupils of compulsory school age, not being a school maintained by the local education authority, a grant maintained school or a special school maintained by the education authority'. The 'five pupils' includes schools which are primarily nursery schools but which happen to have any group of five children of school age. Hence private nursery schools or post-school provision which includes five or more children or young people of school age will come under the provisions of Section 91(1).

The social services departments must take all reasonably practicable steps to enable them to decide whether the child's welfare is adequately safeguarded and promoted in the school (Section 87(3)). If they consider that the child's welfare is not being adequately safeguarded, the social services department must notify the Secretary of State. Social Services may authorise people to enter the school in order to exercise their welfare duty and may (subject to regulations yet to be drawn up) inspect the school premises, records and the children. The right to inspect the *children* is of particular significance with regard to children with special educational needs. They are the most likely to have communication difficulties and to be placed at some distance from their family home. Vigilance from social services departments will offer a significant new protection. HMI duties are unaffected by these new powers for social services.

The Boarding Schools Association has identified 923 independent schools in the United Kingdom, with 127,250 boarder pupils (Anderson and Morgan[27]). They estimate that there are approximately 5,320 pupils (i.e. four per cent) with special educational needs. Inspecting these schools will have major resource implications for both social services departments and education authorities. It should also be emphasised that the new arrangements apply to *all* independent schools and not only to those providing for special educational needs. Although the idea of inspecting Harrow or Eton would seem quite alien to many authorities, *all* residential establishments caring for children need careful monitoring. It is to be hoped that the Children Act will refocus attention not only on the quality of education offered in residential schools, but on the wider needs of children living in them.

The changing policies in local authorities away from residential homes towards fostering children should be positive for children with disabilities. A growing number of children, some with complex needs, are being successfully placed with foster families. However, foster families (like natural parents) will need extra help and resources. An evaluation of the independent adoption agency, Parents for Children[22] suggests that specialist adoption and fostering schemes need:

a) A sufficiently long and supportive introduction period between child and parent.

b) A realisation that 'atypical' substitute families, with unusual backgrounds, may be more appropriate than conventional carers.

c) Ongoing support for the family, which takes account of changing needs as the child grows.

d) A positive expectation that whereas some placements may break down, the majority can be successful with appropriate recruitment, placement and support arrangements and that there are many families in the community who will be happy to accept a disabled child.

Disabled child - handicapped adult?

General improvements in services for young disabled children have led to increasing optimism about the feasibility of ordinary *adult* life experiences and independent living and employment. However, as the Warnock Report noted in 1978,

> We are aware that greater independence particularly for those with severe disabilities will not be achieved simply by administrative measures or the injection of more resources . . . in the end changes in the nature of education, training and supporting services will depend upon changes in *attitude*.

Attitudes, particularly following the implementation of the 1981 Education Act, have become generally more positive and optimistic for *children*. But recent research clearly indicates that the lessons from children's services have not necessarily been successfully applied to adult services and that the transition period is poorly managed and often nullifies earlier progress.

The Prince of Wales Advisory Group (1985), the Royal College of Physicians (1986) and Brimblecombe and Kuh (1987) all examined current research and practice with regard to the management of transition for disabled adolescents and young adults and raised important areas of concern for future work and development. The most substantive (Brimblecombe and Kuh) arose from earlier research within the Exeter Health Authority, which had established the need for a family support centre and parent-orientated services for young disabled children. Honeylands is still the best developed (and the most completely evaluated) of all the centre-based services for disabled children and families. But this evaluation in turn indicated that many children who were well supported until sixteen met a lack of opportunities and sometimes positively harmful absence of treatment when they moved to adult services.

A research study was therefore established in order to examine the needs of *all* the disabled school leavers in Exeter in one year and to compare their expectations, lifestyles and personal satisfaction with a control group of able-bodied peers. The study is unique in not only asking parents and relevant professionals for their opinions, but in also talking directly to the 365 young people themselves. The research indicated important and alarming gaps in services in a relatively well resourced health authority, with particularly good children's services. Less than half the young people (forty-eight per cent) had seen a medical specialist in the previous year, although they had all received regular health care until they moved from paediatric services. Sixty-eight per cent felt that they had insufficient information about the actual medical implications of their disability (including the genetic implications if they wished to subsequently have children). A similar sixty-eight per cent lacked physiotherapy, speech therapy and other specialist medical input. Seventy per cent of the young disabled people and sixty-three per cent of those with a mental handicap lacked any daytime occupation - apart from simply at home, and sixty-two per cent felt that they had limited opportunities for any social life once they had left school. The *carers* indicated a general lack of short term care, help and advice and generally felt unsupported.

When compared to their peers, the young disabled people indicated some major and worrying differences. Thirty-five per cent as against twelve per cent mentioned loneliness as a big problem. Lack of social confidence and poor self-esteem were very conspicuous and a number felt that their problems actually lay in being at home, where their needs were not sympathetically met. It should be noted that there has been almost no significant research (and none in this country) into the changing role of parents as carers of young adults. Indeed we are probably only now moving into a period of growing expectations about 'Care in the Community', where there is an assumption that the traditional institutional forms of residential care will be unacceptable but where alternative local provision is not yet developed. Maintaining an adult child-parent relationship whilst providing for major care needs must present significant challenges. A number of services for young adults (like MENCAP's Home Foundation residential homes) are initiating training for staff working with parents *and* adult children. The provisions of the 1986 Disabled Persons Act enable the needs of carer and disabled persons to be assessed separately. But the recognition of different and sometimes differing needs, and the most effective way of renegotiating parent/adult child relationships need further investigation.

The depression indicated in the Brimblecombe/Kuh research[23] has also been clearly demonstrated in the work of Julie Bargh[28] in evaluating the National Children's Bureau's self-advocacy project for young people with learning difficulties. The project, the first of the self-advocacy programmes to work with *young* people between sixteen and nineteen, found a high incidence of depression, lack of self esteem and a feeling of stigma and rejection because of the disability. As in the Brimblecombe research, the young women from Inner London also felt marginalised. They felt that they had never been able to discuss their difficulties, which they found very painful to articulate. They frequently perceived themselves as being less valued than their siblings and longed for 'real lives' without knowing how to develop the social and vocational skills necessary to achieve them. Both studies clearly demonstrated that young people with a mental handicap can articulate their anxieties and their needs. Both studies also showed the sharp fall off on leaving school and the lack of transitional arrangements to ensure appropriate provision in adult life. The Bargh project had been designed to provide parallel group work experiences for *parents* but had found it almost impossible to persuade parents of the value of group and shared activities. Other attempts to attach parent groups to young adult services have also met with varying fortunes.

The legal framework

The Children Act 1989 offers an important opportunity and a framework within which social work can take a new lead role in:

a) Acknowledging that *all* children are 'children first' and that any services offered should be appropriate to basic child care principles, whatever a child's level of disability.

b) Using the new duties to identify 'children in need' and to maintain a register of disabled children in order to be more pro-active in identifying and planning for children with disabilities and their families. The success of the new community care arrangements will be considerably affected by the extent to which children's needs are adequately met and effective arrangements negotiated for transition to adult services.

c) Using the new legislation to revitalise social services relationships with the Education and Health Authorities and with the voluntary sector. In the end an 'ordinary life' for children with disabilities must be seen as everybody's business.

Many of the principles within the children Act apply to all children, but have been conspicuously lacking in much traditional planning for working with children with disabilities. The welfare principles of the children Act is to 'give first consideration to the need to safeguard and promote the welfare of the child throughout his childhood' and 'so far as is practicable to ascertain the wishes and feelings of the child regarding the decision and give due consideration to them having regard to his age and understanding'. The Act, with its advocacy principle, therefore creates new opportunities for social services to take a more positive lead in working with families. But it also poses major challenges at a time when resources are scarce and when children with disabilities are likely to be a minority group within any local authority.

Local authority support for children and families

The Act introduces a new concept of *children in need*. This is defined as meaning that a child will be regarded as being in need if:

a) he is unlikely to achieve or maintain, or to have the opportunity of achieving or maintaining, a reasonable standard of health or development without the provision for him of services by a local authority under this Part (of the Act);

b) his health or development is likely to be significantly impaired, or further impaired, without the provision for him of services; or

c) he is disabled.

For the purposes of this part, a child is disabled if he is blind, deaf or dumb or suffers from mental disorder of any kind or is substantially and permanently handicapped by illness, injury or congenital deformity or other such disability as may be prescribed, and in this Part of the Act:

- 'development' means physical, intellectual, emotional, social or behavioural developments
- 'health' means 'physical or mental health'
- 'family' in relation to such a child, includes any person who has parental responsibility for the child and any other person with whom he has been living.

The new definition of need provides the basis of a general duty now imposed on local authorities to provide services for children in need and '*so far as is consistent with that duty to promote upbringing of such children by their families*'. This general duty is supported by other specific duties such as facilitation of 'the provision by others (including in particular voluntary organisations or services)' and by schedules which will spell out the nature of these services. It is generally anticipated that these provisions should encourage local authorities to provide respite care and other support services as a means of supporting disabled children with their natural families.

For the first time local authorities have a general duty to provide day care services and supervised activities for *children in need* aged five and under and not at school and for school age children outside school hours and in school

holidays. It is hoped that these general duties may improve the range of holiday
and 'respite care' and other services for disabled children living at home or with
foster families. As Schedule 2 of the Act requires local authorities to identify
children in need and to publish and advertise the services provided (*in addition
to maintaining a register of disabled children*), the Act could result in a wider
range of out-of-school activities for children with special needs, with correspondingly better information on their whereabouts for both parents and professionals.

For disabled children, the Act (Schedule 2, Part 1) requires that:

Every local authority shall provide services designed:

> a) To minimise the effect on disabled children . . . of their difficulties; and

> b) To give such children the opportunity to led lives which are as normal
> as possible.

One major concern which has arisen with regard to support services such as
respite care is the potential deterrent to families if charges are introduced. At
present charging for respite or support services in social services of health
authorities is almost unheard of. Under the Children Act (Schedule 2, Part III,
Para 21), local authorities acquire a new duty to consider whether they should
charge parents. But they 'may only recover contributions . . . if they consider it
reasonable to do so.' The definition of 'reasonable' will vary between authorities
and has parallels with the NHS and Community Care Bill, which makes similar
provisions for charging for certain services. Both the Children Act and the NHS
and Community Care Bill separate assessment, advice and counselling (which
will be free) from practical services such as respite care, laundry or day care which
could be charged for. However, the OPCS Reports (1989) have clearly indicated
(a) the lower level of income in families with a disabled member as compared to
their counterparts in the wider community and (b) the existing additional costs
of caring for a disabled child.

Parental rights - and responsibilities

The Act introduces a new concept of *parental responsibility* as opposed to
parental rights. Clause 3 notes this as 'all the rights, duties, powers, responsibilities and authority which by law a parent of a child has in relation to the child
and his property.' A feature of the Act is that it acknowledges the extended family
as well as the parents. If, for example, the Courts consider that it is better for the
child to make a residence order to a grand-parent or other suitable person, rather
than a care order, they may do so. There is much greater flexibility available in

determining where and who with a child should live. This should be particularly helpful when a child has a disability.

Parents not only acquire responsibilities with the new legislation. The transfer to the local authority of parents' legal powers and status can now only be achieved through a Court Hearing. Otherwise services to the family must be arranged on the basis of a *voluntary partnership*. The concept of partnership is linked to prevention of family breakdown and the removal of the stigma that often associates itself with social services involvement.

This is particularly important in relation to children *not* subject to care orders but who may have been accommodated by the local authority (or health authority) for some time. The local authority will have as its first responsibility a *welfare duty* that takes into account the wishes of the child and his parents, as well as the child's ethnic origin and cultural and religious background. Subject to this principle, regulations will provide *voluntary agreements* between the local authority, the parents and the child (as appropriate). These new arrangements will include a number of provisions but they are not legally binding on parents.

The local authority is placed under a duty to do all that is reasonable in all circumstances to safeguard and promote the child's welfare. If, in the longer term, an agreement does not work, the local authority may seek a care order. If - by the time the courts hear the case - the parents' own circumstances have changed for the better, there may be debate about the degree of harm to which the child is now being exposed. The definition of *harm* can include the child's mental and physical development and advice on the nature of disability will be essential.

Assessment: a new partnership between parents, professionals - and the child

The duty to identify children in need (see section III) will require local authorities to develop assessment arrangements within agreed criteria which take account of the child and family's preferences, ethnic origins and any special needs relating to the circumstances of individual families. The assessment procedures are expected to complement existing statutory procedures of assessment, such as those already operational under the 1981 Education Act. Formal assessment under the 1981 Education Act already involves collaboration between health, education and social services and a child's Statement of Special Education Needs is likely to provide an important component in any social services assessment processes. As with the 1981 Act, social services departments will be expected to involve both parents and children in any assessment and decision making processes.

In some circumstances, more formal procedures may be necessary. In cases which go to court, the court will have to be advised amongst other things of the likely effect on the child of a change in circumstances and the ability of the child's parent to meet his or her needs. The court will further be guided by the assessment of the Report Writer, as to whether the making of an order will be better for the child than making no order at all. A high level of skill will be required to determine whether a child is suffering or likely to suffer significant harm. 'Harm' will be construed not only as actual physical or sexual abuse but also factors arising from the state of the child's health or development.

It is important to remember that a Child Assessment Order does *not* authorise an assessment or examination which the child refuses to undergo if the child is regarded as having sufficient understanding to make an informed decision about this question (Section 43(8)). Discussion around 'sufficient understanding' and the Data Protection Act suggest that children and young people with learning difficulties are not exempt from this right. In cases where there is concern about the child's ability to give an informed decision, a *Guardian ad Litem* may be appointed to act on behalf of the child and to provide an independent voice.

Throughout the new legislation, the theme of listening to children is given major emphasis. The Act contains a checklist of matters to be considered in most court hearings with regard to the child's best interests. As *An Introduction to the Children Act* (1989, HMSO) notes,

> The checklist of particular matters to which the court is to have regard in reaching decisions about the child is headed by the child's wishes and feelings.

The Guide goes on to say that

> The Act in the area of private law seeks to strike a balance between the need to recognise the child as an independent person, or ensure that his views are fully taken into account and the risk of casting on him the burden of resolving problems caused by his parents or requiring him to choose between them.

As well as incorporating his or her views in the Checklist, the Court may permit a child to request an order about his or her own future. If the Court commissions a welfare report, it must ensure that the child's views are included within it.

Because the Courts have new and much wider powers to intervene, it is hoped that they will be able to use these powers to protect children from risk or harm wherever they live, but also to avoid 'unwarranted intervention in their family life' (*Introduction to the Children Act*).

Child protection

The OPCS Reports on the lives of disabled people in the UK (1989) indicated that fifteen per cent of children with disabilities living away from home did so because of physical or sexual abuse. A further thirty-three per cent had 'unsuitable family homes'. Children with disabilities are, therefore, not immune to the risks from adverse family circumstances which affect their able-bodied peers. Although the spirit of the Children Act is one of partnership with parents and voluntary agreements, the histories of Jasmine Beckford, Kimberley Carlile, Tyra Henry and many others show the need to have clear procedures to protect vulnerable children.

Courts may now make an *Emergency Protection Order* 'if, but only if, it (the child) is likely to suffer significant harm'. The Court may also make an order if the local authority shows reasons in suspecting that a child may be suffering harm or if parents refuse access to the child 'unreasonably'. These orders can, however, only last for eight days and can only be extended once for seven days. After seventy two hours parents or *the child* can apply to challenge the order. The order may have a direction regarding a medical examination of the child attached. However, despite considerable debate, a medical examination *cannot be enforced against the wishes of a mature child*. Courts may impose *Child Assessment Orders* (see above) to enable a Court to order such an examination and to take advice from a range of professionals and agencies about the well-being of the child. Local authorities have an active duty to investigate where there is 'reasonable cause' to suspect that a child is suffering or likely to suffer significant harm and can apply for *Emergency Protection Orders* where they encounter difficulty in gaining access to the child or where there is considerable concern about the child's safety.

Children in a multi-cultural society

The Children Act, for the first time in any UK legislation, acknowledges the need to be sensitive to cultural and ethnic issues when providing services. Section 22(5) requires that 'local authorities must also give due consideration to the child's religious persuasion, racial origin and cultural and linguistic background.' This means, for example, that when a local authority social services department exercises its new powers under the Act to provide day care for children and other supervised activities in holidays or outside school hours, the authority must take into account 'the different racial groups to which children in their area who are in need belong' (Schedule 2). As the Act also requires social services departments to review such day care or out-of-school provision with the appropriate education authority, there will be new opportunities in order to ensure that cultural and ethnic differences are acknowledged and that services are acceptable to the families concerned.

Education supervision orders

The Children Act creates a new kind of supervision order which may be made on the application of an education authority. *Education Supervision Orders* are administered by the education authority and last for up to one year in the first instance. Education authorities must consult their services counterparts before making such orders. They can only be made if the child is of compulsory school age and is not being properly educated (i.e. 'is not receiving efficient full-time education suitable to the child's age, ability, aptitude and any special educational needs he or she may have (Section 36(4)).'

The Children Act abolishes the old Truancy Orders. Debating the Children Bill in the House of Lords, the Lord Chancellor noted that truancy should no longer be a primary reason for removing a child from home, because the cause of truancy might be *school*-based rather than *home*-based. Failure to educate a child properly (including sending him to school) is not a sufficient reason to issue a care order under the new legislation. But the Court may make such an order if it finds that the child is suffering significant harm, since 'harm' may be defined as the impairment of development (whether physical, intellectual, emotional, social or behavioural development). Hence Education Supervision Orders can be applied to children with disabilities when there is concern about the quality or quantity of education being provided.

Education Supervision Orders will involve the appointment of a supervisor, who will have the primary duty to advise, assist and befriend child and parents and as far as is practicable to ascertain their wishes. He or she will endeavour to 'secure the child's proper education.' Some commentators have pointed out a potential tension between the new support and advisory role of a supervisor and the punitive powers which still remain to bring parents of non-attenders before a magistrate and impose fines.

But this new role could provide positive support and advocacy for children with disabilities, particularly when problems arise in integrated placements. Social work support in mainstream schools is usually minimal.

Partnership with parents - family dynamics and disability

The birth of *any* child can be a traumatic as well as a happy event for the parents concerned. Parenthood brings alarming new responsibilities, as well as pleasures. When a new baby has a disability, the initial diagnosis may be devastating for the parents. Recent research by Cunningham[1] and Davis[2] and others clearly shows us how important it is to recognise the impact of disability on parental expectations and self-image. But, as Hewett[3] noted,

> the general tendency to characterise parents of handicapped children as guilt-ridden, anxiety-laden ... over-protective and rejecting beings is unfair. They are, rather, vulnerable families faced with a major challenge for which they require practical support as well as counselling, and respect rather than any global assumptions about 'pathological abnormality'.

Many disabled children require high levels of *practical* support in their day-to-day lives. A study by Glendinning[4] found that 50.1 per cent of the 361 severely disabled children in her survey could not be left alone and unsupervised for more than ten minutes at a time in any one day. Wilkin[5] and Baldwin[6] have emphasised the burdens placed upon *mothers*, with little support from neighbours or other relatives. Cooke and Bradshaw[7] found that disabled children in a study of families using the Family Fund were *more* likely than other children to experience at least one spell in a one-parent family.

These spells were longer than for families with non-disabled children and those families with the more severely disabled children were less likely to be reconstituted into new marriages or relationships. It is obvious that physical restrictions of care will limit families' social networks. But the Cooke and Bradshaw research indicates the importance of looking at the *family* networks and structures when there is a disabled child, and at the implications for care and support within that family. Wolkind[8] and others have shown the high incidence of depression and low self-esteem amongst all young parents in disadvantages inner-city areas. The *social* context of disability is therefore of crucial importance in determining whether the more positive approaches to parent support outlined below will be effective for both family and for child. Supporting disabled children and their families will require a range of services. However, ensuring that services are effective, fully used and sensitive to consumer needs requires constant review and assimilation by professionals, carers and managers. The significance of recent research for the development of good quality services is often not appreciated or considered in setting priorities for the future.

References

1. Cunningham, C. *Early Intervention: Some Results from the Manchester Cohort Study*. Department of Mental Handicap, University of Nottingham, 1988.

2. Cunningham, C. and Davis, H. *Working with Parents: Frameworks for Collaboration*. Open University Press, 1985.

3. Hewett, S. *Handicapped Children and their Families, A Survey*. Nottingham University Child Development Unit, 1970.

4. Glendinning, C. *Unshared Care - Parents and their Disabled Children*. Routledge and Kegan Paul, 1983.

5. Wilkin, D. *Caring for the Mentally Handicapped Child*. Croom Helm, 1979.

6. Baldwin, S. *The Costs of Caring*. Routledge and Kegan Paul, 1985.

7. Cooke, K. and Bradshaw, J. 'Child Disablement, Family Dissolution and Reconstruction' *Development Medicine and Child Neurology*. 28, 1986, 610-616.

8. Wolkind, S. 'Depression in Mothers and Young Children' *Archives of Disease in Childhood*. 56, 1, 1981, 1-3.

9. Pahl, J. and Quine, E. *Families with Mentally Handicapped Children: A Study of Stress and a Service Response*. Canterbury Health Services Research Unit, University of Kent, 1984.

10. Younghusband, E. *Living with Handicap*. National Children's Bureau, 1974.

11. Bradshaw, J. and Lawton, D. *Tracing the Causes of Stress in Families with Handicapped Children*. University of York, 1978.

12. Barnardos. *Carraigfole Paediatric Support Unit: The First Two Years*. Barnardos Irish Division, 1984.

13. Hatch, S. and Hinton, T. *Self-Help in Practice: A Study of 'Contact a Family', Community Work and Family Support*. Social Work Monographs/Community Care, 1987.

14. Cameron, R. J. 'Parents as Educators: Learning from Portage'. In Pugh, G. (Ed.) *Partnership Papers III, Working Together with Special Education Needs: Implications for Pre-School Services*. National Children's bureau, 1985.

15. Cameron, R. J. (Ed.) *Portage - Ten Years of Achievement*. NFER/Nelson, 1986.

16. Oswin, M. *They Keep Going Away*. Blackwells/King's Fund Centre, 1983.

17. DHSS Social Work Inspectorate, Banks, S. and Grizzell, R. *A Study of Family Placement Schemes for the Shared Care of Handicapped Children in Norfolk and Oxfordshire*. SSI/DHSS, 1984.

18. Robinson, C. *Avon Short Term Respite Care Scheme: Evaluation Study*. Department of Mental Health, University of Bristol, 1986.

19. Office of Population and Censury Surveys. *Education, Transport and Services for Disabled Children*. HMSO, 1989.

20. Berridge, D. and Cleaver, H. *Foster Home Breakdown*. Basil Blackwell, 1987.

21. Leonnard, A. *Out of Hospital: A Survey of 30 Centrally Funded Schemes Providing Alternative Care for Children with Mental Handicaps*. University of York, 1988.

22. Jackson, S. *The Education of Children in Care*. University of Bristol, 1989.

23. Brimblecombe, F. S. W. *The Needs of Handicapped Young Adults*. Institute of Child Health, University of Exeter, 1987.

24. Brimblecombe, F. S. W. and Russell, P. *Honeylands: Developing a Support Service for Families with Handicapped Children*. National Children's Bureau, 1988.

25. Royal College of Physicians. *Report on Services for Young Disabled People*. RCP, 1986.

26. DHSS. *The Care of Children: Principles and Practice in Regulations and Guidance*. HMSO, 1990.

27. Anderson, E. and Morgan, A. *Provision for Children in Need of Boarding/Residential Education*. Boarding Schools Association, 1989.

28. Bargh, J. *Playback the Thinking Memories*. National Children's Bureau, London, 1987.

Disabled Young People

Michael Hirst, Gillian Parker and Andrew Cozens

Introduction

Childhood is widely accepted as a separate state from adulthood, as a period of human experience in its own right. There is not the same degree of consensus about adolescence, however. Adolescents hover uncertainly between dependency on adults and assertion of their own independence. They also begin to acquire certain legal rights and responsibilities.

Some theories interpret adolescence as a time of growing up physically and sexually and coping with the socio-psychological adjustments those changes demand. Others stress discontinuity: seeing the adolescent as no longer a child who is totally dependent on adults with little influence over the direction of her life, yet not fully accepted as an adult who takes responsibility for carrying out her own decisions. Adolescence may also be regarded as a separate stage in life when the young person has the opportunity to test out a wide variety of roles and identities without necessarily making a firm commitment for the future. Indeed, the maturation of personality, the formation of a coherent set of values, and the adoption of new ways of behaving are not restricted to the years of adolescence and may continue throughout adult life.

However adolescence is interpreted, all young people move from childhood to adulthood. There are certain developmental needs common to all adolescents and many of the social and practical problems they experience - drawing away from dependence on parents, forming new relationships, finding a job, setting up a home of their own, possibly marrying and having children - are the same for all young people.

The road to adult life can be difficult for many adolescents but it is usually harder for young disabled people: the problems they face often have longer lasting effects and their transition to adult status may be prolonged *or* truncated. Many lack the confidence, self-esteem and social skills necessary for a smooth transition to adult life. The difficulties of finding paid work are compounded by poor job prospects and the discriminatory attitudes of employers. The attainment of independence and personal responsibility may present particular problems where the young person is physically dependent on parents in many different and sometimes subtle ways; where mobility and personal independence are limited the development of satisfactory relationships with other people of either sex is hampered.

These difficulties are not due to disability alone. Disabled school leavers are often ill-prepared for moving into the world of work and adulthood; once the young person leaves school, the provision of formal support fragments or is usually lost. The ability of young disabled people to attain adult status, and the extent to which they manage to do so, could therefore be regarded as a measure of formal support and service provision during the transition years.[1]

This chapter looks at the role of social work as young disabled people move to adult life; at current social work policy and practice in respect of young disabled people; at their contacts with and perceptions of social workers; and at the implications of changes in the nature of social work. First, however, we review existing evidence about the difficulties young people with disabilities may encounter as they make the move from childhood to adulthood.

Moving on

Adolescence and the movement towards adulthood involves not one transition but a series. Leaving school, becoming an 'adult' for the purposes of the law, forming long-term relationships, going on to further or higher education, getting a job, setting up home - all are part of the process of 'growing-up'. A combination of inadequate resources and services, lack of understanding, and outright prejudice means that young people with disabilities experience more difficulties and disappointments as they go through these transitions than do their peers.[2]

Employment

Young people with disabilities enter employment from a wide range of settings - some directly from school, some after a period of further education (FE) or training, some after an assessment course, and so on. However, they are substantially less likely than their contemporaries to obtain and remain in employment after leaving school, particularly when their disabilities are physical and/or severe.[3,4,5,6] For young people who have a severe physical impairment the prospect of open employment appears to be particularly bleak. For example, one survey revealed that, by the age of twenty-one, that is, more than three years on average since leaving school, only one-third of young people with severe physical impairments were in open or sheltered employment.[7] Consequently, far too many young people never enter employment at all, going straight from school or further education to a long-term placement at a day centre, or returning home to no structured occupation at all.

If a young person with disabilities is to find employment in a world which seems disinclined to offer it, she needs to leave school with adequate and appropriate knowledge, qualifications and skills to enable her to compete on something approaching an equal footing with her contemporaries. Failing that, the young person needs to go in the right direction to acquire the skills that will be necessary for employment commensurate with her ability. Even if unlikely ever to be able to work, the young person needs to be assessed and prepared for whatever life she will lead after school. Calls for enhanced preparation for the world of work for disabled young people have been made by many researchers and commentators[3,8,9,10] but there is little evidence to suggest that these calls have been acted upon.

Careers education and guidance in schools which cater for pupils with special needs fall short on a number of counts. Young people with disabilities are less likely to have careers lessons or to talk to careers teachers than their peers and are more likely to be dissatisfied with the help or advice given.[3,9,11,12] Young people with physical disabilities seem to be particularly dissatisfied with the careers guidance they have received.[13] Placement in an 'ordinary' school is not likely to make any difference; indeed, as Hegarty *et al.*[14] have pointed out, there is a danger that 'normality' can be emphasised 'to such an extent that pupils' needs [are] overlooked'.

While preparation for leaving school, through leavers' programmes, work experience, independence training, and the like, has undoubtedly improved in the past fifteen years or so, there is still an unmet need for additional help with learning about the world of work.[6,8,12]

However, all the preparation in the world will not help young people with disabilities to combat prejudice in employers' minds. Further education, training, and work preparation appear to make little difference to the proportion of young people with disabilities who obtain employment afterwards.[15,16]

Money and social security

At the age of sixteen years all young people change status in the social security system: under this age they are treated as dependent upon their parents. At sixteen, however, 'adult status is conferred and young disabled people enter, in their own right, a complex and regulated system of cash allowances'.[17] The financial position of young people is particularly complex at this stage and decisions may be taken, often unwittingly, which crucially affect access to work, work-related benefits and disability-related benefits.[18]

Young adults themselves are often ill-informed about their entitlement to benefits of any sort[6,9,17] but those in a position to advise them may be little better informed.[17,19] Consequently, take-up is very poor, with delayed applications most often due to a lack of information or understanding about eligibility.[17]

Decisions about whether or not the young adult is 'able' to take paid employment, or whether she is ever likely to do so, can make a crucial difference to benefit entitlement. If young adults are prepared to resign themselves to being considered 'unemployable', they thereby become eligible for a selection of benefits which enables them to spend their waking hours in more or less any way they like - including doing 'therapeutic' paid work. By contrast, if young adults with disabilities are considered to be 'employable', they find themselves in exactly the same position as their able-bodied peers, with no compensation for the disability-related disadvantages they may suffer.[15] This may be a particular problem for young adults with physical rather than mental disabilities.[18]

As with awareness of the complexity of the benefit system itself, there is little evidence to suggest that those who are in a position to advise young people are fully informed about the options, alternatives and consequences in relation to decisions about 'employability'.

Personal relationships

During adolescence and young adulthood independent social activity assumes great importance, often as a prelude to or in preparation for longer-term emotional and sexual relationships. 'Going out' with a group of friends often gives way to 'going out' with one friend who may then become a special friend.

Available evidence suggests that many young people with physical disabilities are denied access to the social activities and friendships that lead to longer-term attachments. Further, this lack of contact with peers may mean that disabled young people never learn that their fears and anxieties about growing up, about emotions, and about sexual feelings are similar to those of all young people.[9,20] Mobility appears to be a major barrier to social activity for many young adults but lack of social skills may also be a problem.[9,21,22,23]

Other issues centre around young people's anxieties and knowledge about sex and genetics. Both the Court and Warnock reports highlighted the needs of adolescents with disabilities for sex education and sexual and genetic counselling to help prepare them for adulthood, but there is little evidence that this happens. Many of the young people and parents in Anderson and Clarke's study were worried 'by questions relating to relationships, marriage and sex but very few had discussed these issues between themselves or with anyone else, and even fewer had been given specific advice or counselling'.[9]

Independent living

Personal independence is an important issue for all young people. For young people with physical disabilities, however, it is complicated by their continuing need for physical care or assistance with day-to-day activities.[9] Research shows that few of these young people make the transition from dependence on their parents to a more independent form of living.[2,6,9] There are, of course, various reasons why this transition does not occur.

First, there is the issue of the supply of aids to daily living and the provision of adaptations to the young person's home. Poor assessment and, therefore, the provision of inappropriate or unsatisfactory aids, and difficulties with maintenance and repair are perennial problems.[6] Further, between a third and a quarter of young people with disabilities live in housing which is not entirely suited to their needs.[6,20,24]

Secondly, there is the issue of independence training. Few young people with disabilities get the level of independence and skill training that they need. Even when they do, there can be a failure of liaison between home and school so that the young person is not putting into practice at home those things that she has learnt at school.[9,23] This can lead to a self-reinforcing situation where parents do not realise the degree of independence of which their daughter is capable and therefore do not let her exercise new skills.

The third issue about independent living for young people is the availability of alternative accommodation. Most young adults expect to leave the parental home sooner or later. The 1970s and 1980s have seen a hastening of this process, such that most women have left the parental home by the ages of 19-23, while most men have left the parental home by the ages of 20-25.[25] For young people with disabilities to be able to leave home at or around the same age as their peers, however, they not only have to achieve the targets of further or higher education, paid employment, marriage and so on, they also have to find accommodation which suits their needs and, in some cases, alternative sources of physical care and support.

Although comparative evidence is limited, it seems that young people with physical disabilities are much less likely than their contemporaries to move away from their parents,[2,6,17,24] suggesting that these alternatives are not available to them.[26]

Health services

The changes that young adults might experience in the provision of health services are of two broad types: those related directly to changes in their health and those related to the organisation of child and adult health provision. Changing family circumstances and increased independence may also play a part.

Research reveals a mixed picture of transition and transitional problems in the health area. For example, some services such as the supply of incontinence aids appear to be affected hardly at all, whereas there are substantial problems with continuity in the provision of paramedical services such as speech therapy and physiotherapy.[17,27,28] The change from paediatric care - which tends to be all-encompassing - to adult health services - which tend to be fragmented into specialties - can create gaps in overall supervision of health care.[29] Although this loss does not necessarily lead to any major shortcomings in the provision of medical care, it does leave young people without regular support and in some cases with health problems severe enough to warrant hospital care.[30]

GPs do not increase their oversight of young people, or take on the care and supervision previously provided by school doctors and paediatricians when young people reach sixteen or leave school.[29,31] Consequently, there is no one individual to whom the young adult can turn with any confidence when medical or health problems arise.[32]

The role of social work

All that has gone before suggests that many young people with physical disabilities could have a particular need for someone they could turn to for information and advice; someone who could help arrange access to and negotiate with different services and professionals and, if necessary, act as an advocate. The Warnock Committee[8] recommended that the careers officer or specialist careers officer should be the key worker - or Named Person - for young disabled people and their parents. More recently, some researchers have promoted the idea of a resource and development officer owing no allegiance to any particular service who can work across all sorts of boundaries enabling young people to achieve individually and together their own objectives.[33] Post-school placement, access to paid employment, satisfying alternatives to paid employment, independent living away from parents, advice about social security benefits, and guidance in emotional and sexual development are also areas in which there is a role for social work.

In the next section of this chapter we look at the framework of social service provision for young people and subsequently at recent evidence, from young people themselves, about their experiences and views of social workers.

The service framework

While there has been no lack of legislation and government working party activity since 1948, the framework for the provision of services for young people after school lacks coherence and has contributed to a disabling environment of service provision. As a consequence the range and quality of provision vary widely between authorities and are unduly dependent on the enthusiasm and innovation of individual practitioners or the persistence of disabled people, their carers and advocates.

The National Assistance Act 1948 and the parallel National Health Service Act have, until now, formed the basis of local authority responsibility for non-specialist services including residential care and domiciliary provision.[34] Subsequent practice varied widely between local authorities but services provided included training, day care, home helps, meals on wheels, and aids and adaptations. Very few authorities developed specialist residential care for younger disabled people; the main service providers here proved to be in the voluntary sector.[35]

Neither of the two most influential pieces of subsequent legislation were the result of government initiatives. Both the Chronically Sick and Disabled Persons Act 1970 and the Disabled Persons (Services, Consultation and Representation) Act 1986 began life as private members' bills and both attempted to give provision for people with disabilities a higher priority than had previously been the case. The 1970 Act placed a duty on local authorities to determine the extent of need in their area and to publish information about services provided under section 29 of the National Assistance Act 1948, including home helps, aids and adaptations, meals on wheels and telephones.[36]

Despite government guidance that local authorities had a duty (under section two of the Act) to assess the needs of 'individuals determined by them to be permanently and substantially handicapped',[37] this aspect of the Act quickly fell into disrepute. In the absence of any statutory definition of 'need' and the failure of attempts to enforce the Act through the courts, local authorities' enthusiasm for its implementation varied widely.

Despite this, however, the Act did seem to prompt some local authorities into action. There is some evidence that the extent and range of service provision improved in the 1970s[38] but the impact that this had specifically on people with physical disabilities is not known. Indeed, there is evidence to suggest that *non-elderly* people with physical disabilities come at the bottom of the list as regards community health and social services expenditure.[38]

The 1986 Act looks as if it, too, will fail to have the clout and the related resources it needs to force real change.[39] Although local authorities are free to act as if the whole Act were in force, large parts of it remain unimplemented. These parts cover needs assessment, representation, and the assessment of people with mental handicap on discharge from hospital. Of course, young adults with disabilities are covered by all this legislation to the same extent as other people with disabilities. However, there are some elements of current legislation which are particular to the needs of young people.

The 1981 Education Act, based on the recommendations of the Warnock report,[8] requires that school leavers with special needs should be assessed, on a multi-disciplinary basis, in advance of their leaving school. This assessment is intended to help smooth the transition of adult provision. Further, when children are assessed, under the 1981 Act, as having special needs the local authority is now required, under the Disabled Persons Act 1986, to check their eligibility for social services provision. The education authority must notify the social services department at least eight months before the young person is expected to leave full-time education. The social services department must then carry out an assessment of the young person, within five months of being notified, unless the young person (or their parent/guardian if under sixteen) requests otherwise.

This assessment is intended to include advice about educational and voca-tional training, health service provision, social security benefits, housing, em-ployment, and services provided by voluntary organisations and the private sector. These developments mean that social workers working with young people with disabilities must do so within a multi-disciplinary environment, liaising with community health and education services and, more obliquely, with the careers service and the Department of Employment. This section of the 1986 Act was implemented only for those leaving full-time education from April 1990 so there is little evidence about how it is working. If it does work well then, clearly, it could help to avoid some of the gaps and breaks in provision for young disabled people identified above.

Young people's views about social workers

What is actually known about how young people with disabilities see the social worker's role and how they experience their contact with them? In this section we present findings from a survey of 400 young disabled people who were interviewed in January 1987 when they were 13-22 years old. The sample was drawn from the OPCS surveys of disabled adults and children in Great Britain,[40,41] though for present purposes young people with mental handicap have been excluded. A comparable survey of young people in the general population was also carried out.[42] Both samples were identified by screening private households, in the same geographical areas, to provide nationally representative samples of young people.

Most young disabled people have no recent personal experience of dealing with social services or other social work agencies. Only one-in-five (twenty-one per cent) reported direct contact with a social worker in the past twelve months, but this was a significantly higher level of contact than in the comparison group, where only six per cent said they had talked to a social worker in the past year. These findings suggest that social workers do direct their professional support towards young people who, *prima facie*, have greater needs. Other evidence from the survey points to the same conclusion. For example, young disabled people who came from a lower social class background, and those who were not in education, training or paid work were most likely to have talked to a social worker. Moreover, contact with a social worker generally increased with increasing severity of disability: thirty-five per cent of those in severity categories 7-10 compared with eleven per cent of those in categories 1-3 said they had had direct contact with a social worker. (Categories of overall severity were defined by OPCS researchers[40] from information about thirteen types of disability.)

We do not know precisely what these young people had talked about with their social workers but the survey suggests that they had sought advice, information, counselling and practical help for a wide variety of concerns. Thirty-nine per cent said they had discussed two or more issues with a social worker and overall no single issue emerged as dominant (Table 1). The most common problems concerned family life, in particular tension and conflict in relationships with parents and other family members. Matters relating to choosing a career, finding a job, and school work were the next most important areas of concern. Personal relationships, including relationships with the opposite sex, money problems and health matters were also of concern to a substantial minority of young people. The large minority who mentioned 'other' topics suggests that some young people discussed a variety of individual matters with their social workers. Apart from health matters, however, there were no significant differences between the two samples in the proportions of young people mentioning each topic.

Table 1: Matters discussed between young people and social workers

Topic*	Study Group %	Comparison Group %	Significance
Family relationships	32	35	ns
Health/disability	22	2	$t = 2.9; p < 0.01$
School work	22	23	ns
Careers advice	21	25	ns
Money matters	16	10	ns
Personal relationships	12	14	ns
Accommodation	11	6	ns
Further/higher education	4	3	ns
Social activities	4	4	ns
Other	20	33	ns
Base:	*49*	*45*	

* percentages sum to more than 100 because of multiple response

These findings provide some insight into the nature of social work practice among young disabled people. They show that young disabled people discussed, more or less to the same extent, a similar range of topics with their social workers as other young people. Social workers were apparently sources of advice, information and material assistance for any young person - disabled or otherwise. In so far as social workers define 'need' and determine agendas,[43] it seems that young disabled people were treated primarily as young people with the same sorts of needs and concerns as young people in general. The lack of significant contrasts between the two samples in the topics discussed may of course reflect the masking of more subtle differences in the broad categories identified here. Information about the dynamics of social work contact is also absent. We do not know for example whether, and how generally, the topics mentioned by young disabled people stemmed from their experience of disablement or arose from the same sorts of issues that concern all young people. It might be that social workers did not allow disablement and its consequences to surface in their discussions with these young people, reflecting the declining importance of specialist social work practice. But the finding that significantly more young disabled people discussed health matters than their counterparts in the general population does suggest that those who felt sufficiently worried about their health or disability were able to discuss their concerns with a social worker.

Overall the findings show that vocational issues were the most common areas of concern discussed between these young people and a social worker. Matters relating to school, further and higher education, choosing a career and finding a job were mentioned by forty-seven per cent of the young disabled people in regular contact with a social worker. Whether social workers are best placed to give advice and guidance in this area is another matter. Apart from generalised advice, social workers' particular expertise relates to *alternatives* to education, training and work. These young people may, of course, have been talking to teachers, careers officers or job centre staff as well as social workers about training and employment opportunities and career choices. But without a degree of co-ordination with other professionals at the local level, such as specialist careers officers and disablement resettlement officers, the advice and help offered by social workers would, at best, be less effective than it could be. At worst, it might be an irrelevance for the majority of young disabled people about to leave full-time education.

It seems that most young people with disabilities were treated as adults by social workers: fifty-nine per cent reported for example that they usually talked to a social worker on their own, that is without parents or others present. Moreover, most young disabled people (seventy-eight per cent) said they knew how to get in touch with their social worker if they needed to do so.

Social workers were, however, only slightly better at recognising the emergent adult status of young disabled people than were health professionals. Of those in regular contact with a doctor, for example, fifty-three per cent said they saw a GP on their own, a proportion only marginally smaller than that for social work contact. Moreover some uncertainty or ambiguity was apparent in the way social workers treated young disabled people. It might have been expected, for example, that the proportion seeing a social worker on their own would increase with young people's ages, reflecting a growing recognition of their adult status. However this was not the case: fifty-four per cent of those aged nineteen to twenty-two compared with sixty-five per cent of sixteen to eighteen year olds said they saw a social worker on their own. Those with more severe disabilities were particu-

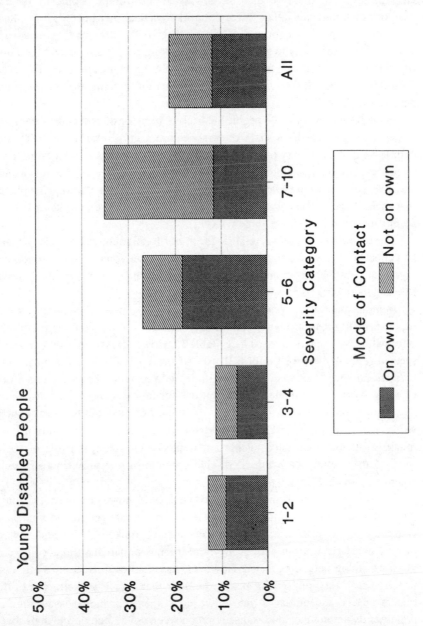

Figure 1. Proportion Talking to a Social Worker by Severity

larly disadvantaged: more than seven out of ten young people in severity categories 1-6 said they talked to a social worker on their own but only thirty-three per cent of those in categories 7-10 did so (Figure 1). It seems then that social workers have some way to go in recognising young people as adults in their own right. In particular, it seems that social work among young people with severe disabilities tends to focus on the family or another group rather than on the young person herself.

What did young disabled people themselves think of their social workers and is there any evidence that social work practice was seen as disabling? Most young people were, in fact, very positive about their contact with social workers. They were generally seen as understanding and approachable, easy to get in touch with, and active on behalf of their young clients. Thus most young disabled people felt that their social worker was *'easy to talk to'* (seventy-three per cent) and *'as helpful as could be'* (eighty-three per cent).

These findings, of course, relate to the minority of young people who actually had direct contact with a social worker. What did other young people - those with no recent personal experience of dealing with social services - think about the role of social workers?

A wide range of views was reported; most young people mentioned two or more specific areas in which they thought social workers could offer advice, information and practical assistance (Table 2). However, young disabled people seemed generally less well-informed: a quarter said they did not know what social workers do and, compared with young people in general, they were less aware of social workers' particular responsibilities for families and child care. Young disabled people also seemed less aware than their peers about the role of social workers in offering counselling and advice on personal matters. Only a small minority of young disabled people apparently knew about the role of social services in meeting the needs of disabled people by the provision of special equipment and holidays.

Comparing Tables 1 and 2 suggests very little mismatch between young disabled people's perceptions of what social workers do for people and what those who were in contact with social workers actually talked about. Social work involvement arising from delinquency and truancy apparently did not figure as much as young people expected. However, the main contrast centres on vocational issues: very few young people thought that social workers could offer careers advice and guidance yet, as we have seen, vocational issues figured prominently among the matters discussed between young people and their social workers.

Table 2: Young people's expectations of social workers

Social work activity*	Study group %	Comparison group %	Significance
Family/child care	32	42	$t = 2.5; p < 0.02$
Delinquency/truancy	13	12	ns
Financial problems	11	16	ns
Personal problems	10	18	$t = 2.5; p < 0.02$
Housing/adaptations	9	10	ns
Careers guidance	6	5	ns
Aids/appliances	5	2	$t = 2.2; p < 0.05$
Holidays/outings	5	1	$t = 3.2; p < 0.002$
School problems	4	2	ns
Alcohol/drug abuse	1	0	ns
Caring for elderly	1	3	ns
Other	6	8	ns
Non-specific help	31	39	$t = 2.0; p < 0.05$
Don't know	25	18	$t = 2.0; p < 0.05$
Base:	*186*	*672*	

* percentages sum to more than 100 because of multiple response

Overall, the findings presented above suggest that most young disabled people were very satisfied with their social workers. Like the young people in Jones' study,[44] these young disabled people's views about social workers were generally positive and suggest that a caring relationship had been established with many of the young clients. Moreover, most of the young people not in direct contact with social workers saw them as someone to turn to for counselling, advice and practical help. Whether social workers will be able to fulfil or develop that role is, however, less clear. In the next section, we look at the ways in which social work service is set to change and consider the implications for young disabled people.

A future role for social work?

There are a number of tensions and conflicts for social workers in relation to their current work with young people with disabilities. For example, the generic model of social work practice adopted after 1971 has meant that there has been a disincentive to develop specialist forms of service, with a parallel lack of specialist training. Yet, as outlined earlier, social workers are now involved in providing assessments of young people, within the 1981 Education Act and the 1986 Disabled Persons Act, which should, to some degree at least, be based on specialist knowledge and skills. Another tension relates to the role that social workers play. On the one hand they are expected to act as advocate or counsellor to the young person, yet on the other they must sometimes act as gatekeepers to or rationers of services which young people need. Above all, the generic social worker's time is limited, resources are insufficient, and there are major competing demands such as child-abuse work.

Major change in the provision of health and social care to all people with special needs is currently (May 1990) in train. The National Health Service and Community Care Act 1990 is the first government sponsored attempt at co-ordinating community care services since 1948. This Act, which follows the publication of the Griffiths report[45] in 1988, places new responsibilities on local authorities to co-ordinate planning, assessment and service provision for all people with special needs, although with an emphasis, for demographic and finance-driven considerations, on older people. The White Paper which preceded the Bill did, however, make a particular point of the needs of young people during the transition to adulthood.[46]

Whether and how the changes implied by the Act will affect young people with disabilities remains to be seen. One possibility is that the emphasis on assessment and the planning of packages of services, and, particularly, on the close involvement of users in these processes, will transform the experience of people with special needs. In the ideal scenario young people will be helping to identify their own needs, social workers will be helping to identify sources of support, and packages will be put together which will 'run' with minimal intervention from anyone other than the young person herself.

The 'ideal scenario', however, depends crucially on resources, on social workers liaising with professionals in other agencies, and on the priority which individual local authorities will place on provision for non-elderly adults.[47] At the time of writing, the resources to be made available to local authorities have not been announced. If they prove inadequate it is difficult to see how service provision for young people will improve merely on the basis of a change of role for social workers. The demands of case management and care planning, without resources, may simply mean that social workers will have even less overall contact with young people, with little to compensate for the reduction.

References

1. Chapman, L. (1988). 'Disabling Services' *Educare*. 31, 5-20.

2. Clark, A. and Hirst, M. A. (1989). 'Disability in Adulthood: Ten-year Follow-up of Young People with Disabilities' *Disability, Handicap and Society*. 4, 271-283.

3. Walker, A. (1982). *Unqualified and Underemployed*. Macmillan, London.

4. Hirst, M. A. (1983). 'Young People with Disabilities: What Happens After 16' *Child: Care Health and Development*. 9, 273-284.

5. Kuh, D., Lawrence, C., Tripp, J. and Creber, G. (1988). 'Work and Work Alternatives for Disabled Young People' *Disability, Handicap and Society*. 3, 3-26.

6. Thomas, A., Bax, M. and Smyth, D. (1987). *The Provisions of Support Services for the Handicapped Young Adult*. Department of Child Health, Charing Cross and Westminster Medical School, London.

7. Hirst, M. A. (1987). 'Careers of Young People with Disabilities Between Ages 15 and 21 Years' *Disability, Handicap and Society*. 2, 61-74.

8. Department of Education and Science (1978). *Report of the Warnock Committee: Special Education Needs*. HMSO, London.

9. Anderson, E. M. and Clarke, L. (1982). *Disability in Adolescence*. Methuen, London.

10. Walker, A. (1980). 'The Handicapped School Leaver and the Transition to Work' *British Journal of Guidance and Counselling*. 8, 212-223.

11. Enticknap, B. (1983). (1) 'Problems and Needs of Handicapped School Leavers' *Health Visitor*. 56, 5, 159-160. (2) 'Handicapped Teenagers in the High Wycombe Area' *Health Visitor*. 56, 6, 210-211.

12. Hirst, M. A. (1985). 'Could Schools Do More for Leavers' *British Journal of Special Education*. 12, 143-146.

13. Corrie, M. (1983). *Leaving Special School: Report of the First Phase of a Study of Leavers from Special Schools*. Scottish Council for Research in Education, Edinburgh.,

14. Hegarty, S. and Pocklington, K., with Lucas, D. (1981). *Educating Pupils with Special Needs in the Ordinary School*. NFER- Nelson, Windsor.

15. Parker, G. (1984). *Into Work: A Review of the Literature about Disabled Young Adult's Preparation for and Movement into Employment*. Social Policy Research Unit, University of York.

16. Hirst, M. A. (1984). 'Education after 16 for Young People with Disabilities' *Youth and Policy*. 2, 37-40.

17. Hirst, M. A. (1984). *Moving On: Transfer of Young People with Disabilities to Adult Services*. Social Policy Research Unit, University of York.,

18. Hirst, M. A. (1985). 'Social Security and Insecurity: Young People with Disabilities in the United Kingdom' *International Social Security Review*. 38, 258-272.

19. Burgess, P. (1981). 'In Benefit' *Community Care*. 2 July.

20. Castree, B. J. and Walter, J. H. (1981). 'The Young Adult with Spina Bifida' *British Medical Journal*. 283, 1040-2.

21. Jowett, S. (1982). *Young Disabled People: Their Further Education, Training and Employment*. NFER-Nelson, Windsor.

22. Thomas, A., Bax, M. and Smyth, D. (1988). 'The Social Skill Difficulties of Young Adults with Physical Disabilities' *Child: Care, Health and Development*. 14, 255-264.

23. Macredie, T. and Bradshaw, J. (1984). 'Teaching Social Skills: Evaluation of and "Independence Week"' *Child: Care, Health and Development*. 10, 181-188.

24. Hirst, M. A. (1982). *Young Adults with Disabilities and Their Families*. Social Policy Research Unit, University of York.

25. Hutton, S. (1990). *Growing up in the 1960s, 1970s and 1980s*. Social Policy Research Unit, University of York.

26. Kuh, D., Lawrence, C. and Tripp, J. (1986). 'Disabled Young People: Making Choices for Future Living Options' *Social Services Research*. 15, 1-30.

27. Benjamin, C. (1988). 'The Use of Health Care Resources by Young Adults with Spina Bifida *Zeitschrift fur Kinderchirurgie*. 43, 12-14.

28. Thomas, A., Bax, M. and Smyth, D. (1987). 'The Health Care of Physically Handicapped Young Adults' *Zeitschrift fur Kinderchirurgie*. 42, 57-59.

29. Parker, G. M. and Hirst, M. A. (1987). 'Continuity and Change in Medical Care for Young Adults with Disabilities' *Journal of the Royal College of Physicians of London*. 21, 129-133.

30. Bax, M., Smyth, D. and Thomas, A. (1988). 'Health Care of Physically Handicapped Young Adults' *British Medical Journal*. 296, 1153-1155.

31. Brimblecombe, F., Kuh, D., Lawrence, C. and Smith, R. (1986). 'Role of General Practitioners in the Care of Disabled Young Adults' *British Medical Journal*. 293, 859-860.

32. Royal College of Physicians (1986). *Physical Disability in 1986 and Beyond*. Royal College of Physicians of London, London.

33. Brimblecombe, F. (1987). 'The Voice of Disabled Young People' *Children & Society*. 1, 58-70.

34. National Assistance Act 1948, section 19 (1).

35. Health Circular HM(68)41 (1968).

36. Chronically Sick and Disabled Persons Act 1970, section 2 (1).

37. Circular LAC 12/70.

38. Beardshaw, V. (1988). *Last on the List: Community Services for People with Physical Disabilities*. King's Fund Institute, London.

39. See DHSS Circulars: LAC(87)6 - Sections 4, 8(i), 9 and 10 of the 1986 Act; LAC(88)2 - Sections 5 and 6 of the 1986 Act.

40. Martin, J., Meltzer, H. and Elliot, D. (1988). *The Prevalence of Disability among Adults*. HMSO, London.

41. Bone, M. and Meltzer, H. (1989). *The Prevalence of Disability among Children*. HMSO, London.

42. Hirst, M. A. (1987). *National Survey of Young People with Disabilities: Background and Methodology*. Social Policy Research Unit, University of York.

43. Robinson, T. (1978). *In Worlds Apart*. Bedford Square Press, London.

44. Jones, R. (1987). *Like Distant Relatives: Adolescents' Perceptions of Social work and Social Workers*. Gower, Aldershot.

45. Griffiths Report, (1988). *Community Care: An Agenda for Action*. HMSO, London.

46. Department of Health (1989). *Caring for People*. HMSO, London.

47. Beardshaw, V. and Towell, D. (1990). *Assessment and Case Management*. King's Fund Institute, London.

The Significance of the OPCS Disability Surveys

Paul Abberley

The recent White Paper on care in the community[1] voices the expectation that there will be 900,000 severely disabled adults living in the community by 2001, whilst the bewildering succession of short-term occupants of the post of 'minister for the disabled' have repeatedly insisted that provision for disabled people will be reviewed on the basis of the OPCS survey data. It is therefore important that social workers working with disabled people have some understanding of this data, both for what it can tell us about the situation of disabled people, to which question I will argue the answer is 'not much', and for how it can illuminate the processes by which government continues to sell disabled people short through the utilisation of so-called objective evidence, official statistics.

Like Max Bygraves, I would like to start off by telling a story. In Greek mythology, the robber Procrustes would invite travelers to spend the night in his wonderful bed, that fitted everyone. If they were too short for the structure he would stretch them, if too tall, cut off those portions of their anatomy that were deemed excessive; they rarely survived the ordeal, but in this way the reputation of his sleeping arrangements was preserved. In addition to this, and most significantly, he was now able to make off with the property of his overnight guests. Whilst some disabled people may see shades of Procrustes in some of the activities of rehabilitative medicine, another area where his practices have found favour is amongst the compilers of official statistics. Indeed it is my contention that they more thoroughly reflect the Procrustean project, since the consequences of their statistical mutilations of the experience of disability is to enable the state to justify its failure to provide disabled people with the necessary resources to exercise our human rights; in a word, robbery.

When confronted with the products of the Office of Population Censuses and Surveys, often referred to as official statistics, it is, then, as important to consider the implications of their being official as to analyse their significance as statistics. So far as disabled people are concerned, Stone[2] has indicated how the legitimacy or otherwise of claims about disability has been a matter of state concern since the concomitant development of the earliest stages of industrial capitalism and the most rudimentary elements of state welfare. The simple distinction between those unable and those unwilling to work, the deserving and the undeserving poor, has, with increased sophistication in the division of labour, similarly become more refined, with new definitions, based on clinical or functional criteria, being employed. Thus the new survey is presented as superior to others, in part because its ten point classificatory schema is subtler than the four categories of its immediate predecessor. The thing it shares with previous studies, however, which far outweighs any differences, is that disability is seen as essentially a property of individuals rather than a consequence of particular social systems. As Oliver[3] points out, a comparison of two different sets of questions on the same subjects, the first from an individual perspective as employed in the OPCS research, the second from a social one, makes this distinction apparent:

1) What complaint causes you difficulty in holding, gripping or turning things?

2) Do you have a scar, blemish or deformity which limits your daily activities?

3) Have you attended a special school because of a long term health problem or disability?

4) Does your health problem/disability affect your work in any way at present?

could be reformulated as:

1a) What defects in the design of everyday equipment like jars, bottles and lids causes you difficulty in holding, gripping or turning them?

2a) Do other people's reactions to any scar, blemish or deformity you may have, limit your daily activities?

3a) Have you attended a special school because of your education authority's policy of sending people with your long-term health problem or disability to such places?

4a) Do you have problems at work as a result of the physical environment or the attitudes of others?

It is a political decision, conscious or otherwise, to employ questions of the first type rather than the second. Since state researchers, whatever party is in power, have consistently asked individualising rather than socialising questions on a whole range of subjects it should come as no surprise that they do this on disability, which is as political a subject as any other. Even for someone who finds this a contentious point, the notion that functional limitation can be investigated without regard to the different social and environmental contexts of people's lives, as the standardised OPCS questions attempt to do, is a dubious one. Any response about difficulties with an activity of daily living, e.g. using the lavatory, getting dressed, eating or drinking, only has its meaning in the context of the facilities available to that individual to carry out the task - an individual able to use the Euro-American pedestal may report severe difficulties east of Suez. An inability to use the right hand for eating will have more severe social consequences for someone from a Muslim than from a Roman Catholic background, for whom in turn the prohibitions of Leviticus will have implications for any aspirations for the priesthood. Gender and age are also important variables to be taken into account in assessing the significance of particular disabilities, whilst class in both financial and cultural aspects also has obvious effects on people's experience of disability.

There are, then, these inevitable limitations to any understanding which fails to relate functional limitation to its social context, even in this limited sense of the word. Functional definitions are essentially state definitions, in that they relate to the major concerns of the state; as regards production, capacity to work, as regards welfare, demands that have to be met from revenue if they cannot be offloaded on some other party; they ignore any consideration of the role of the state in the construction and perpetuation of disability. To say this is to say no more nor less than one would say of any other set of Government inspired statistics: that they reflect the interests of Government.[4]

One question often begged in the discussion of data is 'should it be gathered at all?' Leaving aside the awkward question of whether money spent on research could more usefully be employed in meeting needs which are already quite apparent, there is, for example, an ongoing debate over the very gathering by the state of data on ethnic origin.[5] Certainly most would agree that data gathering in Nazi Germany was not unconnected with the state's project of genocide.

In a less extreme situation, registration as a disabled person is seen as of little if any value in Britain today and it is unlikely that Topliss's[6] explanation of the mere half a million names on the 1978 Disabled Person's Employment Register as 'undoubtedly due to the different definitions of disability employed' is a feasible one. Rather, any possible benefit that might result from registration accrues to the employer, in terms of his meeting his quota under the albeit unenforced Disabled Person's (Employment) Acts. The 'problem' with the figures is then more likely to result from a political source (the disabled person's recognition of the pointlessness to him/herself of registering) than to the 'technical' problem hypothesised by Topliss.

Whilst the proponents of Action Research can adduce some evidence for the beneficial effects of the active involvement of the subjects of their researches in the investigation and transformation of their own situation, the subjects of Official Statistics are invariably the passive objects of the researcher's investigations. Oakley[7] has argued that this is an inherently oppressive process in that it not only does nothing to aid the transformation of the subjects' lives, but may also confirm and reinforce sentiments of ignorance and passivity in those interviewed. Likewise, the spurious objectivity of published findings upon which welfare agencies often rely for evidence, can reinforce, for the whole range of people to whom the research is supposed to apply, oppressive definitions of their reality. Both these aspects deserve consideration as regards the OPCS surveys of disability. The very process of isolated disabled people being asked this kind of individualised question by someone in authority can serve to disempower them, since it reproduces and reinforces, as it ostensibly asks 'neutral' questions, a personal tragedy view of disablement. Similarly, the published findings, which claim to tell us the average cost of particular degrees of disability, or that a disfigurement which 'severely affects one's ability to lead a normal life' has a 'severity score' of only 0.5, must, unless challenged, have their effects on the lives of disabled people.

As Hindess has pointed out[8] there are two kinds of instruments employed in the gathering of Official Statistics, 'instruments of the social survey and "conceptual" instruments, the system of concepts and categories governing the assignment of cases into classes'. In this paper I argue that the OPCS surveys are deficient with respect to both these aspects, that both the kinds of things enquired about are inappropriate and that the way in which the researchers go about trying to find out the answers to these inappropriate questions leaves much to be desired. But, given that a body of data has been gathered, whatever one thinks of the propriety or mode of its accumulation, what also needs consideration is whether, and if so in what ways, such data can be utilised in the interests of the objects of such investigations, in this case disabled people. I thus also try to indicate where I think the OPCS surveys do yield significant information about the situation of disabled people, and how it might be utilised.

The report

The OPCS surveys of disability in Great Britain were commissioned by what was then the DHSS in 1984. The stated objective was to provide up to date information about the number of disabled people in Great Britain with different levels of severity and their circumstances, for the purposes of planning benefits and services. Four separate surveys were carried out between 1985 and 1988, covering adults in private households, children in private households, adults in communal establishments and children in communal establishments, and the results published in six reports. This paper will examine the first two reports, which are of the most general significance.

Previous investigations by the OPCS on behalf of the Ministry of Health nearly twenty years ago culminated in a study of almost 250,000 households, of which 8,538 were followed up and interviewed in depth.[9,10] Degree of disability was operationalised in terms of a series of questions concerning capacity for self-care.

The response to these questions resulted in total adult population projections, in terms of a division into four categories:

		Approx number
1.	very severely handicapped	157,000
2.	severely handicapped	356,000
3.	appreciably handicapped	616,000
4.	impaired	1,942,000
	Total	3,071,000

Approximately 7.8 per cent of total population.

Since one of the main purposes of the survey was to estimate the number of people who might qualify for attendance allowance, impairment, in this survey, is distinguished from handicap, in terms of self-care needs, the former term implying nil or minimal need.

The most obvious feature of the new survey is that it results in the upward revision of estimates of the number of disabled adults in England, Scotland and Wales, from just over three to nearly six million adults. The North of Ireland, for no obvious theoretical reason, but possibly because it was feared that high rates of injury associated with English occupation would become apparent, possibly because of similarly associated difficulties in carrying out research, was excluded from the investigation.

What accounts for this discrepancy? Has life become so much more dangerous that nearly three million more people have been irreversibly injured, or some hitherto unperceived plague maimed them? Has medicine advanced so far it has kept that many more people from dying, albeit with reduced physical capacities? The answer is far more prosaic, and to do with definitions; the 1971 survey was concerned with physical impairments that severely limited activities, the new survey with a much wider definition. We should thus not look for an answer to the question, 'what is the true number of disabled people?'. Rather we should recognise, as Oliver has pointed out in relation to disability[11] and other writers have argued in more general and wide-ranging ways[4,8] that all statistics are constructed by particular people in particular social and historical contexts for particular purposes, and can only be understood as such.

The first report[12] describes the main concepts and methods common to all the surveys and presents the prevalence estimates from the two surveys of disabled adults. This disability survey attempts to be more wide-ranging than the previous one, trying to cover all types of disability whatever their origin, and setting a lower 'disability threshold'. The survey distinguishes thirteen different types of disability and produces a formula to establish severity categories. This procedure gives rise to the following projections for the population as a whole.

Severity category	No. of disabled people in private households
1 (least severe)	1,186,000
2	824,000
3	732,000
4	676,000
5	679,000
6	511,000
7	447,000
8	338,000
9	285,000
10	102,000
Total	5,780,000
Living in establishments	422,000
Grant Total	6,202,000

(Adapted from Table 3.1, Martin and White[13]).

Examples of who fall into categories 1-3 indicate that these individuals, whose daily activities are restricted, but not severely so, may not have been eligible for inclusion in the least severe 1971 survey category of 'impairment'. If we were to subtract these individuals from our total, the estimated total proportion of the population who are 'disabled' would roughly correspond with the 1971 figure.

However a third source, the 1985 GHS estimates, based on the answers to two questions (Martin 1988[12] p.20), gives an overall figure which is considerably higher in total, and for younger (less than seventy) age groups. The OPCS surveys made no attempt to establish the geographical distribution of disabled people, nor is this failure justifiable by methodological difficulties, since the 1971 survey[9] did precisely this. This omission seriously weakens the explanatory and policy-making potential of the data.

Whilst the ten point severity scale is ostensibly a more sensitive measure than previous systems, the procedure used to judge severity is a complex one, which at base rests on the subjective judgements of a panel, an unspecified number of whose members were themselves disabled, on the importance of a somewhat arbitrarily selected subset of incapacities. Essentially, despite protestations of the researchers to the contrary, judges were being asked, in a general way, and thus with no regard to individual situation or social contexts, to judge which conditions are 'worse'. In so far as the results of such procedures mean anything, they merely reflect a cruder version of any pre-existing cultural consensus in the groups from which the panel of judges is culled, cruder since most common beliefs about disability are more sophisticated than to attempt to provide an answer to questions of the 'is it worse to be blind or deaf?' kind. The spurious objectivity implied by complex quantifications and ten-point scales should not fool anyone into believing that 'severity' is identified by the OPCS surveys in anything more than the most general of ways (see Disability Alliance 1988[14] for a fuller discussion).

Age

The report is to be commended for separating ageing from disability. It shows that whilst the vast majority (69 per cent) of disabled people are over pension age, a similar proportion of pensioners (355 per thousand) are NOT disabled. Only amongst those of eighty-five or more are disabled people in the majority.

Race

So far as race is concerned the treatment is woefully inadequate. One question yields the information that disability rates for 'Asians' and 'West Indians' are 12.6 and 15.1 per cent respectively (after adjustment for age distribution) compared to an equivalent figure for 'whites' of 13.7 per cent. The rest of the data is not systematically discussed in race terms, nor is this justified, for example in terms of small sample size, leading to the conclusion that the survey does not take race seriously. Some recent work[15] indicates that the experience of disability for individuals from minorities already oppressed by racism requires separate and detailed analysis. Through its failure to systematically employ a 'race' variable, the OPCS survey has passed up the chance of gathering some general data which could have been of importance to those working in this area.

Sex

The survey (table 3.6) indicates that there are considerably more disabled women than men except in the lowest severity levels, with 3.6 million disabled women compared to 2.5 million disabled men in the country as a whole. This excess is judged by the authors to be significant only in older people (75+) and may in large part be accounted for by greater female longevity. The increased prevalence of a number of functionally defined 'disabling' conditions in ageing, also contributes to the increased 'disability' of any more elderly population. Since women generally live longer than men, they will be disproportionately included within this population.

However, it is also the case that the survey found (Martin 1988,[12] p.22, Table 3.7) an increased prevalence rate (fifty-four male, sixty-three female per 1,000 in private households) in the 16-59 age group, a difference the authors of the report deem insignificant.

This apparently contrasts with the 1971 survey, where rates for males of working age with some impairment were rather higher (Harris 1971,[9] p.5) and numbers greater (ibid, p.4). This led Oliver to argue (Oliver 1983,[11] p.40)

> up to the age of fifty both in sheer numbers and prevalence more men are likely to be defined as disabled than women. Two possible reasons are: i) many more men work and risk disablement through accidents and work induced illnesses and ii) many more young men partake in dangerous sports and leisure activities . . . Consequently these figures reflect sexual divisions within society whereby certain activities, both work and leisure, are dominated by males.

OPCS 2 does not present its data in a form which allows direct comparison, employing a blanket 16-59 age band: one would not expect them to have done so, however, if there had been significant differences within it.

So what accounts for this apparent turn around in the sexual distribution of disability in people of working age over the last twenty years? It cannot be explained through the inclusion of 'less disabled' individuals in the later survey, since the figures indicate differences at all levels of severity. It does then seem to indicate either a) a 'real' change, or b) significantly different methods of measurement between the two surveys, such that they could arrive at reversed rates for sex prevalence. Whichever of these explanations is correct, the implications are of significance, and it is unfortunate that the report does at least not mention the matter. As a growing body of literature shows,[16,17,18] the mode and extent of oppression experienced by disabled women is different in important respects from than of disabled men, and a chance to provide a quantitative dimension to what has up to now been largely, of necessity, a qualitative argument has been missed by the OPCS researchers.

The questions

Any introductory textbook on social research enjoins the reader to address notions of reliability and validity when examining the tools employed in a piece of research. Reliability in a question employed to elicit information in a questionnaire or on an interview schedule refers to whether we have reason to believe that the question is consistently understood in the same way by the interviewee, and is thus measuring the same thing in different respondents. Validity refers to whether there is reason to believe the question is understood in the same way by the researcher and the respondent, and is thus measuring what the researcher thinks it is and not something else. An examination of the questionnaires and interview schedule employed by the OPCS researchers reveals some significant problems as regards validity and reliability.

Repeatedly the notion of 'difficulty' and 'great difficulty' is employed, both in the postal screening questionnaire and the interview schedule. For example,

4) Does anyone in your household have . . .
   a) Difficulty walking for a quarter of a mile on the level? Yes/No
   b) Great difficulty walking up or down steps or stairs? Yes/No

To ask if someone has difficulty is to ask them to make a comparison, which a disabled person is in a particularly unsuitable position to do. For example, the literature informs me (Laurie 1984,[19] p.12) following an explanation in physiological terms that 'polio survivors work abnormally hard . . . to accomplish the same activity'. In this sense everything I accomplish with affected parts of my body is 'difficult'. But, having survived polio some thirty-five years I am in no position to make this judgement experientially, for I have no 'normal' baseline to measure my effort against. Again, by the use of tricks, like wheelies used to get wheelchairs over obstacles, and devices disabled people survive in hostile environments. If you've a trick to get round the problem, do you still have a 'difficulty'?

For people with longstanding disability then, who constitute the vast majority of respondents in the OPCS survey, 'difficulty' is quintessentially a subjective construct, bearing little relation to 'normal' difficulty or to 'difficulties' confronted by someone with a dissimilar disability. As such it is a singularly inappropriate measuring tool for a supposedly objective assessment, and likely to result in systematic underestimation of the problems confronted, and often successfully dealt with, by disabled people.

Financial circumstances

The second report[13] examines the financial circumstances of disabled adults living in private households. It is based on data from a survey carried out in 1985, and so does not take into account changes, particularly those affecting social security benefits, that have taken place since that time. Various writers have argued that these changes have had the effect of worsening, in a variety of ways, the financial situation of disabled people.

Three specific aims are identified by the researchers:

1) to examine the extent to which disability affects people's income;

2) to establish whether extra expenditure is incurred as a result of disability and to establish the magnitude of that expenditure;

3) to evaluate the overall impact of disability on the standard of living and financial circumstances of disabled adults and their families.

Employment

Disabled adults under pension age were found to be less likely to be in paid work than adults in the general population, allowing for differences in age, sex and marital status. Only thirty-one per cent of non-pensioner disabled adults were working, this proportion falling from forty-eight per cent in category one to two per cent in category ten (Martin 1988,[13] fig. 2.4). No attempt is made to relate these findings to the growing body of literature on unemployment and health.[20,21] Unmarried disabled adults were less likely to be working than married in each age, sex and severity group, as were those over, as opposed to under, fifty (Martin,[13] table 2.18). Thus marriage and youth seem to be factors associated with likelihood of employment, as well as the more obvious factor of being in a lower severity category. A number of recent small scale studies[22,23] have indicated the discrimination, direct and indirect, experienced by disabled people in obtaining and keeping jobs, and again it is a pity that the OPCS study did not take the opportunity to explore this further.

Income

So far as earnings from work were concerned, both men and women disabled full time employees earned less than full-time employees in the general population, which could not be accounted for by differences in hours worked (Martin 1988,[13] table 3.1). Some evidence of a decrease in earnings was found with higher severity categories for men, but not for women. In discussing a similar pattern in relation to race, Smith 1984,[24] p.169 suggests that

> part of the explanation for the similarity in the overall levels of wages among white and black women was that the enormous disparity between men and women in this respect left little scope for racial disadvantage to have a further, additive effect.

Whether these facts indicate that low pay follows from disability (discrimination, lower qualifications and thus job levels etc) or that those in low paid occupations are more likely to become disabled (a higher likelihood of impairment in lower social classes) is not determinable via this data. The probability is that the explanation is a combination of the two, that class inequalities and oppression combine to produce general patterns of disadvantage.

For the majority of married disabled adults under pension age, at least one member of the family was earning, but only twenty-two per cent of the total of disabled adults lived in such a unit. The majority of disabled adults (seventy-eight per cent of total, fifty-four per cent of those under pension age) lived in family units containing no earners and thus the significance of State benefits was great. Although half of all disabled adults had another source of income besides earnings and benefits, the most common of these were pensions or redundancy payments from a former employer or income from savings and investments, and were thus most likely to be received by older respondents.

Comparisons with the equivalent incomes of families in the general population showed that disabled non-pensioner families had significantly lower incomes than non-pensioners in general: on average seventy-two per cent. Whilst much of this is due to disabled adults being less likely to have earned income, families with one or more earners still had lower than average incomes than comparable families in the general population.

Disabled pensioners, however, were not readily distinguishable in income terms from non-disabled, and this is again probably related to the general lower average income of pensioners than non-pensioners, which produces a 'flattening' effect on the figures. In 1983 sixty-four per cent of pensioners were living in poverty or on its margins, compared with twenty-four per cent under pensionable age.[24]

Expenditure

It was found that for all severity-categories there was some extra expenditure involved because of disability. This was divided into three types, lump sum expenditure on special items, regular expenditure on special items and regular expenditure on items required by most people but on which disabled people need to spend more.

Occasional costs

Type one, lump sum expenditure, on special items of equipment like special furniture in the year previous to the survey, was incurred by only sixteen per cent of the sample, spending £78 on average, but with considerable variation between individuals. The average for all disabled adults works out at £12.50 a year. Because of the limited time span the OPCS researchers admit this is likely to be a low estimate of true costs.

Regular costs

Regular expenditure on items required solely because of disability, like prescriptions, costs associated with hospital visits, private domestic help, were incurred by sixty per cent of disabled adults. Amounts and proportions increased with severity category, with average expenditure for those incurring it being £2.20 a week, or £1.30 for each disabled adult.

The third type of expenditure, 'ordinary' items on which disabled people need to spend more, e.g. fuel, clothing, food, travel, home maintenance, was reported by seventy-one per cent of disabled adults, with an average cost to those incurring it of £6.70, or £4.80 for all disabled adults. Again, the proportion of adults with expenditure of this kind and the amount they spent rose with severity.

Adding these two together, the average extra expenditure entailed by disability for all disabled adults amounted to £6.10 a week, or, including the lump sum average, £329.70 a year. This is only an arithmetical average, however, and there were considerable variations in actual expenditure, both within and between severity categories.

As well as rising with severity, average extra expenditure rose with income within severity categories, indicating that people may well have spent more if it were available. Altogether twenty-four per cent of disabled adults thought they needed to spend more because of their disability but could not afford to do so.

An effect of having to spend a proportion of income on items associated with disability is to reduce disposable income. The report examines this in terms of 'equivalent resources', which is arrived at by calculating the income remaining after disability related expenditure has been subtracted and using equivalence scales to adjust the remaining income for differences in family composition. This is expressed in terms of £=.

On average net equivalent resources were ninety-two per cent of net equivalent income, that is eight per cent of income was spent on disability-related expenses. Although the average amount of such expenditure was lower for those on lower incomes, they spent a higher proportion of their income on disability-related expenses. Proportion also rose with severity: those in severity category 10 were spending on average fifteen per cent, compared to four per cent for category 1.

The average equivalent resources of disabled non-pensioners were £=91.70 per week, compared to £136.70 for the non-pensioner general population. Forty-one per cent of disabled non-pensioners had equivalent resources of less than half this amount, compared to twenty-three per cent of the general population.

The difference between disabled and non-disabled pensioners was not so marked, probably for reasons mentioned above. The use of the notion of equivalent income in making these calculations, whatever reservations one may have about the calculations themselves, is to be welcomed. It makes clear that there are calculable costs of disability which, given the political will, government has the ability to offset, employing a number of alternative or complementary mechanisms, some of which are more attractive to disabled people than others.

Financial problems

Altogether eight per cent of disabled householders thought they were getting into financial difficulties, but there were significant differences between household types, with thirty-six per cent of the albeit small group of single parents, twenty-three per cent of single childless householders, but only three per cent of pensioners reporting difficulties. Objective calculations tended to confirm subjective views, and both related financial difficulties strongly to equivalent resources.

Standard of living

Measures of standards of living are habitually constructed in terms of the lack of named items or activities, which are deemed to be 'basic', e.g. a warm winter coat, meat or fish every other day or consumer durables, e.g. washing machine, telephone. In terms of 'relative deprivation' some consumer durables are judged luxuries, e.g. video recorder, whilst others considered 'normal' items of living at a given point in time, e.g. refrigerators today, but not in the 1950s. The selection and significance of these items is involved in the ongoing debate about 'absolute' and 'relative' poverty, and the report assiduously avoids employing these terms.

A criticism raised of previous studies, for example, Townsend[26] was that they failed to distinguish between not possessing a consumer durable or basic item because you couldn't afford it, which would be a reasonable indicator of economic deprivation, and not having it because you didn't want it, which wouldn't. This study allows for that, and found a proportion of both 'luxuries' and 'basic items' lacking from choice. However, it found a relationship, strongest when calculated in terms of equivalent resources, between disability and inability to afford desired items.

Responses

It is evident of the growing strength of organisations for and increasingly of disabled people that a number of detailed responses to the reports, particularly report two, were speedily forthcoming. In particular, the Disability Alliance and the Disablement Income Group produced documents[27,28] which, whilst welcoming the reports' highlighting of the link between disability and poverty, were critical of the methods employed, which, they argued, resulted in systematic and significant underestimations of the 'true cost' of disability, which OPCS quantified at an average of £6.10 a week. These reports largely take the individualist methodology of OPCS for granted, but argue that their methods result in them getting the 'wrong' answers to what are tacitly assumed to be the 'right' questions.

Whilst this approach does not address the more profound methodological issues raised in the earlier parts of this paper, these are perhaps not of such a great significance in relation to the attempt to quantify the costs of disablement, and their contributions are certainly of significance in the immediate social policy debate. A number of factors, the critiques argue, combine together to produce systematic underestimation of the costs of disability.

1) The survey was conducted before the benefit changes of April 1988, which resulted in reduced benefits for an estimated one million disabled people.

The survey was thus seriously out of date even before the publication of results.

2) One-off items, such as costs of a car, housing adaptations, electrical wheelchairs etc. are grossly underestimated as a result of the OPCS decision to ask only about items bought in the last twelve months although from their own figures (Martin 1988[13] p.37 whilst sixty-eight per cent of people surveyed had made at least one 'lump sum purchase' only sixteen per cent had done so during the relevant twelve month period.

3) Not enough severely disabled people were surveyed. OPCS employ ten categories of disability, of which 1-3 are those whose 'daily living activities are not severely restricted' (DIG would argue these should not be included at all). OPCS respondents are mostly in the lower categories, with only 1.6 per cent of those surveyed in the highest category.[10] Using other likely indicators of severity of disability in the sample, only thirteen per cent received disability benefit, eight per cent attendance allowance, seven per cent mobility allowance and only a fifth of this thirteen per cent received two benefits. The suggestion is then that the sampling technique was skewed in a way that made the more severely disabled, and thus those most likely to incur greatest additional expenditure, less likely to be included.

4) The form of question, interviewing method and the time taken over interviews. The OPCS interviews lasted about one and a half hours, only a part of this time being devoted to questions about the costs of disability. No prompting or clarification by interviewers was permitted, resulting in a significant number of D/K responses, since, by the researchers' own admission[13, p.35]:

> not surprisingly people found it very difficult to estimate what proportion of the total cost of say heating was incurred because of their disability.

DIG and DA argue that more time needs to be spent on interviews, with clarification and illustration to help people work out the answers. When DIG replicated the OPCS survey with a more lengthy and exploratory interviewing technique they reduced the 'Don't know' category to zero. In the OPCS survey there was at least one item of information missing in at least forty per cent of responses which led them to

> decide to impute an average expenditure for them based on the estimates of those who were able to give an estimate (Martin 1988,[13] p.36).

Disability Alliance argue:

> it is impossible to calculate the effect that this will have on the overall accuracy of the results. (Disability Alliance 1988,[27] p.22)

5) Need and expenditure. The OPCS data indicated seventy one per cent of their sample of disabled people were spending extra as a result of their disability. Twenty-four per cent - 1,387,000 - said they needed to spend more than they did but could not afford to. The items most often cited were basics such as fuel, clothing and food. Shocking though these figures are, DA argue that these figures are likely to systematically underestimate real levels of need. Accurate responses in this area are notoriously difficult to achieve. Coates and Silburn have commented[29] on the unrealistically low estimates provided by their respondents of the level of extra income they would require to be 'comfortable'. West[30] describes how female tobacco workers would describe themselves as working for 'pinmoney' when a detailed survey of household income and expenditure revealed the essential nature of their contribution to family economy. A high proportion of the respondents were elderly, amongst whom discrepancies between their own estimates and those of professionals have habitually been noted.

All this suggests that we should pay particular attention to the apparent contradiction between seventy per cent of disabled people having an income substantially lower than the general population and a similar percentage expressing 'satisfaction' with their standard of living.

What DIG did

The Disablement Income Group has made the study of the extra costs of disability its speciality, with work by Hyman,[31] Stowell and Day[32] and Buckle[33] all producing considerably higher figures than the recent OPCS study. Whilst the OPCS used a large-scale survey technique, the DIG studies employ in-depth studies based on relatively small samples.

To demonstrate what they regard as the inappropriate nature of the OPCS methodology in ascertaining the 'true cost' of disability, DIG followed a two-pronged strategy of

1) administering an OPCS type questionnaire

2) administering a semi-structured unstandardised questionnaire of a type used in small-scale, in-depth studies with running prompts and additional questions to the same subjects, and comparing the results from the two.

DIG, who, unlike some other sections of the Disabled People's Movement, regard a high degree of restriction of activity as definitional of disablement, employed a sample culled from their Advisory Service case files which represented a range of conditions, but all of whom would fall into the two highest (9 and 10) OPCS categories, and were receiving at least one of the two main disability-related allowances. However, they say they deliberately avoided selecting the most severe cases from their files. Their sample was also significantly younger, on average, than the OPCS group, and the only two respondents over sixty-five had been disabled for twenty and forty years respectively.

Employing the OPCS style survey, an average extra weekly expenditure of £41.84 was reported whereas the response of the same subjects to the DIG schedule produced an average of £65.94, a difference of fifty eight per cent between the two methods.

DIG argue that these results support their view of the OPCS survey:

> that the sample they interviewed and the interview schedule and techniques they used have given rise to a much lower figure for the average weekly costs of disability than would have been the case if more significantly disabled people had been interviewed and if a more detailed questionnaire had been used (Thompson 1988,[28] p.28).

Avoiding any discussion of the DIG view that some of those included in the OPCS survey aren't 'really disabled', the discrepancy between the results obtained employing the two types of interview support DIG's more general conclusion:

> We believe we have shown that the results in the OPCS second report cannot be used as the basis for making policy decisions about extra costs. They must be supplemented by other information about the high extra costs of disability. (Disability Alliance 1988,[27] p.29)

Conclusion

For disabled people and for social workers attempting to work appropriately with us, the significance of the OPCS surveys lies in their occurrence and the chance for discussion of disability that they provide, rather than their contents.

Whilst the first report highlights the systematic underestimation of the prevalence of disability which was enshrined in previous government research, and upon which social policies were putatively based, it should by no means be interpreted as providing the 'true' figure. Such a project is an impossible one, since 'disability' is a social construct, and definitions inevitably in contention. They depend upon the interests, intentions and unexamined presuppositions of those with the power to define, and the ability of those so defined to resist inappropriate conceptions of their reality. So far as the severity scales are concerned, the danger is that the spurious objectivity implied by calculations and an elaborate system of judgement panels seduces the social worker into concluding that degrees of disadvantage and suffering are amenable to statistical representation in this way, and that appropriate welfare provision and resource allocation may be determined on the basis of it. In other areas, particularly those related to the growing concern amongst disabled people and their allies to explore the relationship between disability and other dimensions of oppression, such as racism and sexism, the report is disappointingly, but predictably, silent. It largely fails to seek information in these areas, and where it does, gathers and presents it in a form which is not amenable to its contributing to current debate.

The second report, on financial circumstances, does provide recognition that disability causes poverty, although, mindful of the sensibilities of their paymasters, the word itself is avoided by the researchers. Because of the research methods employed, however, they fail to even approach an adequate quantification of the financial disadvantages experienced by disabled people. the danger here is that the figures presented, in the absence of any others and as part of a general strategy of reducing public expenditure, form the basis of government policy towards disabled people, and will be accepted by social workers in their day-to-day work as realistic.

The OPCS surveys constitute a missed opportunity. A rare chance to carry out a large scale study which could provide evidence to support or refute aspects of a growing body of micro-level studies existed. The resources of time, money and technical expertise available to OPCS, despite repeated cuts in the funding of state research since the Rayner review of 1981, dwarf those of individual researchers and organisations of disabled people. But this review also made clear that information should not be collected primarily for publication. It should be collected primarily because government needs it for its own business. That this is the course that has been adopted has become increasingly apparent, with senior government functionaries up to Sir John Boreham, former head of the Government Statistical Services, as well as the more usual critics, expressing their disquiet at the constraint and abuse of the statistical services for political purposes. It is to be expected that the questions asked and the information arrived at should reflect even more directly than before the concerns of the state rather than those of disabled people and social workers attempting to provide appropriate services.

Given this, a critical understanding of the deficiencies of the OPCS surveys, both in terms of overall approach and of method, can provide a salutory example of how not to research issues of disability. Attempts to depoliticise the unavoidably political, to examine the complex and subtle through crude and simplistic measures, indicate by negative example some of the things that good research in this area, and indeed any other, requires.

Disability must be recognised as a political matter, with ramifications in our understanding of work, sexuality, literature, design, humour and all other areas of human life, and discussions of the more obvious and immediate sphere of social policy cannot take place in isolation from a recognition of this. This is not to say that a single piece of research must deal with all these aspects, but rather that it should be designed with and interpret its results in the light of, such an awareness.

Disabled people, in this country and elsewhere, are increasingly conceptualising their lives in political terms and acting accordingly, rejecting the dominant 'personal tragedy' model of our situation. In this context, no conceptualisation of or questions about disability can be seen as 'neutral'.

As with other oppressed groups, for the social worker to operate in a non-oppressive manner, a preliminary requirement is that she develop some knowledge of the nature, extent and mechanisms of that oppression. Part of what that involves is the critique of oppressive practices and 'knowledge'. A critical reading of one of the most recent examples of oppressively structured 'knowledge' of disabled people, the OPCS surveys, is quite a good place to start. And what about following this up by talking to disabled people themselves, after all there are now six and a quarter million of us to choose from - and that's official!

References

1. HMSO (1989). *Caring for People - Community Care in the Next Decade and Beyond.*

2. Stone, D. (1984). *The Disabled State.* Macmillan, Basingstoke.

3. Oliver, M. (1990). *The Politics of Disablement.* Macmillan, Basingstoke.

4. Irvine, M. and Evans, J. (1979). *Demystifying Social Statistics.* Pluto, London.

5. Leech, K. (1989). *A Question in Dispute.* Runnymede Trust, London.

6. Topliss, E. (1979). *Provision for the Disabled* (2nd edition). Blackwell with Martin Robinson, Oxford, 1979, 49.

7. Oakley, A. (1981). 'Interviewing Women: A Contradiction in Terms'. In Roberts, H. (Ed.) *Doing Feminist Research.* RKP, London.

8. Hindess, B. (1973). *The Use of Official Statistics in Sociology*. Macmillan, London, 12.

9. Harris, A. (1971). *Handicapped and Impaired in Great Britain*. HMSO, London, 1971.

10. Buckle, J. (1971). *Work and Housing of Impaired People in Great Britain*. HMSO, London.

11. Oliver, M. (1983). *Social Work with Disabled People*. Macmillan, London.

12. Martin, J., Meltzer, H. and Elliot, D. (1988). *Report 1. The Prevalence of Disability among Adults*. HMSO, London, 20, 22.

13. Martin, J. and White, A. (1988). *Report 2. The Financial Circumstances of Disabled Adults in Private Households*. HMSO, London.

14. Disability Alliance (1988). *Briefing on the First Report from the OPCS Surveys of Disability*. Disability Alliance, London.

15. Confederation of Indian Organisations (UK) (no date) *Double- Bind - To be Disabled and Asian*. Confederation of Indian Organisations (UK), London.

16. Deegan, M. and Brooks, N. (1985). *Women and Disability, the Double Handicap*. Transaction Books, New Jersey.

17. Campling, J. (Ed.) (1981). *Images of Ourselves*. RKP, London.

18. Morris, J. (Ed.) (1989). *Able Lives*. Women's Press, London.

19. Laurie et al. (Ed.) (1984). *Handbook on the Late Effects of Poliomyelitis for Physicians and Survivors*. St. Louis Missouri Gazette, International Networking Institute.

20. Smith, R. (1987). *Unemployment and Health*. OUP, Oxford.

21. Warr, P. (1987). *Work, Unemployment and Mental Health*. Clarendon Press, Oxford.

22. Fry, E. (1986). *An Equal Chance for Disabled People? - A Study of Discrimination in Employment*. Spastics Society, London.

23. French, S. (1988). *'They Weren't Obstructive but They Didn't Go Out of Their Way to be Helpful Either' - Disabled People in the Health and Caring Professions: Professional Attitudes and Personal Experiences*. London South Bank Polytechnic.

24. Smith, D., 1974, cited in Brown, C. (1984). *Black and White Britain - The Third PSI Survey*. Heinemann, London, 169.

25. DHSS (1986). *Tables on Families with Low Incomes 1983*. HMSO, London.

26. Townsend, P. (1979). *Poverty in the U.K.* Penguin, Harmondsworth.

27. Disability Alliance (1988). *Briefing on the Second OPCS Report*. Disability Alliance, London.

28. Thompson, P. with Buckle, J. and Lavery, M. (1988). *NOT the OPCS Survey - Being Disabled Costs More than They Said*. London Disablement Income Group.

29. Coates, K. and Silburn, R. (1970). *Poverty - the Forgotten Englishmen*. Penguin, Harmondsworth.

30. West, J. (1980). *Women, Reproduction and Wage Labour*. In Nichols, T. *Capital and Labour*. Fontana, London.

31. Hyman, M. (1977). *The Extra Costs of Disabled Living*. National Fund for Research into Crippling Diseases, London.

32. Stowell, R. and Day, F. (1983). *Tell Me What You Want and I'll Get It for You - A Study of Shopping when Disabled*. Disablement Income Group, London.

33. Buckle, J. (1984). *Mental Handicap Costs More*. Disablement Income Group, London.

Creating a Supportive Environment: Meeting the Needs of People who are Ageing with a Disability

Gerry Zarb

Introduction

This chapter considers the challenge to social workers and other service workers that is posed by the increasing number of people who are now ageing with a disability. Based on the findings of the first major research project on ageing with disability carried out in Great Britain,[1] we will outline a model for creating an ideal supportive environment and the implications this would have for social workers. In particular, the chapter considers the support needs associated with ageing with a disability; the resources available to meet these needs; and how older disabled people's own ideal solutions compare with existing solutions.

Ageing with disability: a new challenge for social work

The ageing of the population in Britain is having a profound impact on social policy, service provision and professional practice. It is important to keep in mind, however, that the 'ageing population' is a far from homogeneous group; rather, there are important differences between particular groups, sub-groups and age cohorts, which have to be identified, acknowledged, and responded to, if appropriate services are to be provided and individual personal needs adequately met.

One particular sub-group which has been more or less completely overlooked are disabled people who are experiencing the ageing process, and the practical and personal problems which are often associated with this. To be clear, this does not refer to people who may experience disability as a consequence of ageing, but to those who become disabled in childhood or adulthood and who are now beginning to age with their disabilities. Indeed, it is only within the last fifteen to twenty years that there has even been an identifiable cohort of ageing disabled adults, since life expectancy for many types of disability prior to this was so low.

Changing patterns of life expectancy brought about by advances in medical technology, treatment and rehabilitation also mean that the size of this sub-group of disabled people is increasing. Whilst there are no completely accurate figures for this, it is possible to get some idea of the number of people involved from existing sources. The first OPCS survey of disabled people carried out in 1969 estimated that there were 97,000 'very severely', 'severely' or 'appreciably handicapped' people between the ages of thirty and forty-nine in Great Britain.[2] If we assume that half·of this group have survived in the subsequent twenty year period, this would mean there are at least 50,000 disabled people alive today who are experiencing the process of ageing with a disability.

The latest OPCS survey, whilst using a slightly different classification of disability, estimates that there are now 201,000 similarly disabled people (categories 6-10) aged between thirty and forty-nine.[3] These figures clearly indicate, therefore, that the number of people ageing with a disability is likely to continue to increase considerably over the next few years. Indeed, it is quite probable that this group will double in size within the next twenty years.

Next to nothing is known, however, about the experience of ageing with a long-term disability. It is important to consider that, whilst there may be some overlap between the interests of ageing disabled people and other groups in the ageing population, each group will bring its own perspective to the ageing and disability experience. These contrasting perspectives may, in turn, influence expectations and preferences about what kind of support may be required, and how it should be made available.[4] Clearly, then, there is an urgent need to develop recognition of the needs of ageing disabled adults and an understanding of the implications for service delivery, including the impact on residential care, community nursing, personal care assistance and social work itself. Equally, it is essential to consider the impact on families and primary carers who, it should be recognised, will often also be experiencing the ageing process themselves.

The present structure of community services fails to meet the needs of the majority of disabled people, let alone those who may be experiencing the additional problems often associated with ageing. Furthermore, working with disabled people is often a low priority within social services departments.[5,6] Since the same applies to working with elderly people,[7] it is not difficult to see that many social workers will have failed to consider the needs of people who are both ageing and disabled. Most importantly, the lack of appropriate services means that many people in this group will fall through the net of existing support provision.

Whilst the needs of people who are ageing with disability have been largely unrecognised until now, the emerging visibility of this client group will undoubtedly represent an increasing challenge to social workers in the next decade and beyond. As a first step towards responding to this challenge service professionals and planners will need to establish clear principles to guide the development of appropriate policy and practice. Given the lead role of social services departments - and social workers in particular - in implementing the new community care legislation, this need is now more urgent than ever.

It was against the background of these concerns that the research on ageing with disability was initiated. The study discussed here looked at the experiences of one particular sub-group - people who had been disabled as a consequence of spinal injury. However, the research has since been extended to cover other groups.[8] In the next section of this chapter, some of the main support needs identified by the study are summarised together with the resources currently available to meet these needs. After this, a model for the development of a supportive environment is outlined based on older disabled people's ideal solutions for meeting their support needs. Finally, the chapter considers some of the practical steps which need to be taken in order to implement such a model.

Support needs associated with ageing with a disability - a summary

Our study has identified a range of support needs associated with ageing with a disability. An increased need for personal care and domestic support were the areas of most pressing concern to the majority of people in the study. At the same time, these needs were often inextricably linked to people's housing and financial needs, as well as the need for appropriate support from health services - both hospital and community based.

One of the main issues the study highlighted is that there are a wide range of physical problems/changes associated with ageing. Often, however, these physical problems were closely tied to other personal changes people had experienced in their lives, and to a range of material and social factors - particularly the level of support they and/or their carers had available to them.

Not surprisingly, the physical consequences of the ageing process often had significant implications for personal mobility and personal care. Many people found that their daily routines were taking longer and becoming more difficult. Over forty per cent of our sample reported wanting more help with transfers and between twenty-five and thirty-five per cent wanted more help with other aspects of their personal care like dressing/undressing and bathing. Several reported having to make changes in their routines as a consequence of the physical effects of ageing; these ranged from finding new ways to get in and out of a bath, or the car, to simply having to rest more often during the day. Some had made wider ranging changes like having an occasional care attendant, or home help, or in a few cases, changes in living arrangements. Many more expressed awareness that they may need to make similar changes in the foreseeable future.

For the majority of people in the study, the actual amount of extra help needed was, however, fairly minimal. Nearly a quarter reported needing no extra help, whilst for well over half, the amount of help wanted was between one and three hours per day. Some people felt that this might increase in the future but, obviously, were not usually able to say by how much. There was a trend for the amount of help needed to increase slightly both over time since injury and with age, although the oldest group - aged seventy or over - reported wanting double the average amount of daily help.

Whilst the physical consequences of ageing were an important feature of many people's experiences, several people pointed out that the physical problems they had experienced were usually only the 'trigger' for changes in support needs. Often, other personal and social factors - particularly the level of supportive resources available - had a more direct bearing on the amount of extra help they required. Whether or not the physical effects of ageing actually constitute a problem for the individuals concerned is ultimately dependent on such social and environmental factors as their housing environment, their financial resources, the suitability of the aids and wheelchairs they use, and whether or not they and their carers receive enabling and acceptable support.

Another very important issue which the study has highlighted is that the amount of support different individuals need is almost always variable and can increase significantly during periods of temporary difficulty like a spell of ill-health, or when there are changes in family or domestic circumstances. Several people also reported that their need for support can change from day to day depending simply on how they are feeling - physically and/or mentally, or on the kinds of things they might need help with. For example, someone might want help with moving furniture when they are cleaning the house one week, but not the next.

This feature of the support needs associated with older disabled people has particularly significant implications for the delivery of services, which are discussed in more depth in the next section of the chapter. For disabled individuals themselves, the problem many people faced was that it is often difficult to predict when a temporary need for additional help will arise. Most accepted that, if they did want help of this kind, a degree of compromise might be required over timing. At the same time, they were not prepared to accept having to constantly arrange their lives around the routines demanded by service providers.

However, as existing support services - particularly community nursing and social services themselves - are not able- to respond flexibly to this kind of situation, people more often than not had to manage without support at these times, although the gaps were often partially filled by help from informal sources (i.e. friends, neighbours or family).

For the people in the study who were not completely independent in terms of their personal care needs, support was provided mostly by a spouse or other relative (seventy-five percent of those with carers). Many people and their carers expressed considerable anxiety over the long term viability of these support arrangements - particularly as many of the carers themselves were experiencing the physical effects of ageing. Perhaps even more important than the physical strain on ageing carers were the emotional costs involved. We found evidence of considerable problems in this area and several carers clearly felt very unsupported emotionally as well as practically. Some wanted to make more use of respite care facilities, but had found it very difficult to obtain this support. Some specifically identified a need for professional counselling, whilst several others wanted advice and information about carers' support groups. Clearly, these are specific areas where social workers could make a direct contribution, but hardly any of the carers in the study had received any support at all.

Not surprisingly, several people felt that a breakdown in their present support arrangements was at least very likely, if not inevitable. For some, this had already happened and they were consequently already in a crisis situation with little or no support available from alternative sources. This was particularly likely to be the case for people whose main carer was a parent in their seventies or eighties. Also, there were a few individuals whose spouse was also disabled. In these cases, the caring role tended to be reciprocal, with both partners functioning independently as a unit. However, the viability of this type of arrangement tended to be prone to breakdown as soon as either partner experienced any problems. More often than not, people in this situation had already experienced significant crises over their support.

In addition to carers within the family unit, several people received assistance from other informal sources of support like friends and neighbours. The support available from these informal sources was mostly restricted to domestic assistance and, in a few cases, transport. On the rare occasions when informal helpers had been involved with personal care, this was typically on a very temporary basis to cover for an emergency or crisis situation. Also, there was a clear recognition that, as they were themselves ageing, informal helpers like friends and neighbours would not be able to provide more support in any case. Rather, they would be more likely to help less over time.

Given the strains which ageing imposed on many people's informal support, it might have been expected that there would be an increase in the use of statutory agencies. In fact, there was very little regular contact with formal support services amongst the people in the study. The only exception to this was the community nursing service; over a third were using the service currently, and well over half had done so in the past. Whilst most people were generally satisfied with this service, some had experienced significant problems. Particular difficulties concerned the unavailability of nurses at nighttimes and at weekends and the regulations about what duties they were allowed to perform. For example, people reported that their community nurses were not allowed to help with bathing, even though they could and did assist with getting in and out of the bath. Rather, bathing services are supposed to be provided by bathing auxiliaries, who usually visit only once a week. This was considered to be inadequate by practically all the individuals who wanted such assistance.

In some cases, individual nurses simply ignored the regulations regarding duties and regularity of visits in order to provide the kind of assistance wanted. Whilst this meant that the needs of the individuals concerned were being met in the short-term, this was due to quite arbitrary factors such as the personal disposition of individual nurses. From an objective viewpoint this cannot be seen as an adequate basis for support provision as there are no guarantees about such support continuing to be available in the longer term.

It was also clear that the community nursing service was often plugging gaps which could or should have been filled by social services departments or other agencies. In particular, some individual nurses were effectively acting as supplementary care attendants, providing assistance which would normally be described as social support rather than nursing or health care as such (e.g. helping people getting in and out of bed). In a few cases, community nurses were advising people on aids and adaptations, or even making referrals on their behalf. More generally, several people reported that the community nurses were providing important and valued personal support on an ongoing basis - even though no practical help was actually required.

At one level, this situation obviously reflects the arbitrary compartmentalisation of support according to the organisational and professional boundaries imposed by a fragmented and uncoordinated system of community services. This fails completely to recognise the constant overlap between 'health' and 'social' support in the day-to-day reality of disabled people's lives.

At another level, however, the role played by the community nursing service reflects the failure of social services departments to respond to, or even recognise the needs of older disabled people. Further evidence of this is given by the actual level of contact people had with social workers and other professionals other than community nurses.

For example, only seven per cent of the sample were using the home help service, although nearly twenty per cent stated that they wanted to, and a similar number were buying in their own domestic help privately. In some cases, requests for a home help had been turned down. Usually this was on the basis that people's families were able to cope. As noted above, however, this is often a mistaken assumption and in some cases had actually contributed to the strain on people's informal carers. Some people had declined to use the service even though they wanted domestic support. This was either because they could not meet the charges, or because the regulations about what duties home helps could perform meant that the service was inappropriate to their domestic needs. A common complaint was that home helps declined to help with 'heavy' tasks like moving furniture, hanging curtains etc., which were precisely the kind of things people were most likely to want help with.

Less than five per cent of the people in the study were in contact with either a domiciliary occupational therapist or a social worker, although a much larger proportion had dealt with a social worker in the past. Several people had approached their social services departments with specific requests for help which, more often than not, had either been dealt with inappropriately or simply ignored. Some people, for example, had wanted various aids or adaptations; a few had asked about assessments - either for home help or care attendant services. As mentioned earlier, some had wanted help or information relating to support for carers.

As the following extracts from the interviews illustrate, the majority of people who had been in contact with a social worker expressed considerable dissatisfaction about the experience. This, in turn, is also reflected in the low levels of current contact, as many people had been put off approaching their social services departments by the responses they had received in the past:

We just had to make do with what we could manage to sort out for ourselves. The social services were useless. They wouldn't help with finding accommodation - we had to do that ourselves. And as for getting any adaptations done, the social worker chap I saw just said - 'Don't ask me, pull your own strings'. So that was it, I did - and I always have ever since.

They're hopeless - social services and I do not get on. I don't know why they promise you things - why do they ask you what you want, when they've got no intention of providing it? The system doesn't work because there's too many people involved - too many layers.

You can't trust them - I don't bother with them anymore.

We did ask them (social services) about a bath seat - but they never turned up, so I forgot about it.

But, you talk about getting old . . . the social services, or nobody, never offered any help.

Often, the practical difficulties people had experienced with service based support, together with the frustrations caused, only served to increase their feelings of insecurity and anxiety. Several people reported that, whilst the actual amount of extra assistance they needed was minimal, usually they were simply unable to get it. Given this lack of support from statutory community services, it is not surprising that several people had considered using care attendants or personal helpers as a resource for meeting their support needs. Very few people were regularly using care attendants at the present time, however. Usually this was because people wanted to delay having to do this until it was absolutely necessary, or because they could still manage without (with varying degrees of difficulty). Some people also mentioned lack of finance or difficulties in obtaining care attendants (particularly at short notice) as factors preventing them from using this kind of support at present. More than one in five of the people in the study, however, stated that they would definitely use care attendants at some point in the future, and over half reported that they might want to depending on whether or not there were any further changes in their personal circumstances.

Regarding the type of care attendant service people would want to use, less than a quarter reported a preference for permanent care attendants (living in or out); a similar proportion preferred a rota system. The most popular option was for either an occasional or 'on-call' type of service. However, several people added that the type of care attendant service they would want might change if there were changes in their personal and/or family circumstances. For example, some people felt that an occasional service would be most suitable to meet their anticipated needs but that, if they were to experience significant physical decline or ill-health in the future, they might want more regular assistance. Nevertheless, there is a very clear tendency for people to prefer occasional rather than permanent help.

These preferences reflect the fact that existing support services are too inflexible to meet the needs typically associated with ageing. The provision of some kind of flexible care attendant service, on the other hand, was seen by many as an appropriate solution to the problem of short-term support - particularly in situations where a potential crisis could arise if such support was not available. The ideal for many situations - which at present is usually unattainable - would be for a system of local care attendants or personal helpers who could be obtained at short notice via the telephone. The main benefit of this type of service would be to provide the security of knowing that support would be available quickly, if and when it is needed. Several people also mentioned that this would also considerably relieve the strain on their usual carers. Some also felt that a more flexible service could avoid the need for more costly options like having a full-time care attendant, or going into hospital or a nursing home.

Whilst personal care and domestic support needs were usually the most immediate concern, these cannot be viewed in isolation from people's other support needs - particularly the need for an acceptable and appropriate range of living options. Approximately a third of the people in the study had already, or were considering making changes in their living arrangements in response to problems or changes they had experienced with ageing. For a few people, this involved trying to arrange for a relative or personal helper to move in so that support would be available if and when required. Some people had moved into warden controlled sheltered accommodation, or were looking into the possibility of this option. There were problems with this, however, due to the shortage of places for disabled residents; also, most places which are available are for single person occupancy, which effectively rules out this option for married couples.

Many people in the study were concerned at the lack of alternative living options available to older disabled people. Very few people were in favour of the kind of living options often proposed for disabled people (e.g. Fokus housing, group hostels etc.). Usually, this was because such options were seen to be segregationist and opposed to the idea of living an ordinary lifestyle. Regarding more traditional forms of residential care, several people were very critical of the practice of mixing disabled residents with people who may either be very elderly, or mentally ill. Some people who had personal experience of living in such environments reported that they would not wish to repeat the experience under any circumstances, adding that death would be a preferable option. Many others were equally concerned at the prospect of residential care and expressed their anxieties that this often seems to be the only option available to older people if and when they experience a need for extra personal assistance:

> I could never live in an old people's home or anything like that. I've been free for too long - I'd be clawing at the cage bars.

> If they can't find someone to come in and do for me what she's (mother) always done for me, I shall have to go into a Cheshire home or something like that . . . I don't want to because, I think one week in there and I shall be up the pole and round the bend.

> Independent living is still my aim, but I feel it threatened by the lack of sufficient community care of the right type.

Developing an ideal 'supportive environment'

The experiences reported by the people in this study clearly demonstrate that ageing with a disability is often associated with an increased need for support. However, the range of existing responses to this are usually inappropriate or inadequate. Most people neither want nor need the kind of support provided by either residential care or a full-time care attendant, and most of the alternatives to these two options represent only partial or piecemeal solutions to their support needs (see Figure 1). Clearly, a new model of support provision is required which would more closely match the needs of older disabled people and their families and carers. Based on the needs summarised above, the rest of this chapter outlines what an ideal model for a supportive environment would look like, and the practical implications of putting such a model into practice.

The components of the supportive environment model and the ways in which this contrasts with existing models of support are summarised in Figure 2. The model suggests that the type of support which currently exists will be most likely to lead only to partial solutions, whilst the ideal model would be more likely to lead to a truly supportive environment. Obviously, no single model of support provision could cover the full range of needs associated with ageing without taking into account individual circumstances and preferences. Rather, the model is intended to be used as a set of principles against which to evaluate overall support and identify how the support needs associated with ageing could be more appropriately met.

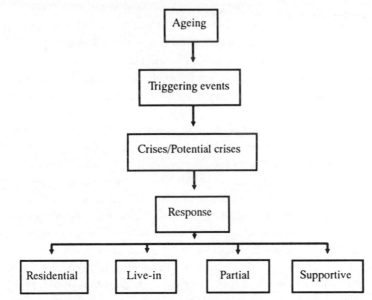

Figure 1: Range of responses to the problems of ageing

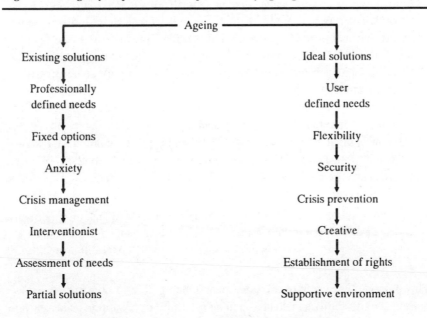

Figure 2: Components of the Supportive Environment Model

i) Professionally vs user defined needs

One of the most fundamental principles of the model discussed here is that the supportive environment must be understood and evaluated in terms of older disabled people's own definitions of resources and needs. In other words, in the provision of appropriate and satisfactory support, the self-defined needs of people wanting support should take precedence over the professionally defined needs of service providers.

In the present structure of support provision, however, this principle is almost invariably reversed and disabled people's own definitions of their needs ignored. The consequence of this failure to take older people's own definitions of their situations and needs as a basic starting point has been that social workers and other service professionals have tended to develop their own set of indicators of what they take to be the 'problems' and 'needs' associated with ageing. In practical terms, this tendency all too often results in a limited range of support options being offered which fail to meet the real needs of older people themselves.

Furthermore, there is a pervasive tendency in social work - which runs right through from training to day to day practice - to view the needs of older people almost exclusively from a problem orientated perspective.[9,7] This same problem - and for more or less the same reasons - has also been noted in relation to the needs of disabled people.[10,11,12,13,14] Again, this usually only results in people being offered inappropriate services. Furthermore, precisely because people's own definitions of their needs do not match the assumptions held by social workers and other service providers, these needs often simply go unrecognised.

The fundamental issue which needs to be addressed, then, is whether or not the structure of service provision is premised on the definitions and issues defined by disabled people themselves, rather than primarily by service professionals. The British Council of Organisations of Disabled People, for example, has argued that existing professional interventions have not benefited disabled people; also, that there is an urgent need for service provision which is initiated and controlled by disabled people themselves:

> . . . new solutions to issues of segregation, inequality and lack of opportunity, which have defied the best efforts of able-bodied people, professionals and 'experts', despite massive inputs of resources . . . which have left many services ineffectual and inappropriate to meet our real needs.[13]

This proposition hinges on disabled people being able to construct their own definition of disability and, hence, their own definitions of support needs and how these should be met. This is more than a semantic issue because of the implications it has for both the provision of services and the ability of individuals to control their own lives. There has been a persistent lack of fit between disabled people's own definitions and those underlying existing service provision and policy formulation, which has consistently failed to involve disabled people to any significant extent - a situation which benefits neither service professionals nor disabled people.[15] Disabled people are often offered services which bear no relation to their own definitions of need, leading to frustration for the individuals concerned and a waste of social and material resources.

Undoubtedly, the roots of this problem are far-reaching; there are a wide range of cultural, political, economic and historical forces influencing the position of disabled people in society, and the present dearth of appropriate supportive services.[16,11] Often it is social workers and other service professionals at the sharp end of social policy who are faced with trying to deal with the consequences of situations which are largely out of their control. At the same time, however, there is an important role for social workers - working in partnership with disabled people - in furthering understanding of the issues which are of most concern to disabled people themselves, and in the development of supportive services which meet their own definitions of need.

A further problem associated with the discrepancy between professional and personal perceptions of need is a tendency to concentrate only on the objective, observable features of individual circumstances, without paying attention to the meanings and values which older people attach to different aspects of their total life experience.[17] This theme was also echoed in our study. Many people had experienced very similar physical effects of ageing; some had almost identical kinds of practical support needs. How these experiences were perceived subjectively, however, varied considerably from individual to individual. The need for increased support, for example, was often the most significant feature of how people perceived the effect of ageing on their lives. For some, needing even the smallest amount of help represented an unacceptable degree of compromise on how they wished to live their lives. This was often a particular problem for people who had spent their early adult years living in institutions and who, consequently, perceived the need for support as a reversal of all their hard work building and maintaining their independence. This is aptly illustrated by the following quotes from people in the study:

> I taught myself to be independent - no one in the residential home even knew I was doing it. It wasn't easy . . . because no-one believed tetraplegics could do anything. I was always falling out of my chair trying to do things for myself. But,

> I just kept crawling back - I wasn't going to give up. It was obvious that no-one was going to help so I just had to do it - and there's no way I'd give it up now.

> I get very depressed - I feel that all the work of years to get more independence was now wasted because I had to have more help.

> When you've been independent . . . you're very reluctant to ask people to do things . . . when it's something you've been able to do, and now you can't, I feel degraded having to ask somebody to do it.

There were other people in the study, however, who took a much more philosophical approach, viewing the need for extra support as the most practical way of maintaining their independence. There were yet others who, whilst not completely happy with their present situations, were prepared to make pragmatic compromises in order to prevent any further loss of independence. The common trend amongst these divergent views is that each individual wanted to maintain control over how their support needs should be met. Rather than deny this, a truly supportive environment would be characterised by support provision and living options which enabled each individual to retain his or her personal autonomy.

Furthermore, nearly all of the people participating in the study emphasised that not only did they wish to retain control over how their support needs should be met, but that they viewed it as their responsibility to do so. Most were prepared to adopt a pragmatic view and recognised that, sometimes, compromises may be necessary. The crucial point, however, is that responsibility for deciding what represents an acceptable degree of compromise must always remain with the individual and can never, under any circumstances, be assumed. Negation of this principle denies personal autonomy and, in practical terms, will often only result in support being declined even where a need exists.

ii) Fixed options vs flexible support provision

It should be clear from the discussion so far that any appropriate model of support must take older people's own definitions of needs as a starting point. Equally important is the need to take account of how an individual feels about his or her situation, as this will have a crucial influence on the appropriateness and acceptability of any particular support option.

On a practical level, this will mean that any social work intervention should work towards the development of each individual's 'ideal' solutions to their own support needs, rather than be restricted by the range of services currently available if these are inappropriate. As one of the women in our study put it:

> We don't really want to have anybody living-in. It is inevitable that we are going to need more help . . . I don't know exactly what we need, but it will have to be something in between the minimal help we get now and actually having someone living-in.

Following on from this, support provision should be flexible enough to respond to people's changing needs with a variety of supportive resources, rather than offering the same range of fixed options to everyone - regardless of individual circumstances or choices. Whilst, for many people, the consequences of ageing may mean that there is an increased need for support, both the amount and type of assistance needed will often vary from day to day, and from week to week. Temporary periods of ill health or intermittent physical and/or emotional fatigue, for example, are both predisposing factors particularly likely to lead to potential crises which could be offset by the provision of short-term support. At the same time, some people may also find that the overall level of support they need increases gradually over time.

The precise components of the support required at any particular time will vary depending on what formal and informal sources are already in place, and on people's present living arrangements. An appropriate model of support, therefore, would be flexible enough to respond speedily to potential crisis situations and provide an adequate choice of acceptable solutions which can be adapted to people's needs as they change. This last point is particularly important. It is a basic premise of our model that support provision should adapt and respond to individual needs; individuals should not have to adapt their needs to suit inappropriate provision. (Although, as noted above, most people may accept a degree of compromise so long as they can retain overall control over how their needs are met).

For example, an individual who presently requires only occasional help from a care attendant or home help may want gradually to increase the amount of help he or she receives over time, and/or place this arrangement on a more regular basis. At some point in the future he or she may even decide to make changes in living arrangements (e.g. have a live-in care attendant, or move to some form of sheltered accommodation). Whichever of these options particular individuals decide are most appropriate/acceptable, they should be able to make any changes to their support arrangements with the minimum disruption to how they wish to live their lives. This would mean that a flexible range of support and living options should be generally available so that each individual can choose those which are most appropriate to their evolving needs. In a truly supportive environment, people should most definitely not have to make a choice between managing with inadequate support, or unacceptable and unnecessary 'solutions' such as moving into a nursing home.

The lack of this flexibility in support provision can often result in the escalation of a temporary crisis to a more long-term problem, or even a permanent breakdown in support arrangements. Furthermore, this can often lead to a counter-productive increase in demand on health and/or personal social services if an individual finds that he or she can no longer cope due to the lack of appropriate support.

Most importantly, it was clear from the experiences reported in the study that the lack of flexible support can often lead the individuals concerned to feel that they have lost control over how they wish to live their lives. The lack of choices over what kind of support is available, and how it is provided, can often represent an unacceptable degree of compromise and, for some, the options of either suicide or euthanasia may even be preferable to being forced to accept inappropriate support:

> If you are in reasonable conditions then you are alright, you don't want to commit suicide. But if you're in conditions you haven't got a lot of control of, where people couldn't care less about you, then you do want to commit suicide.

> If I ever get to that stage (needing help with personal care), I'd rather just sit here in my chair and wait to die - it wouldn't be tolerable to go through all that . . . I can't see the point in keeping going when it gets that bad.

iii) The need for security

As we have already noted, many people in our study expressed varying degrees of concern about the future viability of their support arrangements. This points towards the next major component of an appropriate model of support provision - namely, security. The lack of adequate support at times of crisis is obviously an immediate and practical problem for the individuals concerned. More often than not, however, anxiety over whether or not this kind of problem will be experienced at some time in the future is of equal significance, even in the absence of any immediate need. Most people were aware that, if the existing range of support and living options were not adequate to meet even their present needs, the prospects for the future, when they would be likely to need more support, were less than optimistic, to say the least.

Appropriate social work intervention, therefore, should be concerned not only with responding to needs as and when they arise, but also with promoting a secure supportive environment. In other words, it is equally important that people feel secure in the knowledge that - if their personal circumstances should change, or if they should experience any of the physical or personal problems often associated with ageing - appropriate and acceptable support and living options will be available to them. The fact that some people stated quite explicitly that they would prefer the option of suicide or euthanasia to reliance on existing support services, is an indication of the gap between this ideal and the provision which currently exists.

Just as physical well-being is interdependent with emotional well-being, the provision of practical support cannot be complete without equal consideration to the subjective levels of security (or insecurity) this creates. This lack of security - and the consequences that people have to live with - are summed up very well in the following quote from one of the women in our study:

> As long as the community services do their bit, I'm sure I'll manage somehow. It is a bit worrying though, because you just don't know if the help is going to come through. It's ghastly trying to cope in a situation which is so difficult. I don't see my life as ever being level again because I'm leaping from one minor crisis to another and it is on a knife edge whether or not these crises are coped with in the right way.

Clearly, the kind of support available and whether or not this provides this kind of subjective security will often be one of the major factors determining the quality of an individual's life. Security, therefore, is a fundamental and essential component of the ideal supportive environment. Any social work intervention which fails to take this fully into account will have little chance of meeting the real needs of people who are ageing with a disability.

iv) Crisis prevention vs crisis management

The need for security goes beyond building confidence in the ability of supportive services simply to be able to respond to needs as they arise. Rather, true security would mean that existing supportive resources were sufficiently flexible to prevent the kinds of problems many people had experienced with their support arising in the first place. One of the main features of the ageing experience is that there are several potential 'triggering' events and/or situations which are likely to lead to varying degrees of crisis for older disabled people and their carers. The experiences of the individuals in our study clearly illustrate that responses to these crises from social workers and other agencies are nearly always reactive rather than preventative. Furthermore, the provisions made or offered are - in many cases - incoherent and piecemeal and, in consequence, often rejected by the very people they are intended to assist.

At the same time, many people were able to outline - with varying degrees of certainty - their own alternative solutions as to how their needs should be met. Some had already taken steps to put these plans in motion. Most people, however, even if they have an alternative solution, often find that they are unable to move towards its implementation due to lack of personal or social resources.

Some people, for example, wanted additional support from a statutory service to supplement their own informal arrangements, but had been unable to obtain it. Others wanted to make changes in their living arrangements but were prevented from doing this by lack of financial resources and/or suitable living options. Consequently, in contrast to the ideal of a supportive environment, the reality of their situation had been anxiety over their ability to retain control over how they wish to live their lives.

Most people were attempting to plan ahead and construct satisfactory support arrangements designed to avoid crisis situations arising. As the following example from the interviews highlights, several people also felt that social workers and other professionals who may need to have an input into such support arrangements should be helping in this planning process rather than waiting for a crisis to develop before making any response:

> . . . the set-up I have now would not be any good on a long term basis. If I'm to stay here, the time's going to come when I'm going to have to have combined help from the nursing people, the home help people and the care attendant people isn't it? When I need everything done if I'm going to stay here and I want to get them all in on it before I actually fall that low - because it won't be very far off at the rate we're going . . . I thought that this was the whole purpose of community care - to keep people in their homes. Basically, I would hope to live out the rest of my life here and if I can't I'm going to kick and scream.

For social workers and professionals in other support agencies the development of a more supportive environment would, therefore, entail a move away from the 'crisis management' approach (which has its roots in the problem orientation to needs described earlier), towards a 'crisis prevention' approach. Such a model of support would be sensitive to both the potential practical crises associated with ageing, and to the significant levels of subjective insecurity these can create.

v) The need for creative solutions

The need for a more preventative approach to support is closely related to the need for a more facilitative role for service providers. One of the most important implications of the kind of model we have outlined is that the needs of older disabled people would be met much more effectively if support provision was based on the solutions which individuals defined as most appropriate to their own particular situation. This means that support should be geared towards enabling people to move towards the attainment of their own solutions; building on the resources they already have; and, if necessary, enabling them to define and implement appropriate solutions through the provision of an adequate and flexible choice of supportive resources and living options.

An important part of this enabling process would be to ensure not only that an adequate range of resources is available, but also that people are aware of the choices they have. In the course of carrying out this study, it was noticeable that several people did not know what sources of support might be available to them - even amongst the limited range which currently exists. A few individuals, for example, had not heard about care attendant agencies, or thought that they would be ineligible to use them. Some people had experienced difficulties obtaining information on entitlement to benefits or allowances, or on assistance with housing adaptations. Several did not know about the (albeit limited) alternatives to residential care which might be available if they chose to make changes in their living arrangements. Clearly, without this kind of information people will be unable to make informed choices about how their support needs should be met.

A model of support which enables people to construct their own creative solutions does not mean, however, that there is no role in this for professional social workers; only that, in an appropriate model of provision, that role would change towards facilitating the implementation of disabled people's own ideal solutions, and away from intervening with the provision of inadequate and inappropriate piecemeal services.

This would require social workers to take a longer-term and more holistic view of needs and solutions. However, given the higher probability of a successful outcome, this would presumably be a more satisfying and creative way of working. More important still, this kind of approach would help to facilitate a genuinely secure supportive environment for older disabled people and their carers.

Such support would be all the more secure because the model on which it is based anticipates potential crises associated with ageing, rather than simply reacts to them. The experiences of several people in the study clearly illustrate that, under the models of support which currently exist, by the time a crisis is recognised it is - by definition - too late to prevent it. It is precisely this inherent weakness in existing provision which is largely responsible for the high levels of insecurity which people expressed.

At the same time, for the minority of people who already had completely satisfactory support, it was noticeable that this was almost invariably based on solutions which the individuals had constructed for themselves (even though statutory services may have been a part of this). Flexibility and being able to plan ahead for any changes in circumstances were also noticeable features of their support arrangements. Creative solutions, then, are most likely to be successful solutions and clearly point towards the ideal which an appropriate model of support should seek to attain.

vi) Rights vs assessment

So far we have discussed the main fundamental principles on which an ideal supportive environment would be based. The final component of this model concerns building guarantees that such a model could become a reality rather than merely an ideal. As Fiedler puts it - 'the language of good practice does not replace good practice itself'.[6]

Many organisations run by disabled people themselves have argued that the provision of supportive services which are enabling to people seeking to live independently and create their own solutions to their needs should be made available as of right - for example, reference 18. Indeed, it could be argued that, logically, the only way to ensure real security would be for the provision of support to be made available on demand as of right.

The building in of rights to support into a new model for a supportive environment clearly implies the implementation of solutions to the problems associated with ageing as they are defined by disabled people themselves. This would include the right to choose where and how to live, and who with; the right to choose what support is needed and how and when this should be provided; it would also include the right to decline any support which compromises an individual's sense of independence and (if he or she wishes), the right to demand alternative options which retain the individual's personal autonomy; ultimately, this may even extend to the right to decide when to die. In short, the right to a supportive environment means allowing people the right to control their own lives. However, before this move to a rights based model of support can be made, there is another aspect of support provision which would need to be re-evaluated - the question of 'assessment' of needs.

The need to question the notion of assessment has two important dimensions. Firstly, the very term 'assessment' is clearly ideologically loaded. It reflects the basic logic underlying current social work practice - i.e. 'professional assessment of need' - into which both social workers and their clients become locked. This fundamental relationship which only allows needs to be defined by professionals, rather than allowing disabled people to define their own needs, is clearly antipathetical to the ideal supportive environment which we have been discussing.

Far from facilitating the kind of supportive environment which would allow disabled people to retain control over how they wish to live their lives, this relationship actually contributes to the limiting of the options available to them, and to the denial of their legitimate rights. Indeed, by definition, assessment implies 'rationing' of resources which is the opposite of support provision according to 'rights'.

Furthermore, the logic of assessment only serves to reinforce negative images of disabled people's assumed 'dependency' on (able bodied) professionals to meet their needs. This ideological and cultural construction of dependency has already been widely discussed in relation to older people in general. More recently, similar critiques have highlighted the ways in which existing social policies work towards the construction of dependency amongst disabled people - young and old alike.[19,20] Unless this forced dependency is removed it would be impossible to move towards a more facilitative environment which would allow older disabled people to move towards the creation of their own solutions to their needs.

Secondly, on a practical level, the notion of assessment also leads directly to the provision of inappropriate and wasteful services. This can be illustrated very clearly by considering the amounts of support different individuals may need at different times. Reflecting the ideology of dependency noted above, there is a tendency amongst both planners and service professionals concerned with the needs of older people to categorise individuals and groups according to assumed levels of 'dependency'; these range, for example, from 'high dependency' to 'low dependency'. One major problem with this kind of external assessment of need is the assumption that levels of dependency - even if they are reliable indicators of need (which is questionable) - will remain constant. The findings from this study illustrate very clearly that this is not the case. An individual may only need one hour's help per day in a 'typical' week, yet the same individual may require several hours help per day when - for example - he or she is feeling particularly tired, or unwell, or when usual sources of support are not available.

More importantly, perhaps, whilst most of the older disabled people we interviewed typically only needed fairly small amounts of assistance, the presence or absence of such assistance can make a crucial difference to the quality of an individual's life. However, the problem with current support provision which is underpinned by the logic of assessment is that the kinds of solutions available are almost always too inflexible.

This inflexibility means that service providers can only offer solutions from the pre-existing range of options. In practice, this usually involves the provision of fixed amounts or 'units' of assistance rationed at so many hours per week regardless of expressed need, or, twenty-four hour 'care' either from a care attendant or in an institution. More often than not, neither of these kinds of options actually match the variable needs of individuals themselves. Consequently, rather than provision being adapted to meet these needs, many people have to manage with no support at all.

The final example from our study neatly illustrates how the logic of professional assessment can completely fail to meet the needs of older disabled people. The following quote is from a woman whose eighty year old mother is now finding it increasingly difficult to carry on in the role of carer; her specific practical needs are for help getting in and out of bed, and with washing and dressing - amounting to one hour in the morning and half an hour at night. Unlike the majority of people in the study, this woman was receiving some support from statutory services; however, despite the intervention of four different professionals including a social worker, existing resources were still unable to meet her needs:

> I get the district nurse to come in. Of course she has to come in to do the catheter but she's not the person to help give me a wash down below and help get me into the chair you know - it has to be another person. Now the other person that comes in to get me into the chair is not allowed to wash me. I've never heard anything like it in my life. We had a meeting here on Thursday of the social services person, the home help person, the physiotherapist and my district nurse and each one had a different job and one can't go over and do the other person's job. And when she said that the person who's coming to help me, she's coming Monday to Friday - she can dress me, she can get me out of bed but she's not allowed to wash me. And I said well who's allowed to wash me then? . . . So if ever you're out and you smell something it will be a smelly paraplegic. Oh dear, oh dear, these rules and regulations.

Some final conclusions - the way forward

This chapter has outlined the main principles involved in developing a supportive environment capable of meeting the needs of people who are ageing with a disability, and discussed some of the practical implications this would have for social workers. We have termed the model an 'ideal supportive environment' in recognition of the fact that the kind of changes proposed could not realistically all become a reality overnight. That they *should* become a reality, however, is not in any doubt. Outlining what a truly supportive environment would look like, therefore, is only the first step. In the final part of the chapter we suggest some of the ways in which it would be possible to move forward, and recap the most urgent practical measures required.

Obviously, social workers cannot be expected to be accountable for all of the changes in support provision which our model would imply. As we have already seen, there is an urgent need for coordination of provision which would require a much greater degree of genuine inter-agency collaboration than currently exists. Social workers will, nevertheless, have a central role in this. Most importantly, there are several ways in which individual social workers can make a start in helping to create an environment which is enabling to people wishing to implement their own solutions to their support needs.

First, many older disabled people experience occasional crises over their support arrangements requiring a temporary increase in support from alternative sources. There is a very clear need for more short-term support provided on a flexible basis. This support will often need to be available at short notice to be of any real value, as individuals will often be unable to predict when such a need will arise.

Depending on the precise needs of different individuals, this short-term support could sometimes be provided by existing statutory agencies (e.g. district nurses or, in the case of domestic support, home helps). More often, however, people's needs may be more general and the greater flexibility provided by short-term care attendants or personal helpers would be a more appropriate option. Under present arrangements, it is likely that this would also be cheaper than using professional service based support. Most importantly, however, the kind of service offered by a care attendant or personal helper affords the individual much greater control over exactly how his or her needs will be met. This option would, therefore, be much more compatible with the principles of the supportive environment model we have outlined.

Second, some people may find that, in addition to temporary inputs of increased assistance, they will gradually need to increase the level of support they receive on a more regular basis. Some people will prefer for any assistance they receive on a regular basis to be provided from a number of different sources in order to ensure that back-up is always available if required, and/or to avoid dependence on a single worker or carer. Others may want more continuity of support and, consequently, prefer their support to be organised around a single worker or carer, perhaps with occasional back-up from other sources.

Clearly, there is considerable potential for creative social work which would help individuals to construct their own ideal solutions around the kind of options described above. For some people, this would be likely to involve liaising between the disabled individual, informal carers and other agencies involved in each individual's preferred package of support. In some cases, help could be given on obtaining information on how to get in touch with other agencies or services, or giving advice on financial needs or problems involved in constructing suitable support arrangements.

Most importantly, under the new community care legislation, social workers will often have a key role in ensuring that all of the components of an individual's support arrangements are in place, and that these are suited to their changing needs.

The common principle in this would be that any support arrangements an individual requires should be both acceptable and secure. In practical terms, there are a variety of ways in which this could be achieved, but much would obviously depend on individual circumstances - particularly choice of living arrangements. The basic principle, however, would be very similar to the 'Grove Road' model of support described by Davis.[21] Grove Road is a variation on the 'tenant/carer' model where residents in a small community provide support to their disabled neighbours on a mutually arranged basis. The support system at Grove Road itself is made up of five 'tiers' as follows:

1. Local statutory services (e.g. home help).

2. 'Supporting families' providing assistance not covered by statutory services.

3. Local Voluntary groups (e.g. WRVS).

4. Friends, neighbours and relatives.

5. Selective hire of agency nurses.

We are not suggesting that the Grove Road scheme is itself necessarily the most appropriate means of meeting the needs of older disabled people. Indeed, amongst the people participating in our study, hardly anyone would choose to live in such a community. What it does provide, however, is a very important practical illustration of how the various supportive resources which people might wish to use could be organised in order to provide both choice and security. As Davis emphasises in the description of the Grove Road scheme, the basic principle is to 'spread the load'. Also, precisely because of the flexibility and security which this provided, it was hardly ever necessary to resort to the fifth tier of hiring an agency worker.

There is no practical reason why the same principles could not be adapted to a variety of other kinds of living arrangements. Equally, the balance between privately arranged assistance and statutory service based support could be altered to suit individual circumstances and preferences. Some people, for example, may wish to rely on their existing main carer for most of their needs, but have an arrangement either with a rota of paid helpers or with a statutory agency to provide back-up either on an occasional or a regular basis. Others may wish to employ a part-time care attendant or personal helper and rely on informal helpers only to provide any additional support as and when required.

Whichever particular arrangements different individuals choose for meeting their support needs, statutory services should be organised around these arrangements in such a way as to enable people to construct their own supportive environments. The common principle to the kinds of alternative arrangements outlined above is that they are built around ordinary lifestyles rather forcing people to fit into a 'structure' of support provision which requires them to organise their daily lives around the way in which particular services are provided.

Third, as we have already seen, some people may want to change their living arrangements in order to increase the options available to them for meeting their support needs. In some cases, this involved a similar arrangement to Grove Road itself by having a lodger or a relative living in another part of the home and provide additional support as and when required. Others, who perhaps wanted more regular or structured support, had or were considering moving to warden controlled sheltered accommodation. Only a tiny minority of people in the study, however, would contemplate a move into a residential or nursing home.

It is essential, therefore, that social workers consider the living options available to older disabled people as part of a complete package along with the other components of the supportive environment. Again, given that people's options were often even further restricted by not knowing about what alternatives may be available, social workers could play an important role in exploring the living options available in their area and placing this knowledge at the disposal of their clients. This would enable people contemplating changes in their living arrangements to make a more informed choice and help them to find a living environment compatible with how they wish to live their lives.

Fourth, it is a basic premise of the supportive environment model that each individual is the person most qualified to define both his or her needs, and how these should be met. So long as social workers fail to recognise this expertise, the services they provide will fail to meet people's real needs. At the same time, the collective expertise of different groups of disabled people has also been consistently under-utilised (if not ignored altogether) in the planning of service provision. This has been most apparent at the level of national policy, but more often than not, at local level also. This situation is both unimaginative and counter productive as it only results in ineffective services which are often rejected by the people whom they are intended to assist.

Clearly, more real participation by disabled people in the planning of support provision will be an essential prerequisite to establishing a genuinely supportive environment. At a practical level, social workers in the community should make more use of local organisations of disabled people as a resource for their own work. There is also the potential for an important facilitative role for social workers in pressing for greater consultation between social services departments and local disabled people.

All of the steps discussed above would make a positive contribution to the development of the ideal supportive environment we have outlined in this chapter. However, it is important to emphasise again that none of these will be completely effective unless they are underpinned by the right to support which enables people to retain control over how they wish to live their lives. Ultimately, only the security which a rights based model would produce can lead to the kind of supportive environment we have described.

Any evaluation of support for people who are ageing with a disability (and any other groups wanting support, for that matter) must, therefore, be based on the distance between this ideal and the reality of existing support provision. The experiences of many older disabled people suggest that the gap between the two is still considerable. Helping to close this gap, and creating a truly supportive environment to meet the needs of people who are ageing with a disability, remains one of the most important challenges facing social workers, among others.

References

1. Zarb, G., Oliver, M. and Silver, J. (1990). *Ageing with Spinal Cord Injury: The right to a Supportive Environment?* Thames Polytechnic/Spinal Injuries Association, London

2. Harris, A. (1971). *Handicapped and Impaired in Great Britain*. HMSO, London.

3. Martin, J., Meltzer, H. and Elliot, D. (1988). *OPCS Surveys of Disability in Great Britain: Report 1 - The Prevalence of Disability Among Adults*. HMSO, London.

4. De Jong, G. (1986). 'Evaluating Housing and In-Home Service Alternatives for Persons Ageing with a Physical Disability.' Paper presented at Annual Meeting of American Congress of Rehabilitation Medicine, Baltimore, 24th October.

5. Beardshaw, V. (1988). *Last on the List: Community Services for People with Physical Disabilities*. King's Fund, London.

6. Fiedler, B. (1988). *Living Options Lottery: Housing and Support Services for People with Severe Physical Disabilities*. Prince of Wales Advisory Group on Disability, London.

7. Marshall, M. (1990). *Social Work with Old People* (2nd edition). Macmillan, London.

8. Oliver, M. & Zarb, G. (1982). 'Ageing with a Disability: The Dimensions of Need.' Research proposal prepared for Joseph Rowntree Memorial Trust, 1989.

9. Goldberg, E. and Connelly, N. *The Effectiveness of Social Care for the Elderly*. Heinemann, London.

10. Blaxter, M. (1980). *The Meaning of Disability* (2nd edition). Heinemann, London.

11. Oliver, M. (1983). *Social Work with Disabled People*. Macmillan Press, London.

12. Zarb, G. (1987). 'Physical and Personal Consequences of Ageing with SCI: Some Implications for Community Care in the UK' *Paraplegia News*. 41, 10.

13. BCODP (1988). 'The British Council of Organisations of Disabled People'. BCODP, London.

14. Oliver, M., Zarb, G., Silver, J., Moore, M. and Salisbury, V. (1988). *Walking into Darkness: The Experience of Spinal Cord Injury*. Macmillan Press, London.

15. Davis, K. (1986). *Developing Our Own Definitions - Draft for Discussion*. British Council of Organisations of Disabled People, London.

16. Oliver, M. (1990). *The Politics of Disablement*. Macmillan Press, London.

17. Johnson, M. (1978). 'That Was Your Life: A Biographical Approach to Later Life'. Ch. 14 in Carver, V. and Liddiart, P. (Eds). *An Ageing Population: A Reader and Sourcebook*. Hodder and Stoughton/OU Press, Sevenoaks.

18. BCODP (1987). 'Comment on the Report of the Audit Commission - Making a Reality of Community Care'. BCODP, London.

19. Oliver, M. (1988). 'Disability and Social Policy: The Creation of Dependency' *Tidskrift for Rattssociologi*. 5, 1.

20. Barton, L. (Ed.) (1989). *Disability and Dependency*. Falmer Press, East Sussex.

21. Davis, K. (1981). '28-38 Grove Road: Accommodation and Care in a Community Setting'. In Brechin, A., Liddiard, P. and Swain, J. (Eds.) *Handicap in a Social World*. Hodder and Stoughton/OU Press, Sevenoaks.

Research Highlights in Social Work

This series examines areas currently of particular interest to those in social and community work and related fields. Each book draws together a collection of articles on different aspects of the subject under discussion, highlighting relevant research and drawing out implications for policy and practice.

Social Work and the European Community:
The Social Policy and Practice Contexts
Edited by Malcolm Hill
ISBN 1 85302 091 5
Research Highlights in Social Work 23
The creation of the Single European Market in 1992 will have major implications for social problems and social services. There is likely to be increased movement of social service users, of social workers and of practice ideas. This book analyses the similarities and differences in approaches to public welfare, social service organisation and social work education within the social and political contexts of the member states of the EC. It outlines the institutions of the European Community and their impact on social policy and social work. Finally, attention is given to a number of social work issues to examine how these are tackled within the EC. Such topics include community development, juvenile justice, child abuse, family policy and services for elderly people.

Poverty, Deprivation and Social Work
Edited by Ralph Davidson and Angus Erskine
ISBN 1 85302 043 5
Research Highlights in Social Work 22
CONTENTS: 1. The social fund and debt, Gill Stewart. 2. Employment and unemployment, Angus Erskine. 3. Regional divides, Stephen Maxwell. 4. Women and poverty, Jane Millar. 5. The elderly and poverty, Professor Alan Walker. 6. Ethnic groups and poverty. 7. Social work response with individuals and families, Ralph Davidson. 8. A community work response, Phil Bryers. 9. The role of voluntary organisations, Ann Stafford.

Privatisation
Edited by Richard Parry
ISBN 1 85302 015 X
Research Highlights in Social Work 18
Privatisation is a major issue in British social policy in the 1980s and 1990s and practitioners must come to terms with the practical and philosophical questions concerned. This volume covers both theoretical and practical issues involved in the privatisation of social services and health care, and highlights some of the challenges posed by privatisation to those who have to make social welfare services work.
'This is a useful publication'

– Community Care

Jessica Kingsley Publishers, 116 Pentonville Road, London N1 9JB

Social Work and Health Care
Edited by Rex Taylor and Jill Ford
ISBN 1 85302 016 8
Research Highlights in Social Work 19
This volume explores the interface between social work and health care in institutional and
field settings. Three chapters provide overviews of the changing relationship between
social work and health work, four chapters assess different aspects of social work in
hospital and health centres, and four are concerned with the contribution of social work to
community health care.

Living with Mental Handicap:
Transitions in the Lives of People with Mental Handicap
Edited by Gordon Horobin and David May
ISBN 1 85302 004 4
Research Highlights in Social Work 16
This volume presents the lives of people with mental handicaps as a series of transitions -
from home to school, from school to work, from hospital to community, from child to
adult, from adulthood to old age – and offers us a view of a world that is as complex and
changeable as any.

Evaluation
Edited by Joyce Lishman
ISBN 1 85302 006 0
Research Highlights in Social Work 8
This volume attempts to discover exactly what research can tell a planner, manager, or
practitioner, who wishes to evaluate a service, project or piece of work, about methods of
evaluation in general, and which method might be most appropriate for this specific task.
The second edition brings up to date findings of the first edition, published in 1984.
'This short book is full of concentrated vitamins. It describes what research can tell a
planner manager, or practitioners who wish to evaluate a service or project, how an
evaluation is carried out, and which method may be appropriate to the task in hand.
Although the canvas is the social services, the principle can apply anywhere.'
                                                                    – *Managerial Auditing Journal*

Jessica Kingsley Publishers, 116 Pentonville Road, London N1 9JB

**Performance Review in
Social Work Agencies**
Edited by Joyce Lishman
ISBN 1 85302 017 6
RHSW 20

Why Day Care?
Edited by Gordon Horobin
ISBN 1 85302 000 1 hb ISBN 1 85302 049 4 pa
RHSW 14

New Information Technology in Management and Practice
Edited by Gordon Horobin and Stuart Montgomery
ISBN 1 85091 022 7
RHSW 13

Child Care: Monitoring Practice
Edited by Isobel Freeman and Stuart Montgomery
ISBN 1 85302 005 2
RHSW 17

Sex, Gender and Care Work
Edited by Gordon Horobin
ISBN 1 85302 001 X
RHSW 15

The Family: Context or Client?
Edited by Gordon Horobin
ISBN 1 85091 026 X
RHSW 12

Working with Children
Edited by Joyce Lishman
ISBN 1 85302 007 9
RHSW 6

Social Work Departments as Organisations
Edited by Joyce Lishman
ISBN 1 85302 008 7
RHSW 4

Developing Services for the Elderly 2nd ed
Edited by Joyce Lishman and Gordon Horobin
ISBN 1 85091 002 2 hb ISBN 1 85091 003 0 pa
RHSW 3

Jessica Kingsley Publishers, 116 Pentonville Road, London N1 9JB

of related interest

How to Get Equipment for Disability
Compiled by Michael Mandelstam
ISBN 1 85302 095 8
Jessica Kingsley Publishers and Kogan Page for the Disabled Living Foundation

'Any health care professional requiring in depth or general information about equipment
for the disabled is catered for... The book clearly explains the legislation, costs, whose
responsibility it is, how to obtain it, maintain it and dispose of it... It is packed with useful
and essential information from cover to cover and presented in a user friendly format... I
would recommend it for any hospital ward or unit and any primary care team.'

– Bare Bones

'At last, an authoritative single guide to the complex system of provision of equipment for
people with disabilities. This unique guide provides an essential reference source...a must
for anyone working in this specialist field.'

– Disability News

'The book...must now be considered a part of the necessary equipment for everyone
advising people with disabilities...a pre-eminent guide.'

– Journal of the Royal College of Physicians

Disability Studies
A Reader
Stuart Carruthers and Jim Sandhu
ISBN 1 85302 189 X

People with disabilities have special needs, and these are now being met and recognised by
an increasingly wide community. *Disability Studies* has been written to meet the lack of
readily available information which might provide a general introduction to the issues
facing the disabled and their service providers. *Disability Studies* covers the following
issues: history; disability, handicap and impairment; demography; legislation; equal
opportunities; support services; assistive technology; employment; education; leisure;
transport; environment; and the future of disability. It will be an invaluable text for
students studying disability, and will provide professionals with a source of readily
accessible reference material.

Disabled People and Buildings
Ian McKee
ISBN 1 85302 207 1

Demand for accessible building is increasing. The implementation of the Community Care
Act is highlighting the need for accessible and adapted housing as people with disabilities
move from hospitals into ordinary dwellings. This book fills the need for a non-technical
guide to the issues involved in designing and adapting buildings for disabled and elderly
people.

Jessica Kingsley Publishers, 116 Pentonville Road, London N1 9JB

The Disability and Rehabilitation series, published with the Rehabilitation Resource Centre, City University

Approaches to Case Management for People with Disabilities
Doria Pilling
ISBN 1 85302 099 0
Disability and Rehabilitation 1
Is there a need for case management? What is case management? Why is it on the map? The author answers these questions and provides an in depth survey of current and recent case-management and co-ordination projects and services in Britain describing their main features and the differences between them and what is known so far about their successes and failures. She also discusses the evaluation of case management and explores the experience of case management from both the clients' and the service providers' point of view.

Managing Disability at Work:
Improving Practice in Organisations
Brenda Smith, Margery Povall and Michael Floyd
ISBN 1 85302 123 7
Disability and Rehabilitation 2
'...managers will undoubtably find the recommendations...useful in formulating satisfactory disability polices and training schedules...and by achieving this, *Managing Disability at Work* serves well those members of our society who, through no fault of their own, often get a very raw deal in the world of work.'

– Library Management

Information Technology Training for People with Disabilities
Edited by Michael Floyd
ISBN 1 85302 129 6
Disability and Rehabilitation 4

Jessica Kingsley Publishers, 116 Pentonville Road, London N1 9JB